DATE DUE

TOLERANCE AND MOVEMENTS
OF RELIGIOUS DISSENT
IN EASTERN EUROPE

Edited by

BÉLA K. KIRÁLY

EAST EUROPEAN QUARTERLY, BOULDER
DISTRIBUTED BY COLUMBIA UNIVERSITY PRESS
NEW YORK AND LONDON
1975

EAST EUROPEAN MONOGRAPHS, NO. XIII

BROOKLYN COLLEGE

THE CITY UNIVERSITY OF NEW YORK

SCHOOL OF SOCIAL SCIENCE
DEPARTMENT OF HISTORY

STUDIES ON SOCIETY IN CHANGE, NO. 1

EAST EUROPEAN MONOGRAPHS

The East European Monographs comprise scholarly books on the history and civilization of Eastern Europe. They are published by the *East European Quarterly* in the belief that the studies contribute to the knowledge of the area and serve to stimulate research and scholarship.

To the Memory of Henry L. Roberts

PREFACE

This book contains the proceedings of a series of discussions of the subject held in various institutions of higher learning over a period of several years. The first such session was held on May 8, 1971 at the Sir George Williams University in Montreal; several sessions were held at and sponsored by the East European Section of the Center of European Studies at the Graduate School and University Center of the City University of New York. The resulting studies were compiled and edited at Brooklyn College of the City University of New York during the 1974-75 academic year as the first volume of a projected series, "Brooklyn College Studies on Society in Change."

This work, edited by Béla Király, Professor of History at Brooklyn College, provides a basic sourcebook of materials not normally presented together. The grouping of studies on religious intolerance in Christendom, Hasidic-Mitnagder polemics in the Jewish communities of East Central Europe and religious tolerance in East Central Europe present a historical perspective which has previously been lacking in the treatment of Eastern European religion.

The contributors include the leading American and Canadian scholars in the field of Slavic and East Central European history. Besides Professor Király, they are Robert Kann, Frederick Heymann, Peter Brock, Marianka Fousek, Mordecai Wilensky, Norman Lamm, Abraham Duker, Ezel Kural Shaw, Stanford J. Shaw, and Stephen Fischer-Galati.

The projected series, "Brooklyn College Studies on Society in Change," represents an important facet of Brooklyn College's continuing commitment to academic research. We are grateful to the Graduate School and University Center of the City University for their sponsorship of the studies represented in this volume and we look to many equally successful cooperative efforts to bring our own faculty and other distinguished scholars together in future research enterprises of this nature.

JOHN W. KNELLER
President
Brooklyn College

CONTENTS

Hans J. Hillerbrand

RELIGIOUS DISSENT AND TOLERATION: INTRODUCTORY REFLECTIONS

The several essays collected in this volume depict a variety of aspects of Modern European History. As the overall title indicates, their explicit focus is on problems of religious dissent and toleration, two related matters of considerable significance for the history of European intellectuality during the Early Modern period. The geographic focus is on Eastern Europe.

Movements of religious dissent and the notion of toleration are to be seen as phenomena in their own right and as integrally related to each other.(1) As regards the former, the existence of dissent, in the variety of ways to be described below, need not be accompanied by toleration. As regards the latter, toleration clearly presupposes the existence of dissent. Only if there prevails an unacceptable diversity of religious sentiment does the question of toleration arise.

Moreover, the category of religious dissent presupposes the existence of normative religious and ecclesiastical standards. Dissent is here not a synonym for mere diversity. It means that a normative position exists, that it is officially enjoined and encouraged. The notion of religious dissent also presupposes the utilization of some means to enforce these standards, generally by way of the secular authorities. The goal is to maintain and safeguard these norms. A close connection, as well as harmony, thus exists between church and state.

Religious dissent must be understood in the broadest possible form. It need not assume empirical form. Any exposition of religious ideas, no matter how mute or cursory, not in harmony with prevailing orthodoxies brings the issue of dissent into focus. It may simply be the voice of a lone outsider; it may be a mighty army of restlessness and disagreement. In either case, they are chapters in the history of dissent.

If the latter, isolated sentiment turns into a torrent of opinion and into an impressive school of thought. By the same token it may also vanish.

Theoretical dissent, of course, may also assume empirical form; the lone dissenter will turn into the founding father of a large movement. His call is echoed by numerous disciples, a movement emerges. The issue of toleration and religious freedom arises in both instances. That is to say, the question is answered — both by those in political and ecclesiastical control — as to whether such dissent should be tolerated.

It is somewhat more difficult to speak with precision of the meaning of "toleration." Sometimes the term is used interchangeably with that of "religious freedom." A careful differentiation is, however, necessary. Or, to put it differently, one may differentiate between an aspect that has to do with the policies of the body politic, the "openness" of a particular society, the severity with which the ecclesiastical and religious uniformity in a society is enforced.

We shall presently note the complex convergence of factors that make for a particular policy in this regard. In any case, the policy of a society is influenced by certain assumptions and presuppositions. We may call this *political* toleration and we mean by it that a social policy is enforced as a political instrument, quite likely for political reasons.(2)

"Religious" toleration may be distinguished here. It refers to the delineation, in cogent intellectual argument, of categories to advocate the notion of toleration. In one way or another all advocates of *religious* toleration pursue one of two lines of argumentation.(3) One is to assert that certain religious affirmations are unimportant or of no incisive difference. They are relegated to insignificance and thus overlooked in the quest for final metaphysical truth. The assertion is that men of sincerity may well disagree concerning them. The other line of argumentation, equally integral to the position of the proponents of religious toleration, is the concession (or insistence) that there is no final certainty concerning the truth or falsehood of specific theological assertions. Truth, in its fullness and detail, in other words, is beyond definitive apprehension. In the eighteenth century Voltaire quipped that it was not worth sacrificing one's life for a metaphysical conjecture. While it took a while for such sentiment to become ubiquitous (its growth indeed being the history of the rise of toleration), it does express the basic argument of most proponents of toleration.

The existence of intolerance, by the same token, entails the converse of what has just been noted. The proponent of religious intolerance is pursuaded that he is in full possession of the truth; he also is convinced that the point of disagreement between orthodoxy and dissent is a major one, that it pertains to the crucial affirmations of the faith, and that divergence cannot be ignored or tolerated. Frequently, such intolerance turns into persecution. Religious dissent, far from being intellectually "tolerated", is suppressed with outright measures with the help of the secular authorities. The dissenter is silenced not so much by the logic and persuasiveness as by the executioner's block or the hangman's noose.

In a way the story of religious dissent and toleration is the story of Western civilization. Christianity, the dominant intellectual force for centuries, was in its beginning itself a movement of religious dissent, first within Judaism, subsequently within the Roman Empire. The persecutions suffered by the Christian Church in the first three hundred years of its existence form a major ingredient in the early chapters of its history. Such persecutions (and atmosphere of intolerance) were, however intermittent, ruthless and cruel. Concomitantly, during the first period of its existence, the ideology of the Christian Church was that of a movement not allowed freedom of expression, a fact made all the more striking in view of the general spirit of toleration prevailing in late Antiquity and the Roman Empire.(4)

Medieval society was, however, quite a different matter.(5) The establishment of Christianity as the nominative religion in the West, as well as the emerging relationship between what we call church and state, turned the original movement of dissent into the pivotal guardian of intellectual orthodoxy and societal law and order. No matter how lively and diverse the theological discourse during the Middle Ages, a clear boundary always existed between permissible and prohibited discourse — the latter, of course, was what we here call "religious dissent". And there was plenty of it. Heresy, to use the technical term for the deviation from accepted standards and canons of orthodoxy, was ubiquitously present, even as it was perenially suppressed. To be sure, the dominical dictum "semper sunt haereses" constituted a chronic if irritating stumbling block for any efforts at complete suppression inasmuch as it seemed to doom to failure all attempts to weed out religious dissent. Such gloomy prognoses did not paralyze those charged with the maintenance of the purity of the faith or of society.

At issue was, of course, the close alliance between secular and ecclesiastical authority. The medieval emperors, at their coronations, promised the popes to defend, secure, and further the church. This put the weight of the secular arm squarely at ecclesiastical disposal. In principle, in any case, the ecclesiastical and secular authorities worked hand in hand. To be excommunicated by the church meant to be a civil outlaw. This convergence of the two authorities received no more telling symbol than the medieval Inquisition, formalized in the 13th century by

Pope Gregory IX. It surely is telling that Pope Gregory and Emperor Frederick, otherwise locked in mortal battle concerning the priority of place of the two "swords", concurred in the notion that heretics had to be persecuted and punished. There were precedents for such rigidity toward religious dissent — the stipulations pertaining to blasphemy in the Old Testament; the Justinian code, St. Augustine's exposition of the role of truth and heresy, and others. The crucial question was, of course, if the use of external force could ever change inward sentiment. Could fire and sword extinguish the flames of conviction? We must not assume an innocence and naivete on the part of the medieval polemicists with regard to this question. The answer they generally gave was negative. There was wide acknowledgment that force could not convince. Internal conviction was beyond external force.

This acknowledgement did not lead, as history-telling shows, to the abrogation of any involvement of external means of enforcing uniformity. Quite the contrary, other arguments were advanced and they focused on different aspects of the matter — foremost the notion of the disturbance of the public peace, of law and order. From that stance, the intimate cooperation between church and state was both understandable and inevitable. Moreover, the Inquisition increasingly assumed certain functions (the skeptic might say out of lack of full preoccupation with its major assignment) and dealt with heresy less than with witches and general morals.

This is not the place to discuss the role of extra-theological factors, notably, of course, political and economic ones, in the emergence of religious dissent. They assuredly were present, though only detailed research will establish the specific extent.

The notion of toleration was nowhere found in the vocabulary of the 16th century, while the fact of religious dissent was present throughout Europe.(6) In its paradox of ideology and empirical reality, the 16th century thus proved to be an important epoch. In particular the Reformation posed dramatically the questions of religious freedom and religious dissent, and became thereby a turning point, through its development of toleration, of European intellectuality. To be sure, scholars have called attention to the discussions of various pre-16th century figures, such as Nicolaus of Cusa, Ficino, Pico della Mirandola, and others. The ideas concerning religious freedom and toleration propounded by them were striking and in discontinuity with the prevailing and normative patterns of the 15th century. The increasingly forceful infusion of new aspects of the thought of Classicial Antiquity unmistakably suggested this possibility. Still, the Reformation of the 16th century deserves a significant place.(7)

We shall presently return to the fundamental question as to the motivations underlying the assertion of the postulate of religious toleration. At this point the similar question must be asked with respect to the postulates of intolerance and religious persecution. Do ideologicial considerations suffice to explain the fact as well as persistence of religious persecution? Its crucial significance arises out of several considerations. Clearly, one of these was the significance of the controversies of the Reformation. These controversies, unresolved as they were in terms of an eventual conciliation of views, dramatized the prevailing empirical diversity. The notion of one Christendom disintegrated. No longer was there the imposing splendor of the one Catholic Church geographically extending across Europe and, despite a wide variety of expressions and emphases of doctrine, a monolithic body recognizing the Pope as supreme head. The Reformation changed all this. What used to be called Christendom turned into no less than five separate and distinctive bodies (Catholics, Lutherans, Calvinists, Anglicans, and Anabaptists) all of which wavered little in their emphatic assertion that theirs alone was the true faith. Needless to say, no one was persuaded by such claims.

Since governmental authority was utilized to establish and maintain one of these bodies as normative in a given realm, there was no ecclesiastical diversity, a few Protestsant radicals excepted, within a particular commonwealth. Most of the people, illiterate as they were, knew little of the diversity of ecclesiastical and religious sentiment that prevailed throughout Europe. To some, however, such empirical reality was known and thus the claim to the sole possession of truth was one that, no matter how emphatically made, carried with it a hollow ring and less than that utter self-evidence which prior to the 16th century had been universal.

Not surprisingly, then, the 16th century proved to be an age of hardened religious persecution. With the notable exception of the Anabaptists and other left-wing figures, the prevailing ecclesiastical parties pursued and persecuted dissent with an eagerness worthy of a greater cause. The irony of the matter was that dissent in one commonwealth was the normative expression of religion in the other — a fact which could not help but add to confusion and uncertainty. Statistics from the 16th century are notoriously unreliable, but the evidence seems clear that the century deserves its infamous reputation for being the high-water mark of persecution. Neither before nor after the sixteenth century were there as many victims of religious jealousy. The authorities, both political and ecclesiastical, were determined to effect uniformity by force.

This ambivalence of diversity and persecution raised the voices of those who objected to the insistence upon uniformity. Some were compelled by pity, others by self-defense; all spoke with courage and conviction. The list of proponents of religious freedom and toleration in the 16th century is lengthy and distinguished. It began with Erasmus of Rotterdam and continued with Sebastian Castellio and Dirck Coornhert; it reached its culmination, in the 17th century, with John Milton, Roger Williams, and John Locke. Beyond these figures, prominent in the annals of any history of European intellectuality, were many others, Jacob Acontius, for example, or David Joris and Bernard Ochino, whose names history has long forgotten.

The scholarly attention paid to both major and minor figures in the history of toleration has been extensive. A variety of classification schemes has been proposed, most notable that of Johannes Kuhn in a book *Toleranz und Offenbarung* (1923) which attempted to relate the theories of toleration to the concepts of revelation.(8)

This is not the place to attempt to summarize this extensive historiography. Suffice it to say that the field of study has been dominated by intellectual or religious historians. Their studies have thrown a great deal of light on the individual figures.(9) The present scholarly desideratum, which exists despite such enormous and prolific scholarship, lies in the relating of ideas propounded, in a more plausible and persuasive manner than has been the case, to the realities of societal life, both political and economic, of the 16th and 17th centuries.(10) To some extent historians of the idea of toleration have accepted that interrelationship as a fact of life, as our comments concerning the impact of the Reformation as a political phenomenon would indicate. And even the acknowledgement that a writer's personal concern for his own safety may have played a role in the formulation of ideas concerning toleration, indicates that ideas themselves did not always lead to the exposition of notions of religious freedom and toleration.

Surely more must be said. A more careful look needs to be taken at the political realities of 16th and 17th century society.(11) The question must be asked how political, social and economic developments influenced the rise of toleration. The establishment of the organizational and ideological division of Christendom as an unalterable fact, however regrettable, was paralleled by the emergence of political ideas no less than economic aspirations; these, in turn, had to adjust themselves to the division, even as they had themselves influenced it.

These observations are not meant to traverse the full range of issues. On the contrary, they seek to argue that the flood of publications both major and minor, on the theme of toleration in early modern European society has not exhausted the topic. If anything, some of the most crucial questions remain desiderata for future scholarship. Now that the texts have been explicated and the ideas analyzed the question remains as to the societal embedment of these ideas.

And something else. The scholarly attention to the problems of toleration and religious freedom has been almost exclusively on matters pertaining to Christianity. In particular, the concerns expressed by Protestant radicals have received extensive attention. Any study of the religiosity of Europe in the late medieval and early modern period needs to recognize, however, the presence, variously significant, of two additional traditions, one ubiquitously spread across Europe, the other nestled in its south-eastern corner — Judaism and Islam. Both related to established Christendom, the former through a painfully lengthy history of intolerance and persecution, only gradually modified in the 18th and 19th century and ruthlessly reversed in our own day and age, the latter through a complex political and ideological pattern. Several of the essays in this volume address themselves to the issue of Jewish and Mohammedan toleration.

In a way, the history of religious dissent as well as that of religious toleration reach their conclusion with the end of the Early Modern period. Such was the case with respect to religious dissent because the separation of church and state prompted the latter to be increasingly disinclined to view religious uniformity as a major social good relegating diversity and dissent to the status of intra-ecclesiastical squabbles. If anything, dissent could also play the role, as has been argued for 18th century Methodism, a socially comforting role.(12)

The principle of religious toleration, on the other hand, was firmly established by the end of the 18th century; the arguments had been put forward and the points made.

Wearing different labels, however, dissent and toleration continued to be major elements in the course of European intellectuality for the past 150 years. And their story is as painful and ruthless as the earlier one pertaining to religion.

FOOTNOTES

1. On toleration in general see the entries in the *Dictionary of the History of Ideas* and the *Religion in Geschichte und Gegenwart*. Religious dissent is dealt with under the rubric of ''heresy'' (with which it is not completely

synonomous). An interesting study which seeks to relate religious dissent to social issues is S. Ozment, *Mysticism and Dissent* (New Haven, 1973).

2. van Schelven, A.A., "De opkomst van de idee der politieke tolerantie in de 16de eeuwsche Nederlanden," *Tijdschrift voor Geschiedenis* 46 (1931), 235-247, 337-388, distinguished between "dogmatic" and "political" toleration, the former the true acknowledgment of all expressions of faith as equal ("aan indifferentisme en scepticisme verwant"), and the latter the pragmatic concession of equality within the political commonwealth. Interesting consequences derive from that distinction: "Political" toleration, being part of the political realities of a society, tends to abrogate concessions of toleration as soon as the initial political conditions change. The history of the Edict of Nantees could serve as an appropriate illustration in this regard.

3. There are useful observations in R. H. Bainton, *The Travail of Religious Liberty* (New York, 1958).

4. On Augustine, a major figure in the discussion, see H. A. Deane, *The Political and Social Ideas of St. Augustine* (New York, 1963) as well as the earlier book by H. X. Arguillière, *L'Augustinisme Politique* (Paris, 1955).

5. On the medieval situation see B. Tierney, *The Crisis of Church and State* (Englewood Cliffs, 1964). An extensive bibliography on the Inquisition is E.V.D. Vekené, *Bibliographie der Inquisition* (Hildesheim, 1963).

6. Lecler, J., *Histoire de la tolérance au siècle de la réforme.* 2 vols. (Paris, 1955) offers the most comprehensive survey of the exponents of toleration in the 16th century. H. Kamen's recent *The Rise of Toleration* (London, 1967) is brief and factual. Lecler has extensive literature.

7. Hassinger, E., "Religiöse Toleranz im 16. Jahrhundert. Motive — Argumente — Formen der Verwirklichung", *Vorträge der Aeneas-Silvius-Stiftung an der Universität Basel,* VI (Basel, 1966), offers a splendid summary of the various issues. See also K. Aland, "Toleranz und Glaubensfreiheit im 16. Jahrhundert", *Reformation und Humanismus* (Witten, 1969), 67-90.

8. Kühn, J., *Toleranz und Offenbarung.* (Leipzig, 1923).

9. M. Heckel, "Staat und Kirche nach den Lehren der evangelischen Juristen in der ersten Hälfte des 17. Jahrhunderts", *Zeitschr. f. Rechtsgeschichte. Kanon. Abteilung* 42 (1956), 117-247, 202-308, has shown the significance of the reflections of the jurists in the 17th century who increasingly separated the matter of ultimate truth (i.e. the theological question) and the public exercise of religion.

10. "La tolérance religieuse et les hérésies à l'époque moderne." *XIIe Congrès international des sciences historiques. 1965. V. Actes.* (Vienna, 1968), pp. 84 ff. with significant observations of O. Halecki on the *political* component of the Polish situation in

11. On the economic element in the pursuit of toleration see E. Hassinger, "Wirtschaftliche Motive und Argumente für religiöse Duldsamkeit im 16. und 17. Jahrhundert," *Archiv f. Reformationsgeschichte* 49 (1958). 226ff. W.K. Jordan, *The Development of Religious Toleration in England,* (Cambridge, 1941), IV, 159f., 275f. and 340ff. has comments on the same aspect.

F. Dickmann, "Das Problem der Gleichberechtigung der Konfessionen im 16 und 17. Jahrhundert." *Historische Zeitschrift* 201 (1965), 265 notes that the history of theology and ideas does not suffice to explain the phenomenon.

12. E. Halevy, *The Birth of Methodism in England* (Chicago, 1971). See also E. Itzkin, "The Halévy Thesis — A Working Hypot'.esis? English Revivalism: Antidote for Revolution and Radicalism 1789-1815," *Church History* 44 (1975), 47-56.

PART I

RELIGIOUS IN TOLERANCE

IN

EAST CENTRAL EUROPE

Robert A. Kann

PROTESTANTISM AND GERMAN NATIONALISM IN THE AUSTRO-GERMAN ALPINE LANDS(1)

In the following, the thesis will be defended that the influence of Protestantism on the evolution of modern German nationalism in the Austro-German Alpine lands was only of very limited significance. Frequently argued opinions to the contrary are more often than not based on a post-hoc, propter-hoc conclusion. Unquestionably German nationalism in the Alpine lands rose vigorously and became ever more radical in particular from the 1880's to the Anschluss in 1938. Without seriously attempting a satisfactory clarification of this evolution, certain factors were adduced to illustrate but hardly to explain this development. The tradition of Protestantism and its suppression by the Counter Reformation rank high among them.

Such reasoning has been strongly influenced by political considerations. However these considerations do not apply any longer to the purely denominational aspects of the problem which are not nearly as emotionally charged today as they were at least until a generation ago. This does not mean though that today's political scientists and in particular politologists have altogether dropped the issue; they have merely changed its thrust inasmuch as attention is now focused on the question to what extent — if any, one might interject — the Protestant tradition in the Austrian Alpine lands had influenced the liberal national vote in these lands.(2) Contrary to this approach, we will try to evaluate the problem outside of the political sphere.

As seen from the vantage point of the presence, the potential political significance of the problem is greatly reduced when approached from the statistical angle. The only Austrian land of today where Protestantism represents more than 10 per cent of the population (13%) is the Burgenland; even this is less than one seventh. Undoubtedly the history of Protestantism in the Burgenland presents most interesting ecological and biological problems, for instance in regard to the consequences of religious differences and non-conformism. Isolated Protestant communities developed where inevitable inbreeding for centuries had harmful effects. Yet the population of the Burgenland shared the historical experiences of the Counter Reformation only to a very limited degree with those of the Austrian Hereditary Lands inasmuch as the Burgenland remained a part of Hungary until 1919.(3) Accordingly, what occurred in this territory of less than 4000 square kilometers and fewer than 300,000 people had little influence on events in the Alpine lands and will therefore remain outside of our discussion.

As to the other eight Austrian lands of today *(Bundesländer)* there are, according to the 1960 census, roughly 3.2% Protestants in Lower Austria, about 6.5, 5.8 and 5.5% respectively in Upper Austria, Salzburg and Styria, all lands with a dynamic and dramatic history of Protestantism in the 16th and early 17th century. There are ven fewer Protestants in Tirol and Carinthia, namely less than 1%, while there are less than 3% in Vorarlberg and about 7.5% in Vienna.

While none of these figures point to a major problem of religious division it is true that compared to the last census in imperial Austria, that of 1910, the number of Protestants in the territory of the Austrian republic has increased considerably. In 1910, 2.9% Protestants lived in this area (without the Burgenland); fifty years later it was 6%.(4) No doubt, this increase was influenced — though not influenced exclusively — by the tragic events in the history of the first Austrian republic, the confrontation between a declared Catholic and a socialist movement.(5) One might add, however, that denominational shifts like political ones may be influenced also by events and experiences which have no direct connection with the religious issue. To take just two examples from the Austrian sphere: Lueger's success in the late 19th and early 20th century which revigorated religious life considerably, was related to his campaigns against big bankers, major industrialists, and liberal intellectuals, his embracing of anti-Magyarism and above all anti-Semitism, all issues which in themselves had no manifest connection with the question of faith. The same is true for the fact that the priestly character of the Austrian chancellor Dr. Ignaz Seipel in the 1920's prompted many Socialists to leave the Church although opposition to Seipel's policies had no rational relationship to his priesthood. Neither could conversion from Catholicism to Protestantism be considered a rational manifestation of a *grossdeutsch,* that is pro-Anschluss ideology. To assume the existence of clear reasoning in matters of this kind is generally a fallacy. True enough, one must not bypass historical experience but one must not overrate its impact either. We face precisely this kind of overrating if actions and attitudes of today are related to events which took place centuries ago and have lost most of their divisive impact in the course of time. This pertains directly to the assumption that the bitter experiences of the Counter Reformation have created an undelible psychological trauma which allegedly favors Protestantism today.(6)

This does not mean that various studies which intend to establish a relation between the vote for parties or party candidates of German nationalist tendencies, the spread of Protestant communities (notably in Salzburg and Styria), and the memories of religious oppression are necessarily without significance. It must be kept in mind however that only the possibility of a relationship between the political events of the present and the religious experiences of the past can be demonstrated; no such decisive influence can ever be proved. To be sure, there exist a variety of reasons why the voter in a certain region supports one or the other political party. The same holds true for religious conversion or dropping church membership altogether. Political, social, historic-traditional factors, new emotional associations, plain expediency, but also purely spiritual considerations enter the scene and frequently overlap. It just is not possible to separate the spheres although complex techniques of public opinion research may lead to at best probable but still problematical deductions. Yet, assumed — but not admitted — that public opinion research could establish correlation to a single factor, in our case the nationalist one, the practical value of such finding would still be questionable. It would, after all, not apply to the large majority of the 400,000 Protestants in Austria but only to the vote of a fraction of the Protestant population of Upper Austria, Salzburg and Styria where the tradition of the religious struggle of the past penetrated deeper than in the other Austrian lands.

It is certainly correct though that the influence of a minority on important ideological questions cannot be measured simply on the basis of its significance in size. To refer to just one example in this context, Schönerer had tremendous influence on the Pan-German movement in Austria even though he was supported only by a handful of deputies who were involved in bitter interparty struggles. The Huguenots in France, the Presbyterians in England, or the Calvinists in Hungary have exercised great and continuing influence quite out of proportion to the number of their adherents within the entire population. The reason is simple. Religious issues will be influenced by social ones and may in turn lead to all kinds of social dissension. Thereupon the original religious conflict will not be of great consequence any longer. Yet the ideological camps were shaped by it, in part or in full. Social as well as ideological restructuring thus remains anchored in the churches.(7)

This applied fully to the conflicts — not necessarily violent conflicts — between Calvinism and Catholic Church in Western Europe but it was not the real issue in the Alpine lands. A very sketchy historiographical survey may help to elucidate the point.

The opinion that the clash between Church and Protestantism in the Alpine lands created unbridgeable ideological tension in a purely religious frame belongs to the past. The last major German historian who presented this view without any qualification was to my knowledge Johannes Janssen in his *Geschichte des deutschen Volkes vom Ausgang des Mittelalters* which came out almost a century ago. A similar view can be deduced indirectly from the works of Ludwig von Pastor, the historiographer of the Holy See,(8) but modern Catholic historians such as Zeeden, Lutz and others have expressed genuinely enlightened viewpoints.(9) The historiographical situation is admittedly not comparable where not the overall issue of Reformation and Counter Reformation but biographical works are the issue. Obviously, in biographies of Luther or Loyola, to take only two significant examples, the problem of identification with the hero of the study and the corollary bias is of great importance. Here the religious issue is only indirectly involved.

The majority of German historians in modern times were by and large Protestants, a factor which played an important but declining role until the end of the First World War. The very fact that they were Protestants made them possibly take a less serious view of the consequences of the religious rift than did the Catholic minority of historians. But on either side clear-cut intolerance only played a minor role within the last generations. This does not mean that it disappeared entirely. One is of course reminded of Treitschke and his far-reaching identification of Austrian policy with a misunderstood tradition of 'popism', rule of the Jesuits, disloyalty toward the German nation, and finally the reproach of a Catholic reactionary spirit *a limine*. These and other prejudices were if not intentionally cultivated at least preserved even in the late 19th century. Still, there is no contradiction here. One must not forget that the *kleindeutsche Frage* and its triumph in regard to the exclusion of Austria from the German political nation stood in the center of attention of Treitschke and his school. Playing up the religious issue here meant actually only a means to a *kleindeutsch* end. Genuine questions of faith did not really interest the Prussian historical school.

The religious prejudice is much clearer on the Protestant side in the work of Janssen's contemporary Gustav Droysen, a historian far from equal to his great father.(10) Gustav Droysen did not yield to Janssen in intolerance. But by and large it was not the zeal of a Droysen but the magisterial would-be objectivity of a Ranke which determined the future direction of Protestant historiography.(11) True, one can still find traces of the old views in the writings of the well known contemporary Protestant church historian Grete Mecenseffy who credits Protestantism with all cultural progress in the Alpine lands and relates all cultural decline in the 18th century to the expulsion and forced conversion of Protestants.(12) Similarly structured views still exist also here and there on the Catholic side but they no longer have authority within either Catholicism or Protestantism. What distinguishes Catholic and Protestant interpretations today is the perfectly legitimate different evaluation of the ideological premises of predominantly spiritual movements, not a differing judgment concerning the tragic social and political consequences of the conflict itself. Catholic historians do not any longer defend Philip II as a matter of principle and Protestant historians do not see any necessity to glorify Gustavus Adolphus.

For these reasons I have to dissent from the view that the counter reformatory expulsions of Protestants and their deplorable reoccurrences in 18th century Salzburg and even 19th century Tirol in the Ziller valley have exercised a lasting, still continuing influence.(13) It seems that the repercussions of the persecutions and in particular of the expulsions were more than balanced by the general influence of the Austrian Enlightenment and of Josephinism.

True, the problem of reconversion by means of direct and perhaps more often indirect pressure is far more complex. Assuming that the clash between Reformation and Counter Reformation in the Hereditary Lands could have been solved by way of forced conversions or by means of the principle of the religious peace of Augsburg, *cuius regio eius religio,* the problem then would have been indeed that of clear-cut suppression and corresponding protest movements. This in all probability would have furthered and accentuated German nationalist tendencies in the future.

Here we must remind ourselves, however, that the center of Protestantism in the Habsburg empire of the 16th and early 17th century until the end of the Bohemian phase of the Thirty Years' War was in Czech territories. Concurrently and thereafter it moved to Hungary east of the Tisza river, in particular to Transylvania. Due to the belated offensive of the Counter Reformation after the reconquest of Buda in 1686, conflicts in Hungary were by no means peacefully adjusted but usually resolved by the force of imperial military intervention. Consequences can be seen in the second Rákóczy risings. Only the peace of Szatmár between the emperor and the Hungarian rebels provided a precarious compromise. The real conflicts were only reconciled by a clear break with the past in the second half of the 19th century.

But in the Austro-German Alpine lands the Protestant issue was in substance settled neither by force of arms nor by treaties. The religious provisions of the Westphalian peace treaty did not apply to the Hereditary Lands. In this respect their validity was already strongly challenged in the religious peace of Augsburg.(14) Thus actually a decision concerning the religious issue was not made but evaded.

Obviously the Catholic orthodoxy was greatly strengthened throughout the reigns from Rudolf II to Maria Theresa and in particular from Rudolf II to Ferdinand II. By and large this meant neither a reconfirmation of articles of faith based on the decisions of the Council of Trent nor a change of faith for the broad masses, except for those in Inner Austria who were threatened with expulsion by Ferdinand II as archduke and later as emperor. There, direct pressure took place, limited however in time and place. beyond this the problem was one of statutory and judicial determination on the one hand and of social and political interpretation of actual conditions on the other. The latter approach proved to be far more important in the long run.

The question who was to be considered a Protestant in the Hereditary Lands was answered in a clear-cut way primarily for the nobles, far less clearly for the burghers and peasants. It is well known that during the reign of Ferdinand I neither a priest's rejection of celibacy nor a layman's partaking of communion in both kinds was considered evidence of his Protestant affiliation. Protestant but also Catholic historians frequently state that the population of the Hereditary Lands in the second quarter of the 16th century was predominantly Protestant. (15) Yet proof is impossible. For the nobility, it is true, much changed during the reigns of Matthias and Ferdinand II. As noted before, the religious rights of the nobles in relation to the sovereign according to the provisions of the religious peace of Augsburg were always contested. The victorious Counter Reformation was in no way ready to offer concessions. The situation changed also for a sizable number of burghers and for an even larger part of the peasantry. On the basis of stricter interpretation of affirmation of religious principles and of religious liberty, such persons were with increasing frequency apprehended as open heretics. In this case the only choice was between enforced formal reconversion or expulsion.(16)

Yet, considering the still relatively limited number of directly affected persons(17) the conclusion is warranted that the large majority of the population neither reconverted nor were they bound formally to declare their obligation to the traditional religion. Most people simply gave up previously adopted or at least tolerated practices and rites. They did not have to renounce them solemnly. The overwhelming majority of the population adjusted to the new situation by way of a conformism which under existing conditions proved to be conducive to the welfare of the individual.

By and large but with major exceptions — such as the peasant risings in Tirol and Salzburg in the 1520's and those under Stephan Fadinger's leadership in Upper Austria a century later — the religious dilemmas, like to a lesser degree the social dilemmas, were circumvented. This in turn frequently led to the conclusion that dodging a problem is easier than tackling and solving it, that staying away from dangerous controversies is the safest and most prudent policy. To put it in a nutshell, if a critical problem rises above the horizon it is wise to look the other way. To mind only one's own business, not to worry about what may be fair or unfair to others, this is the genuine philosophy of life which evolved from the experiences of the Counter Reformation for the majority of the population, though certainly not for all of them. This outlook, aptly formulated in the German proverb *"was dich nicht brennt, das blase nicht"*, is generally associated with the Restoration and pre-March era from 1815 to 1848. But such unheroic approach was practiced long before that era and still exists today. To be sure, similar views and conduct can be found also in other countries. It would not be fair to evaluate them as symptoms of overall opportunism or even of outright cowardice. What we face here is simply a psychological reaction to centuries of absolutism and has been even more marked in the cultural field than in the purely political one. It proved difficult and pointless if not impossible to fight lasting but by no means always visible pressure with heroic gestures or sporadic protests. It was perhaps difficult to choose a path out of the bind between indirect oppression and easy accommodation. But after the choice was made, the convenient exit certainly proved to be more attractive. Eventually it became the rule.

In this context it should be said that there exist many examples of very different, forthright and determined attitudes of social groups in Austrian history, to the present. Generally courageous protests arise when people are faced by suddenly emerging external or internal dangers. No comparable situation existed in the era of declining but still noticeable impact of the Counter Reformation, roughly from the middle of the 17th to the middle of the 18th century. Consequences, conditions and experiences of the movement which remained for several generations relatively stable, exerted an unhealthy influence on the climate of public opinion. It is therefore perfectly consistent that the struggle deriving from the clash between Reformation and Counter Reformation in the Alpine lands has furthered the evolution of attitudes leaning toward compromise and unwillingness to accept risks. The notion that tyrants' violence creates undelible traumas just is not applicable here. The atmosphere of opportunistic compromise represents a semi- if not fully conscious flight from the harsh reality of the religious conflict. This attitude was in all likelihood of much greater significance for the delay in the intellectual evolution of the masses throughout the Austrian Enlightenment .han the alleged victory of reactionary Catholicism over a progressive Protestantism.(18)

As is well known, a sizable number of Protestants emigrated from German states to Austria at the beginning of the 18th century where they were welcomed as merchants and skilled craftsmen. Yet they could not officially settle, they were merely tolerated. This holds true even for the first decades after issuance of the Tolerance Edict of 1781 although restrictions were much relaxed by then. To take just one example, the case of Friedrich von Gentz at the beginning of the 19th century is still the exception which confirms the rule. He was able to compensate for his Protestant creed by practical zeal and extraordinary ability; in other words by puttinghis genius into the service of the good cause as the government saw it.

On the basis of the new legal situation between the end of Joseph II's reign and the revolution of 1848 one might summarize conditions as follows. Absolutist government did not consider Protestantism outright as a black mark against an office holder. In fact, the unqualified adherence to orthodox Lutheranism was considered decidedly preferable to suspected liberal tendencies of Catholic intellectuals. Febronianism during the Enlightenment, and the philosophy of Bolzano and Fesl during the Restoration era may serve as examples that unorthodox Catholicism was considered far more dangerous than orthodox Protestantism. Yet inasmuch as Protestantism deviated after all from established rules, its adherents were obliged to compensate for the deficiencies of their faith by special loyalty to the government beyond the ordinary call of duty. The same held true also for converts, whether Jewish or Protestant, such as Joseph von Sonnenfels under Maria Theresa and Adam Muller under Francis I. To put it differently, the presumption of loyalty existed for Catholics, Protestants had to prove it. Apart from this there was little discrimination against Protestants during the Restoration era until 1848 and hardly a trace after the revolution. Obviously Neoabsolutism and the Concordate of 1855 hurt Protestant interests, but not any more than those of others during this period of outright repression of intellectual freedom. In a sense Protestant interests were in fact less affected. Throughout the Concordate era from 1855 to 1870 Catholics were more severely scrutinized and, due to the power of the Catholic church, more restricted in their freedom than Protestants. Nevertheless the religious question in its narrower sense, as far as it related to public service, had become an academic issue even under Neoabsolutism. The national German issue on the other hand, that is Austria's relations to the German states, began to become a problem of widespread, powerful, emotional impact only with the revolution of 1348. Yet neither at that time nor afterwards did it have any direct influence on the problem of Protestant-Catholic interrelationship in Austria.

How can it be explained then that the *Los von Rom* movement, mightily inspired though not created by Schönerer, pushed Protestant poncerns into the foreground of the demands of Pan-Germanism in the late 1880's and the 1890's? The movement identified German nationalism with a model of political Protestantism. The parallel case is, of course, the early Christian Social party movement which propagated its own thoroughly political interpretation of Catholicism much to the displeasure of the Episcopate.

It would be an inadmissible oversimplification to say that Pan-Germanism merely erected here a fraudulent front. Naturally the Pan-Germans were little or not at all concerned with religious questions per se, a fact which to a lesser degree applied also to a sizable fraction of the Catholic Christian Social petty bourgeoisie. We also have to remember that the proclamation of the dogma of infallibility at the Vatican Council in 1870 was not only repudiated by Protestants but also by many Catholics. Whether and if so to what extent this affected the large numbers of the faithful on either side is impossible to determine. Yet the possibility of such influence can by no means be gainsaid. In any case, not Protestantism but the new Old Catholic movement profited directly from this situation.

Concerning the relationship between political parties and churches, the Christian Social movement's close tie to Catholicism was centered more on the Church as organization than as community of the faithful. Less direct was the connection between Pan-Germanism and Protestantism. The political movement considered it expedient not to neglect the religious bonds to Protestantism. In a sense both movements, the Christian Social and the Pan-German, appealed to overlapping strata of voters of the urban middle class. While the Christian Socials criticized the ruling system sharply, they fully approved of the Habsburg empire as such, while the Pan-Germans rejected not only the regime but, far more important, the state concept itself. This is, of course, a generally known fact which does not need to be emphasized any further. Yet, we have to add a new consideration. The Catholic Church belonged to the very pillars of a system which is frequently summarized as a combination of crown and altar. Pan-German opposition against the Catholic Church was therefore so to speak mandatory. Protestantism per se was by no means a symbol of opposition to regime and state, but it had no close emotional ties to them either, certainly none comparable to the Christian Social ties to both Church and state. Accordingly Protestantism could serve as convenient front for irredentist activities for which, to be sure, the creed could not be held responsible.

The strangest factor of this syndrom of Protestantism, opposition to regime and state, liberalism, anti-clericalism, and anti-Semitism was the deliberate identification of Protestantism with Pan-German, anti-Habsburg nationalism. What are the historical foundations of this unwholesome equation?

It is well known that the French Huguenot emigrés in Prussia have preserved a national and in several instances even regional idenity. Not so the Protestants expelled from the Alpine lands.(20) For this reason alone it is difficult to connect the truly or allegedly pro-Protestant German national movement in Austria directly with descendants of the Protestants who were expelled during the Counter Reformation.

What occurred was something entirely different. Notwithstanding the endeavors of the Pan-German movement to incorporate the Austro-German lands into the second German empire, clear-cut symbols of national identification were lacking. Language did not suffice in this respect since it embraced all those German speaking individuals who affirmed the Austrian state and in their majority adhered to different political creeds. While many Austro-German liberals wished for clear identification with Germany, the Pan-Germans could not join them in this respect on account of the racial question. The increasing affiliation of Jews and Jewish descendants with Austro-German liberalism made it impossible now to unite all *Grossdeutsche* under this flag. But an alternative existed, namely the appeal for religious identification with the German national movement. Since more than three fifths of the population of Germany were Protestants, Protestantism was primarily identified with Germany, particularly Prussia east of the Elbe with its old Protestant tradition. It was so identified — and this is important for our analysis — more outside than inside of the boundaries of the German empire. Inasmuch as genuine liberals did not like pseudo-religious, actually political affiliations, the Pan-Germans thus could conveniently get rid of unwelcome liberal and racially suspect allies.

Naturally, this artificial, prejudiced identification was in various ways highly problematical. The majority of German Protestants were by no means German nationalists in a party sense and even of those who were, not all wished for incorporation of the Austro-German lands into Germany. Farther reaching conclusions can hardly be substantiated. Denominational membership was assigned in official statistics according to the baptismal certificate. This does not allow conclusions as to political sympathies and racial criteria which were so vital for Pan-Germanism. Yet even if one disregards this last mentioned racial factor, it is impossible to determine how many Protestants in Germany were truly faithful to their church and at the same time strove for incorporation of the Austro-German lands. It is relatively easier to evaluate the true religious feelings of the Catholics organized in the Christian Social party since here local statistics, however imperfect, make at least an estimate of the number of practicing Catholics possible.(21) Catholics with Pan-German tendencies also existed, of course, on both sides of the German border; but it is impossible to estimate their percentual share in the Pan-German movement in any fairly reliable way. Mere failure to attend church services and to partake of the sacraments regularly gives no indication in this respect.

Yet it is a fact that integral German nationalism, particularly in Austria, identified Protestantism largely with the notion of a German religion and a Great-German empire comprising all ethnic Germans. Concepts of this kind preceded the rule of National Socialism by at least a generation. One might well point here to the analogy with the Irish problem of our days. The difference between the Irish in the sovereign republic of Eire and those in the six nothern counties of Ulster of the United Kingdom is, in terms of history, rooted in religious causes: a strong Catholic majority in Eire, a Protestant majority in Ulster. Yet the religious issue, while still a distinguishing factor, has lost much of its significance in our days. The present conflict between Catholics and Protestants in Ulster is based on the fact that, for centuries, Catholics have been discriminated against in their daily lives. Gradually a social center has evolved within the denominational frame of the conflict. The ideological issue is still alive but it has changed its direction. German nationalism in the Alpine lands may, to a measure, have religious roots; but to what degree they surface today is quite a different question.

No analogy is perfect. Religious dissension between Catholics and Protestants in the Alpine lands was neither as lasting nor as comprehensive as that in the Irish territories. Social discrimination occurred seldom after the 18th century apart from the frequent failure of elevating Protestants to top positions of mostly ceremonial nature. Even in the 18th century such discrimination rarely touched the private life of the burgher who was not engaged in purely intellectual pursuits. It is true that only a very small number of Protestants belonged to the genuine aristocracy. Yet, more important, after the end of the Counter-Reformation they were much more strongly represented, percentage-wise, in the middle class and particularly in the upper strata of the middle class than in the overall population. At least in the cities very few Protestants were to be found among the paupers.

Admittedly, this has not changed the fact that Protestantism in the age of integral nationalism was frequently identified with Germany and Germandom. It is further true that a perhaps only semi-conscious feeling of alleged discrimination also played a role here. Anyway, to facilitate and to strengthen the identification of Protestantism and Germandom, attempts were made to associate the genuine German nationalism in the Alpine lands with the wrongs suffered there by the Protestants at the time of the Counter-Reformation.

These attempts failed. Pan-Germanism could count on little confidence in regard to its respect for religious feelings. It could rely even less on memories of the historical past. The roots of German nationalism in the Alpine lands are certainly strong and widespread but also in more than one way linked to the non-political tradition of the Holy Roman Empire. The same holds true for the community of language and indirectly probably also for the multi-national character of the Habsburg empire in which after the middle of the 19th century the Austro-Germans increasingly took a position which, particularly in the Sudeten lands after the Slavic renaissance, may be called that of a quite understandable, defensive aggression.

Yet as to the struggle between Reformation and Counter Reformation in the Alpine lands, those who trace German nationalism back to this centuries-old past have created a myth. Considering the lack of conclusive evidence and in view of various different possible explanations for the rise of such nationalism, this myth is not tenable any longer. Many former adherents of this view therefore ceased to propagate it prior to the turn from the 19th to the 20th century. They turned to more rational ideologies. Others remained unconvinced although they too realized that playing up and reviving the issue of religious dissent got them nowhere. Instead, the former advocates of such tactics turned their attention increasingly to the racial problem. It proved to be far more auspicious than the Protestant slogan to promote German nationalist tendencies in Austria.

NOTES

1. The text of this essay is a somewhat extended version of the original report given at the Graduate Center of the City University of New York. It includes

observations made in a lecture at the University of Graz, Faculty of Law, in spring of 1973.

2. Just a very recent example, G. Bingham Powell, *Social Fragmentation and political hostility. An Austrian case study*, Stanford, 1970, 23 ff. 31 ff.

3. Edmund Zimmermann, *Burgenland*, Vienna, 1966, 41-44.

4. See *Statistisches Handbuch der Republik Österreich*, vol. IX, Vienna, 1928 and *Statistisches Handbuch für die Republik Österreich*, vol. XI, Vienna, 1960, where comparative figures can be found.

.. 5. See the following chart (from *Statistische Handbücher für die Republik Österreich*, since 1934 *für den Bundesstaat Österreich*, (1925-1938) which gives rounded off figures for Roman Catholics and Protestants (Lutherans and Calvinists) for the years 1869 to 1934. The figures for Niederösterreich (Lower Austria) up to 1918 are to be understood, like those from 1918 on, with the exclusion of Vienna.   CHART P. 24

These figures show a stronger numerical increase of Protestants mainly between 1890 and 1910. Only during the first half of this period the number of Pan-German members of parliament increased and increased rather fast. Then inner conflicts in the Pan-German camp stopped the increase. However, membership figures in national associations such as Schulvereine, Turnvereine, Touristenvereine, were not touched by in-party conflicts and are of greater importance.

The figures for the First Republic are incomplete. Available statistics for 1923 show no increase in the Protestant population of the lands of Vienna (Wien) and Carinthia (Kärnten). Such an increase is, however, shown for all lands (Bundesländer) between 1923 and 1934. This could be interpreted to a degree as protest against the authoritarian system in existence since 1933. This protest, however encompassed the majority of the republic's total population. It cannot be proved that the influence of German nationalism is more than just a component (see especially the comparative figures for Vienna and Carinthia between 1923 and 1934, the only ones available).

6. See in this respect Eugen Lemberg. *Geschichte des Nationalismus*, Linz, 1950, 102-11; Heinrich Bornkamm, *Luther im Spiegel der deutschen Geistesgeschichte*, Göttingen, 1970, 168-82; Friedrich Hertz, *The development of the German public mind*, London, 1957, 453-56.

7. Friedrich Hertz, *Nationality in history and politics*, New York, 1950, 121-34; Eugen Lemberg, *Wege und Wandlungen des Nationalbewusstseins*, Munster, 1934, 106-11.

8. See especially Johann Janssen, *Geschichte des deutschen Volkes seit dem Ausgang des Mittelalters*, Freiburg i.B., 1891, vol. IV, 467-87; Ludwig Wühr, *Ludwig Freiherr von Pastor, Tagebücher, Briefe, Erinnerungen*, Heidelberg, 1950, 57-62, 100-108.

9. Hugo Hantsch, *Die Geschichte Österreichs*, Graz-Cologne, 1968-69, vol. I, 236-359 *passim;* Ernst W. Zeeden, *Das Zeitalter der Gegenreformation*, Freiburg i.B., 1967, 288-92.

10. Gustav Droysen, *Geschichte der Gegenreformation*, Berlin, 1893, see especially 143-72.

11. Leopold v. Ranke, *Deutsche Geschichte im Zeitalter der Reformation* Vienna, reprint of the 1879 edition, vol. III, 418-23.

Bundesland	Church Affiliation	1869	1880	1890	1900	1910	1923	1934
Vienna	Catholic	569.000	623.000	1,197.000	1,516.000	1,767.000	1,521.000	1,478.000
	Protestant	21.000	27.000	42.000	55.000	76.000	89.000	110.000
Lower Austria	Catholic	1,325.000	1,554.000	1,261.000	1,331.000	1,449.000	—	1,450.000
	Protestant	9.000	13.000	8.000	10.000	17.000	—	33.000
Upper Austria	Catholic	720.000	742.000	767.000	790.000	830.000	—	868.000
	Protestant	16.000	16.000	17.000	18.000	21.000	—	27.000
Salzburg	Catholic	153.000	163.000	173.000	191.000	211.000	—	238.000
	Protestant	—	1.000	1.000	1.000	3.000	—	5.000
Styria	Catholic	713.000	766.000	816.000	872.000	932.000	—	960.000
	Protestant	7.000	9.000	10.000	12.000	20.000	—	39.000
Carinthia	Catholic	298.000	307.000	318.000	323.000	346.000	343.000	369.000
	Protestant	18.000	17.000	19.000	20.000	24.000	26.000	33.000
Tirol	Catholic	237.000	244.000	249.000	265.000	301.000	—	342.000
	Protestant	—	—	1.000	1.000	3.000	—	5.000
Vorarlberg	Catholic	102.000	106.000	115.000	128.000	143.000	—	152.000
	Protestant	—	1.000	1.000	2.000	2.000	—	3.000
Burgenland	Catholic	211.000	223.000	234.000	244.000	245.000	242.000	255.000
	Protestant	37.000	41.000	42.000	43.000	42.000	39.000	40.000
TOTALS	Catholic	4,327.000	4,727.000	5,129.000	5,660.000	6,226.000	—	6,116.000
	Protestant	108.000	125.000	140.000	163.000	207.000	—	295.000

12. Grete Mecenseffy, *Geschichte des Protestantismus in Osterreich*, Graz-Cologne, 1956, 173 f.

13. G. Mecenseffy, *ibid.* 190 ff., 211. A for his time well informed presentation of Reformation and Counter Reformation in Inner Austria is given by Johann Loserth, *Die Reformation und Gegenreformation in den innerösterreichischen Ländern im XVI. Jahrhundert*, Stuttgart, 1898, see espec. 287-572. Loserth's moderately pro-Protestant views are, however, revised in a Catholic sense by the recent study of Helmut J.Mezler-Andelberg, "Erneuerung des Katholizismus und Gegenreformation in Innerösterreich" in *Südostdeutsches Archiv*, vol. XIII, Munich 1970, 97-118. Gerhard Florey, *Bischöfe, Ketzer, Emigranten. Der Protestantismus im Lande Salzburg von weinen Anfängen his zur Gegenwart*, Graz-Cologne-Vienna, 1967, examines the situation in Salzburg. As to Upper Austria see Hans Sturmberger, *Georg Erasmus Tschernembl*, Graz-Cologne, 1953, 81-226 and Georg Grull, *Bauer, Herr und Landesfürst*, Graz-Cologne, 1963, 1-9.

14. Karl Brandi, *Deutsche Geschichte im Zeitalter der Reformation und Gegenreformation*, Munich, 1960, 284-91, 540 f.; Hugo Hantsch, *Die Geschichte Österreichs*, Graz 1959, vol. I, 262-67, vol. II, 7-16.

15. H.J. Mezler-Andelberg, *op cit.* 109-11; Robert A. Kann, *The problem of Restoration*, Berkeley, 1968, 238-41.

16. Ernst W. Zeeden, *Das Zeitalter der Gegenreformation*, Freiburg i.B., 1967, 18-80, 95-112; H.J. Mezler-Andelberg, *op. cit.* 117.

17. J. Loserth, *op. cit.* 431-56; Hans Sturmberger, *Kaiser Ferdinand II* und das Problem des Absolutismus, Munich, 1957, 15-31; H.J. Mezler-Andelberg, *op. cit.*, 116 f.

18. Robert A. Kann, *A study in Austrian intellectual history. From late Baroque to Romanticism*, 2nd ed., New York, 1973, 47-49, 105-109.

19. Paul Molisch, *Geschichte der deutschnationalen Bewegung in Österreich*, Jena, 1926, 157 f., 179 f., 196 f., 211 f.

20. In a limited sense one can here allow for an exception regarding the Salzburg emigrés in Prussia under the reign of Friedrich Wilhelm I. See Thomas Carlyle, *History of Friedrich II of Prussia, called Frederick the Great*, London, 1900, 8 vols., see vol. III, 35-50.

21. See for instance Josef Wodka, *Kirche in Österreich. Eine religionssoziologische Studie*, Vienna, 1959, 353-63 where one finds some pointers. Erich Bodzenta, *Die Katholiken in Österreich*, Vienna, 1962, comes much closer to the problem; see 72-78.

Frederick G. Heymann

THE ROLE OF THE BOHEMIAN CITIES
DURING AND AFTER THE HUSSITE REVOLUTION

We take it for granted that in the period of the German reformation, with all the many difficulties and conflicts, the Imperial cities — or at least many of them — played a considerable role in the reforming process with its far-reaching changes in the Holy Roman Empire. From those cities, we derive a good deal of information on the events which occurred during the less than forty year period from the 95 Theses to the Peace of Augsburg. In the earliest of those years, down to the end of the so-called Peasants' War, the role of the greater cities was of special weight. We have only to think of Nuremberg, Augsburg, Ulm, Frankfurt, Strassburg (at that time a purely German city), but also the three great Swiss cities, Zürich, Basel and Bern, soon followed by the half-autonomous Geneva, in order to see that without those cities the Reformation, though especially influenced by Luther, Zwingli and Calvin, would hardly have developed so fast and so effectively. In Bohemia and Moravia, the two Czech territories within the realm of St. Wenceslas, the earlier reformation, usually called the Hussite Movement, had begun a hundred years before the first actions of Luther. Bohemia, of course, did not have Imperial cities within her borders. Yet, apart from the truly great city of Prague, the country had a considerable number of medium or minor cities which had the right to be called Royal cities, and which were normally not under the possession and the influence of the high nobility as were other cities and towns. In the Hussite reformation, and especially during the revolutionary war (1419-1436) the role of these cities had an effect which was probably greater than in any of the other reformatory movements.

During the early phase, especially up to 1421, it was the capital, Prague, which spoke for the people of Bohemia, directing her policy on the one side against her enemies and on the other side establishing some contact with friendly powers (e.g. Venice in the south, Poland in the north.(1) During the following years, not one but three groups of cities had been organized: those following the city of Prague at that time consisting only of the two separate boroughs on the right of the river: the Old (or Great) Town, and the New Town, built by the King-Emperor Charles IV (the ''Small Side'' had been largely destroyed). For a decade and a half, Prague had been not only the capital of Bohemia, but the whole Czech land had had no ruler, as King Sigismund, Charles IV's younger son, Hungary's King and since 1410 also the King of the Romans, had not been acknowledged by the great majority of the cities and their people.(2) There were a rather small number of essentially Czech Royal cities which had maintained (or in one case regained) their Catholic policy, and this was also true in the case of a few ethnically German cities near to the north or west border of Bohemia. But among the far greater numbers of Bohemian Royal cities there were many which had accepted Prague as their leading political (and religious) centre. In the further development of the Hussite Wars the Prague claim of being the only decisive leading centre was not fully maintained (even though Prague, or at least the Old Town of Prague, as the seat of the University, could declare that theirs alone was the true basis for understanding, organizing and deciding those acts which would present the real religious truth as created in the earlier Hussite development.) The capital city, in these years, lost a considerable number of those cities which had at first been under the direction of Prague. The reasons were that the more radical reformers were not willing to follow the more conservative elements, especially those who represented the majority of the priests who were also teachers at the University. A few had been personal friends of Jan Hus and Jerome of Prague, and were not yet willing to cut off completely the potential relationship to Rome. Some of them went so far in their intention as to limit the reformation to the one single demand: the permission to give the chalice with the blood of Christ to laymen. Others, especially the great figure of Jakoubek of Stříbro (Jacobellus of Mies)(3) went much farther in the ideas of reform, but later he, too, was not willing to accept the more radical thoughts of the Taborite revolutionaries. Only one great leader of Prague, Jan Želivský, organized to a considerable degree a close co-operation with the Taborites. His antagonists, however, among them some members of the nobility, had him and his close friends killed in March 1422(4) and though there were still a good many of his Prague people (especially in the New Town) following his ideas, the Old Town, with the University, maintained its cautious policy.

I cannot go into a description of all the important differences between Prague and Tabor, and especially the ideological and religious thoughts and activities in Tabor. We do not necessarily have to go into Czech historiography, since an American specialist, Howard Kaminsky, has given us an excellent knowledge and understanding of the origins and the development of the Taborite movement within the framework of the early Hussite Revolution and Reformation.(5) It is, probably, sufficient to emphasize that the Taborites went far beyond Hus himself and his close friends and followers: that they cut the weak relations with Catholicism by electing, in the person of Nicholas of Pelhřimov, their own bishop without feeling the need of the permanent law of episcopal ordination;(6) that they were, in their majority, Chiliasts, Puritans and Iconoclasts; that they did not believe in Transubstantiation; and that they did not use the Bible and the liturgy in languages other than the Czech. The centre of the Taborites, after a short time organized by Jan Žižka and other leaders in Plzeň (Pilsen), was established at the former town and castle Hradiště which was then renamed Tabor, its name to this day. At the first of the five foreign Crusades they sent Žižka with his army from Tábor to Prague to defend the capital. But in the longer run the Taborites and the Prague Utraquists got repeatedly into difficulty.

The city of Tábor did not remain alone. By 1421 no less than ten cities had taken the side of Tábor, forming the first effective brotherhood, whereas Prague had at that time still the great majority among the cities under her direction. But soon afterwards, another brotherhood, originally developing in one city of the eastern part of Bohemia, called Hradec Králové,(7) began to establish its special character. The movement was called the Orebites, after the biblical name of Mount Horeb.(8) For some time the cities in which the Orebites developed their Hussitism stood somewhere between the more cautious policy of the Old Town of Prague and the Taborites who in those years tended toward an even stronger radicalism. The priest and fighter who was most important among the Orebites was Ambrož (Ambrose) of Hradec.(9) But the most effective strengthening of the Orebite Brotherhood resulted from the fact that Jan Žižka, now by far the greatest among the Hussite leaders, had for religious reasons left Tábor and moved to Hradec Králové. This Orebite city shook off its dependence on Prague and soon added a steadily increasing number of other cities, especially in the east of Bohemia, which no longer remained under Prague's direction. In 1424, while Žižka was still the greatest military leader, the cities under Prague had been reduced to nine, and the only ones in direct contact with Prague were in the north, mostly along the Elbe river. Three years later, only five were left, and throughout the years in which the two brotherhoods dominated the existence of Hussite Bohemia the role of Prague had been considerably reduced. This was true all the more since the conservatives in the

University as well as some of the active members of the high nobility based their influence, apart from those few northern cities like Mělnik, Roudnice and Litoměřice, on the Old Town of Prague only whereas the New Town developed a very close relationship with the Orebites. The Lithuanian Prince Sigismund Korybut(10) who, in 1422 and again from 1424 to 1427, played at first a rather important role, hoping to become Bohemia's King, was eliminated when it became clear that he wanted to move Bohemia back into the Catholic organization without maintaining the elements of the Hussite reform. In the following years the war which had for too long been fought on Bohemian ground was now moving across the borders. These active military actions were led by the brilliant successor of Jan Žižka, the Taborite Priest-General Prokop the Bald (or "the Great"), in close co-operation with the Orebites who, after Žižka's death in 1424, called themselves the Orphans.(11) Both brotherhoods which for a few years had shown relatively little common action, except in responding to invasion of German troops, began in 1427 to operate closely together, and the great successes of the so-called "spanilé jízdy" (magnificent rides), in large parts of Germany, in Austria and in Hungary, were just as effective as the destruction of the last two Crusades sent into Bohemia at the demand of Rome and many of the German rulers. The mode of operation was based on an organization which made it possible in each of the cities, and sometimes also the remaining five cities under Prague, to use the well-trained members for the permanent service as men "working for God in the field" ("exercitus laboritorum in campis pro nomine Dei laborantes"). While this service willingly engaged in prolonged military activities, a limited number of potential militia was kept in the cities to do normal work but could be called in case their cities were in danger of attack. Thus the overwhelming number of cities, during the years up to 1434, felt that they belonged to the Hussite world and therefore would maintain their strength. In the diets which took place from time to time and which were organized in three curias: lords, knights and cities, the cities could feel that they were standing on the same level. To some extent they were actually stre..gthened by the fact that so many of the knights had joined with the brotherhoods in terms of religious as well as military co-operation. Among the lords there was still a considerable split, for a number of the leading lords, even some who had accepted the four Articles, had contacted King Sigismund and hoped to be again in his graces if and when the war should end with the acceptance of "the natural king". For a long time they had, with few exceptions, played a remarkably weak role — only some especially rich and powerful families not merely maintained their possessions but had even gained a good many lands and villages which, before the outbreak of the revolution, had belonged to the clergy, among them the bishoprics and the many monasteries. A process of secularisation went, in those years, very far.

The brotherhoods, at this time, had begun to hope for peace, and this was also true on the side of King Sigismund as well as the great majority of the Germans, especially in those regions of the Holy Roman Empire where they had been near to the Bohemian border. The peace negotiations began first in the Bohemian city of Cheb, then in the city of Basel where the great Council was getting together. But the peace had been prepared at the very time when a fierce battle began. It was a Civil War between the majority of the lords, many of the knights and the old Town of Prague with one other city (Mělník), all of them led by a Hussite general who himself was a Utraquist Knight against the brotherhoods of the Taborites and Orphans, who were defeated, losing their best leaders. The relation between the three groups, lords, knights, and cities, was again changed with the lords having regained much of their old strength.(12)

The battle of Lipany was a blow for those cities whose more radical religious leaders, especially the Taborites and their closest co-operators lost much — but by no means all — of their strong position. Yet Tabor, though no longer the dominant leader of the radicals, was strong enough to maintain much of its religious strength. Her position was still remarkable when the Emperor Sigismund in the short time during which he had assumed his Kingship of Bohemia (15 months until his death in 1437) gave to Tábor the status of a royal city. In the following years, the city of Tábor functioned as a fairly normal town, but her old traditions did not easily disappear.

During the years which followed the Hussite revolution, and the short rules of Sigismund and his son-in-law, Albert of Habsburg, ending in 1439, there was a long period of interregnum in which there was no king and no order. The high nobility did their best to fully regain their earlier position, but had difficulties because the difference between Catholic and Hussite began again to be very active. For a few years the most powerful among them, the Lord Oldrich of Rosenberg, who had seized enormous lands in the south of Bohemia, tried also to overwhelm the Hussite elements, from the nobility to the cities. If he had been successful the so-called Compactata — the peace arranged in Basel and finally and solemnly accepted at the Moravian city of Jihlava by Emperor Sigismund — would not have been maintained. In the early forties of the fifteenth century the situation in Prague was doubtful and it did not seem quite certain that the Utraquist church would survive, let alone strengthen herself. But Jan Rokycana, the greatest among the

reformers who had followed the Hussite ideas, whom the Bohemian
Diet had elected as Archbishop of Prague but who never received the
promised confirmation by the Papacy,(13) had worked several years
with many of his friends in Hradec Královè. It was at least the second
time that this important east Bohemian city showed her value. But in
1448, the young George of Poděbrady who represented the third
generation of Hussite nobles, conquered the capital of Prague and
overcame the attempts of the Catholic lords, especially Oldřich of
Rosenberg, to do away with the Hussite Church.

In 1452, the lord of Poděbrady became the real ruler of Bohemia. At
first he was regent and then, at the death of the young Habsburg boy-
King, Ladislas Posthumus — George himself was elected as King of
Bohemia. During these years down to the later sixties, George gave his
country a period in which not only the bitter religious antagonism
between the Hussite majority and the Catholic minority seemed to be
overcome, but in which also the political and economic situation seemed
to be in a remarkable healthy state. George did not attempt to force the
Hussite Utraquism upon any of the Catholic parts of the Bohemian
realm. He was wise enough not to force the Hussite reformation on such
lands as the duchy of Silesia or the Margraviates of Upper and Lower
Lusatia. Nor did he try to do this in those border regions where some of
the cities as well as their surroundings were ethnically German and
mostly Catholic. Among the six Royal cities of Moravia there were four
ethnically mainly German ones: Brno, Olomouc, Jihlava and Znojmo,
cities which had maintained their Catholic majority while the gentry as
well as the peasantry had been in their majority Hussites.(14)

Among the Royal cities in the central part of the realm, that is the
Kingdom of Bohemia proper, there were, after the Hussite Wars, no
less than 45 royal cities. The great majority of these cities either had
been religiously Hussite even before the outbreak of the revolution and
the war, or had in those years undertaken the reformation, occasionally
as the result of pressure but in the majority as the effect of a powerful
religious influence.

George of Poděbrady, the one and only Hussite King, did not want to
go too far in his Utraquist reformation and yet was willing to defend this
reform, especially in the laws of the Basel Compacts without which
there could have been no peace. The cities which had earlier fought for
the Hussite reformation could feel that they could continue in their
religious as well as in their political thoughts and actions. In the way in
which the cities of Bohemia had developed (to some degree under the
influence of German city laws such as those of Magdeburg or Augsburg)
they could usually expect the King's support. The Royal cities had

gained the right to elect their own judges whereas in earlier times, before the Hussite revolution, the city judges had been officials appointed by the King. By and large, King George had most contact with the patricians, some of whom had only gained their position when German patricians had lost their position before or during the Hussite wars. But in most of the cities the masses, whether they belonged to the lower guilds not represented in the council or in a general city commune, usually got along quite well with the great King's policy. There were, of course, exceptions. One of them occurred at an early time, immediately following George's election as regent in April 1452: George as well as the elected Archbishop of Prague, Jan Rokycana had repeatedly demanded that the Utraquist Church should be accepted by all Hussite groups, including the radical Taborites. Already in 1443, at a diet held in Kutná Horá, the issue of the real presence of Christ at the Eucharist had long been discussed. Eventually, the overwhelming majority of the representatives had decided that the Utraquists' views were "safer, better and more reliable".(15) Tábor, however, refused to accept this decision, and by 1452 the newly elected regent decided that the Taborites had to be forced to accept the Utraquist policy. With some difficulties — especially on the part of the old leaders, the Bishop Nicholas of Pelhřimov and the radical priest Václav Koranda the Elder who were imprisoned — the Taborite opposition was, at least in the form of an official representation, eliminated, and the great majority of the Utraquist Church, especially in the cities, could feel safe from internal fights.(16) On the other side, however, (apart from the northern, partly German towns) at least two Royal cities, although mainly Czech, were strongly active Catholic centres: one of them was Plzeň (Pilsen) which had shifted from Hussitism to Catholicism at the very early time of the Hussite Wars (1420);(17) the other was Česke Budějovice (Budweis). Both went along with the general policy throughout the greater part of George's rule but turned against him (as did the four leading Royal cities in Moravia and especially the Silesian capital of Breslau)(18) when the papacy as well as King Matthias Corvinus of Hungary and some German princes declared a sort of Crusade and with it forced upon Bohemia a "Second Hussite War".(19) But this policy was by no means followed by the few other (mostly German) Royal cities and the overwhelming majority of the Czech-ethnic Royal cities were and remained quite active in feeling and fighting for Hussite Bohemia. The enemies, on the whole, did not dare to attack those generally well fortified cities. Among the few which had been attacked by the Hungarian King, two, in Moravia, were Royal cities which had accepted the Hussite religion: Uničov, in the north and Uherske

Hradiště, in the south. They were not as great as the Four Catholic cities which had taken the side of the Pope and the Hungarian ruler. But those two remaining Royal cities of Moravia were effectively defended by King George's troops, and Uherske Hradiště especially(20) showed remarkable strength through a long siege during which that city was able to defend herself until the Czech army could relieve the city. In Bohemia another Hussite city, Chrudim, was attacked by a strong Hungarian army under Matthias Corvinus, but this attack turned out to have been a mistake. The cities as well as the villages of this part of Eastern Bohemia fought against the Hungarian, with results which had almost destroyed King Matthias' army and his hopes for gaining both the possession of the Bohemian realm and the right to become King of the Romans.(21) After the long continuing war between the Papal and Hungarian side against the Hussite Bohemia, King George died just as it looked as if he had gained a decisive success in defending his country and his Hussite Church.(22)

In the following years when a Bohemian branch of the Jagiello dynasty ruled from 1471 to 1526, the Royal cities of Bohemia continued among that majority who supported and believed in the Hussite-Utraquist Church. The first among the two Jagiellons, King Vladislav II, had promised to maintain the Compacts, but was himself a Catholic and was, on the whole, on the side of the Catholics. During his long rule, after some destructive wars with King Matthias of Hungary, he accepted a painful decision. This was the Peace of Olomouc (1478-79) which permitted both Kings their right to call themselves "King of Bohemia", but reduced Vladislav's possession to the central, proper Bohemia, whereas Matthias maintained the dependencies, including the mainly Czech Moravia. It was an arrangement which, in this form, could not survive for long.

The great majority of the cities, in this period, tried to strengthen the position of the Utraquist Church against the Catholics. In September 1483 this policy, mainly in the capital of Prague, resulted in a fierce rebellion of the people against the Catholics and also against the members of the city council who were claimed not to be sufficiently strong in their Utraquist ways, and some of whom were killed.(23) The King, as a good Catholic, wanted to punish the Praguers but did not find sufficient support. The only positive result, but indeed a great one, was the meeting of the Diet of Kutná Hora in March 1485. As usual there were the lords, the knights and the cities, and the final result was that the three curias accepted the Statutes in which members of both churches, Utraquists and Catholics, should guarantee each other on the basis of the Compacts, mutual tolerance and freedom of worship, even for subject people, for instance peasants, without regard to the religion of the lord. One can say that those Statutes of Kutná Hora were more advanced in the field of religious freedom than the Peace of Augsburg or the Edict of Nantes.(24) Only the third reforming religious group, the Bohemian Brethren, had begun to develop under King George but had been treated by him with little understanding. Now the Church of the Brethren had grown noticeably and had received considerable help from some of the nobles.

The history of the Brethren, in itself of the greatest significance, will not be treated in this short discussion. There were, indeed, some cities in which the Brethren found a sound basis for their development, and the religious significance of the Brethren was at least as important as that of the Utraquist Church. In the later fifteenth and early sixteenth century the Church of the Brethren was certainly more productive than was at that time the older Utraquist Church, even the so-called Neo-Utraquist Church which, however, was often considerably underrated. But most of the cities which made it relatively easy for the Brethren to establish themselves there were comparatively small places and not Royal cities. An important exception was Mladá Boleslav, a royal city which developed in the time of King Vladislav especially owing to the help of a Utraquist family of lords: the brothers Tovačovský of Cimburk.(25) Among these cities was also Litomyšl, not a Royal city but before the Hussite Revolution the seat of a bishopric. The influence of Litomyšl was largely directed by the Lords Kostka of Postupice, who had played a great role during the Hussite revolution and later under King George.(26) The cities which were active, religiously as well as politically, had to maintain a considerable degree of strength throughout the rest of the fifteenth and through almost the first half of the sixteenth century — a time when eventually the Hussite-Utraquist Church had become one of the number of separate but to some extent related churches which spread the Reformation all over Europe.

But there were some developments which were far from easy for the cities. During the time in which George of Poděbrady was King, and also under King Vladislav, at least his earlier sixteen years from 1471 to 1487, the cities could usually expect to get, if necessary, support from the knights in the meetings of the Diets, and these two curias together could be fairly sure that they would not be overwhelmed by the lords. In 1487, however, the two curias of the higher and lower nobility got together and decided that the peasantry had no right to leave the land of their masters, a decision marked by the beginning of the serfdom which, in the late fifteenth and early sixteenth century, was to be found also in Poland, in Hungary, and in parts of Germany (with bitter rebellions in

Hungary in 1514, and in Germany in the Peasant War of 1524-26). Among the Bohemian parts only Moravia maintained, for some time, the peasants right to leave their land.(27) The partial freedom of the peasantry had for a long time been considered as a benefit not only for the peasants themselves but also for the cities in which they might have wanted to establish themselves. This was now eliminated, to the disadvantage of the cities.

But this was only one issue which put the cities into a somewhat separate position. There were difficulties about the claim of the nobility to have the right to brew beer in addition to the old, traditional rights of the cities. There were other such differences, for instance the cities' right of taxation, their free use of the city judges, and many others. King Vladislav who, since the death of King Matthias Corvinus (1490), had also been King of Hungary, intended to spend most of his time in the eastern land and left Bohemia — which by now had regained her dependencies — for long periods in the hands of leading nobles.(28) For the lords this v. as in several ways a gain, but the cities were often annoyed and did their best to maintain their strength by close co-operation. In 1500 no less than 32 Royal cities, among them as leading ones the Old and the New Towns of Prague, Kutná Hora, Hradec Králové and Žatec, all of these strong Utraquist (among the rest were only one or two Catholic ones) declared themselves as a firmly co-operative association ready, if necessary, to build an army. Later they elected an organizing political and religious body which, if necessary, would fight against the lords.(29) But one of the leading princes, Duke Bartholomew of Münsterberg, a grandson of King George, took the side of the cities, and another grandson, Charles, had to undertake to support the young Louis whose father Vladislav II had died in March 1516. In the years of his kingship, to 1526, Louis showed himself to have somewhat better understanding and more will to act, and during the short visit to Prague (in 1523) he showed his strong interest and warmth in relation to the cities, and his will to reduce the high nobility with its dangerous selfishness. It was party because of this selfishness of the high nobility in both countries, Bohemia and Hungary, that the young King entered the war against Suleiman the Magnificent with inadequate forces and died, with thousands of the troops of his loosely mixed army, at the battle of Mohács in August 1526.

Although the immediate sufferers of this tragic event were the Hungarians, the year 1526 was also of the greatest influence upon Bohemia and her cities. The Jagiellon dynasty no longer supplied a king for Bohemia, and in its place the Habsburg prince and brother of the Emperor Charles V, Ferdinand I, was accepted by all three curias as the

King of Bohemia. From now on the throne was occupied by members of the Habsburg dynasty alone (with the exception of the two short attempts of the Wittelsbachs). But is was the time from the early sixteenth to the early seventeenth century during which the great majority of the Bohemian cities maintained the basic ideas of the Reformation, even when the Utraquist Church would, in the period of the Kingship of Ferdinand I, accept many new elements of the reforming thoughts which came from Luther as well as Calvin. We have no space in this short sketch to go into these details, and will have to be satisfied with the fact that Luther declared himself a true Hussite, and that indeed there were mutual influences to both reforming works and events.(30) On the other hand, King Ferdinand himself, though not a religious fanatic, would have liked to keep the Lutheran influences away from the Bohemian land. He had few objections to some of the Czech people being attached to a minority of the Hussites who declared themselves to be the ''Old Utraquists'', people who wanted nothing more than permission to receive the chalice at the Communion even when they were laymen, but who in every other way would follow the Catholic thoughts and doctrines with all their liturgical acts. There were some short phases in which, at least in parts of Prague and in the University, the tendency toward the policy of those ''Old Utraquists'' seemed to be gaining strength, and King Ferdinand was not the only one who was willing to support it. But the great leaders of the Utraquist Church did not go along with the ''Old Utraquists,'' and the active representatives of the Hussite religion were, with much justification, called the Neo-Utraquists. Their policy was still based upon thoughts which could, in the earlier years down to the end of the rule of King George, be best represented by Jan Rokycana, and during the following years, down to the end of the fifteenth century, his thoughts and his religious policy were faithfully maintained and to some extent developed by the man who had been elected as administrator of the Utraquist Consistorium: Wenceslas Koranda the Younger.(31)

The later developments of the Utraquist Church are usually discussed in the first place as events which have occurred in Prague, and it is understandable that in this great city with its separate boroughs many events and many changes occurred which we could not possibly discuss within this paper. But it would be wrong to omit the role of the other leading and religiously active cities, not only under King George and the Jagiellons, but also at the beginning of the Habsburgs. We have already mentioned some of these cities and it is remarkable that they never ceased to play some part in their religious policy. However in the later history the cities of Bohemia were to play a role which showed a remarkable degree of courage but which led to a most painful result.

This bitter story began with the decision of the Emperor Charlves V to destroy the Protestant principalities which, in 1531, had organized the Schmalkaldic League. In 1546 the Emperor felt sure that he would be able to mainly eliminate Protestantism in Germany. The Emperor's brother, King Ferdinand, should supply additional armies which Charles needed. Ferdinand gave the order that the Bohemian Estates should put together a very considerable force. The troops would, in their majority, have to be recruited from the cities.

At this time, as long before, the overwhelming number of the Bohemian cities was still Utraquist, although Lutheran and, to a lesser extent, Calvinist influences had begun to play a role.(32) In some of the cities the Bohemian Brethren had also played a highly interesting role, and none of the reformed churches were more unwilling to go into war. But the masses of the Utraquists and the related Protestants were just as determined not to fight for the Catholics against the Protestants, especially not against their neighbours in Saxony. Yet clear orders were given by the King not once but several times that the Bohemian troops should be present at the beginning of 1647 in the city of Litomerice from where he intended to cross over to Saxony. In the meantime, the cities had, in Prague, organized a league specifically against any war which would go against Saxony. Of all the many royal cities only three, all of them still Catholic, answered the King's order: Plzeň, Budějovice and Ústi (at the Elbe). Among the leading cities, apart from the capital, one of the most active among the Royal cities was Žatec whose contribution during the Hussite revolution had been extraordinary, among whose reforming figures were, with their Czech majority, also some important early reformers of German origin. In 1521 one of the radical reformers, Thomas Müntzer, visited in the first place Žatec before going to Prague. At this time during the Schmalkaldic War, the people of Žatec went so far in the attempt to prevent any help to the Emperor that the city made it impossible even for the King with his entourage to enter the city.(33)

The hopes to help the Saxon Elector against the two Habsburg rulers were soon destroyed. In April 24, 1547, at Mühlberg, Charles totally defeated the Saxon army and for some time it looked as if the Emperor's overwhelming Catholic position in Germany was permanently established. After the victory King Ferdinand returned with Spanish and Walloon troops put at his disposal by his brother.

For Bohemia, and especially the cities, this event was very serious. In Prague four leading people were executed, and no less than 24 cities which were considered to have acted against the King were severely punished by taking away parts of their walls and all their guns and other war materials. They had also to pay considerable amounts of money as punishment. There were cities whose role was considered to be especially dangerous and whose councils had been put before a sharp judgement. Apart from Prague they were, in the order of having been dangerously active, the cities Žatec, Litoměrice, Tabor, Hradec Králové and Klatovy. The last of this group had, already, played a role in the presence of members of the Bohemian Brethren, and the King acted in an especially harsh way against this church for which he (much like King George earlier) had no understanding and no readiness to leave them in their places. Even a few members of the high nobility who had supported the Union of Brethren could not save themselves from this treatment. The result was the first emigration from Bohemia (75 years later, in the Thirty Years War, such an emigration was to be enormously larger). Some of the emigrants went to Moravia but many others to Poland and Prussia. The other, greater number of essentially Utraquist-Protestant cities were generally permitted to return to their earlier official positions. After a part of the punishment had been paid, some were stopped. The King tried thereby to show that he was not too harsh with his subjects.

But the originally active religious and political attitude of the cities was now far weaker than it had been before. By now the role of the nobility in the Bohemian realm was greater, the role of the cities correspondingly poorer than it had been in the time of the Luxemburgs and their successors. In this way the events, from the "Confessio Bohemica" of 1575 through Rudolf II and his Letter of Majesty to the catastrophe of the battle of the White Mountain, have had some historical connection with the events of 1547. But perhaps it was remarkable enough that the Boehmian cities had worked for so long for their Hussite religion and had even shown influence upon the neighbouring countries who felt the same need for a living reformation — an event which, with its ups and downs, could live through almost a century and a half.

NOTES

1. See V.V. Tomek, *Dějepis města Przby* Vol. IV, 2nd edition, Prague 1899, 26 ff.; Palacký, *Urkundliche Beiträge zur Geschichte des Hussitenkrieges*, Vol. I, Prague 1872-73 (reprinted in Osnäbruck 1966), 39-43, 78-84, 96-98; *Archiv český*, III, 210, 213, 217, IV, 382; in English Heymann, *John Žižka and the Hussite Revolution*, Princeton 1955, 114ff., 131f., 220 ff.

2. See Heymann, "The National Assembly of Čáslav," *Medievalia et Humanistica*, VII, 1954, 32-35.

3. See H. Kaminsky, *A History of the Hussite Revolution*, Berkeley and Los

Angeles 1967, 180-204, 314 ff. F.M. Bartoš, *Husitská Revoluce (České dějiny,* II 7, vol. I, 113 ff).

4. See Kaminsky, *op. cit.*, 271-78, 377-383, 436-460, and Heymann, *John Žizka and the Hussite Revolution,* 214-217, 240-252, 307-318.

5. Apart from Kaminsky's work and that of Bartos there is the very valuable work by Josef Macek, *Tabor v husitskem revolucnim hnuti,* 2 vol. Prague 1955-56.

6. Kaminsky, *op. cit.*, 385-390, and later.

7. See Karel Michel, *Husitství na Hradecku,* Odbor KNV, Hradec Králové, 1956, and Alois Kubiček and Zdenek Wirth, *Hradec Králové,* Spořitelna Kralovehradecká, 1939.

8. See J.B. Čapek, "K vývoji a problematice bratstva Orebského", in *Československý časopis historický,* Prague 1966.

9. On Ambroz see Heymann, *Žižka,* 131 ff., 361-363.

10. *Ibid.,* 319-341, 417-421, 425, 460-61.

11. See Josef Macek, *Prokop Veliký,* Prague, 1953.

12. Macek, *op. cit.,* and R. Urbánek, *Lipany a konec polních vojsk,* Prague 1934.

13. See Heymann, "John Rokycana - Church Reformer between Hus and Luther" *Church History,* Vol. XXVIII, 1959, 240-280.

14. See e.g. F. Hoffman, *Jihlava v husitské revoluci,* Havlíčkuv Brod 1961, and C. D'Elvert, *Geschichte der Bergstadt Iglau,* Brünn 1850; also I.W. Fischer, *Geschichte der kgl. Stadt und Grenzfestung Olmütz,* Olomouc 1808.

15. See Z. Nejedlý, *Promeny k synodám strany Pražké a Táborské 1441-1440,* Prague 1900, pp. 32-38, and O. Odložilík, *The Hussite King, Bohemia in European Affairs 1440-1471,* New Brunswick 1965, 41 ff.

16. See Heymann, *George of Bohemia, King of Heretics,* Princeton, 1965, 60-63.

17. Bělohlavek, Kovář, Svab and Zeman, *Dejiny Plzně,* Vol. I, Plzeň 1965, 75 ff.

18. Heymann, *op. cit.,* 117 ff. 230 ff and R. Koebner, *Der Widerstand Breslaus gegen Georg von Podiebrad,* Breslau 1916.

19. Heymann, *op. cit.,* 476 ff.

20. *Ibid.,* 543-46.

21. *Ibid.,* 513 ff.

22. *Ibid.,* 572-585.

23. See e.g. Adolf Bachmann, *Geschichte Böhmens* Vol. II, Gotha 1905, 664-672.

24. See e.g. Heymann, *George of Bohemia,* 603-608.

25. See J. Th. Müller, *Geschichte der Böhmischen Brüder,* Herrnhut 1922, 164 ff. (also in Czech published by Bartoš, Prague 1923). A valuable early chronicle by Jiří Bydžovsky, *Kronika Mladoboleslavská,* originally published July 1645 (after the forced emigration of tens of thousands during the Thirty Years War), now again published by Zdeněk Kamper at Mladá Boleslav in 1935.

26. A very detailed and interesting history of Litomyšl was published by Zdeněk Nejedlý in Litomyšl, 1934.

27. See e.g. Kamil Krofta, *Dějiny československé,* Prague 1946, 296 ff.

28. Regrettably there exists, so far, no detailed work about the history of the period from the Jagiellons to the age of Ferdinand I. Of the Czech works, we

should mention Kamil Krofta's work just quoted (251-253); further *Přehled Československých dejin* part 1, Československá akademie věd, Prague 1948, 1958, 283-298, 313-335, and in western historical works Adolf Bachmann, *Geschichte Böhmens*, vol. II, Gotha 1905, 673-814, and Ernest Denis, *Fin de l'indépendance bohêmienne*, Paris 1890 and other editions in French (but also in Czech), Vol. I, second part (Les Jagellons).

29. See Bachmann, *op. cit.*, vol. II, 742 ff.

30. See Jaroslav Pelikan, Three articles in *Concordia Theological Monthly*, pp. 747-63, vol. XIX, 1948, and 496-517 and 829-843 in vol. X, 1949. Further S.H. Thomson, "Luther and Bohemia", *Archiv für Reformationsgeschichte*, vol. 44, (1953), 160-81, finally Heymann "The Hussite-Utraquist Church in the 15th and 16th Centuries," *Archiv für Reformationsgeschichte* vol. 52, 1961, 1-16, and "The Impact of Martin Luther upon Bohemia," *Central European History*, vol. I, No. 2, 1968, 107-131.

31. See K. Krofta, "Václav Koranda mladší z Nové Plzně", in his book *Listy z náboženských dějin českých*, Prague 1936, 240-287.

32. See above, n. 30.

33. The events which occurred in the years 1546-47 are presented not only in the works about the Bohemian history but also in all the many books and articles relating to the specific history of the many Bohemian cities. (Remarkably the corresponding German works discussing the events of the Schmalkaldic War do not mention the Bohemian events at all). One of the best reports can be found in the article by W. Katzerowsky, "Beteiligung der Stadt Saaz (Žatec) am böhmischen Ständestreite", *Mitteilungen des Vereins für Geschichte der Deutschen in Böhmen*, vol. XXIII, 1885, 228-245.

Peter Brock

THE HUTTERITES AND WAR, 1530-1800

Sixteenth century Anabaptism contained a violent as well as a nonviolent wing. Scholars have argued, not always conclusively, whether certain prominent figures in the movement should be reckoned as supporters of nonresistance or as its opponents. However, there is no doubt as to the communitarian Hutterite Brethren. From the outset they took an uncompromising stand against war and various forms of violence in society.

The group had originated in Moravia around the end of the 1520's and the beginning of the 1530's. Its members were all German-speaking; most of them were Anabaptist refugees from persecution in other lands, who had sought religious freedom in tolerant Moravia. Dwelling in the midst of a linguistically and ethnically alien population and shut off from their Czech neighbours by their special way of living, the Hutterites were able to insulate themselves from their surroundings more effectively than any other branch of the Anabaptist movement or of its Mennonite successor. The Hutterites experienced no patriotic urges; they felt no intimate ties with the people and region. Their members' overwhelming sense of group solidarity and the knittedness of their lives go far to explain the boldness with which they presented their witness to the world.

After a period of ideological confusion the group, in 1533, had accepted the leadership of an emigré from the Tirol, Jakob Hutter, a simple hatter by trade. Expelled from Moravia in 1535 on account of the Münster troubles, the Hutterite Brethren, as they now called themselves, were permitted to return shortly afterwards, the Moravian nobility who had harboured them being unwilling to lose permanently such model tenants as the Hutterites proved to be. In 1536, however, the Brethren lost their leader Hutter, who was arrested and executed while visiting his native Tirol.

It was the second half of the sixteenth century, in particular, that marked a golden age in the history of the Hutterite Brethren. Secure in the protection of powerful Moravian magnates and bound together by a strong sense of community, they prospered economically. They did not cease to be essentially a body of farmers and artisans. Yet their educational level — and e en their cultural achievement — was no mean one, especially if we compare it with the level reached by the indigenous rural population. At its height the fellowship numbered between 20,000 and 30,000 members, scattered among some 100 *Brüderhofe*. From 1546 on, a few communities came into existence in northern Hungary (i.e., Slovakia). Indeed, at this period the Hutterite brotherhood did not yet constitue the closed sect it was eventually to become, but was filled with missionary zeal to carry its message to other parts of central Europe. If ''the whole world were like us'', Jakob Hutter had said, ''then would all war and injustice come to an end''.

What distinguished the Hutterites from other Anabaptists was of course their religious communism, the belief that holding all things common was no mere counsel of perfection but an essential article of the Christian faith. Those who failed to do this acted falsely: true Christians should not hold fellowship with them. For the rest, Hutterites modelled their faith very largely on the pattern of evangelicial Anabaptism, from which indeed they had derived their origin. They practised adult baptism on confession of faith. They rejected oaths, courts of law, and the magistracy, while recognizing the office of the sword as an institution ordained by God which, although outside the perfection of Christ, remained essential, because of man's sinful nature, for the continued existence of the world. But between the ''world'' and the ''kingdom of God'' an unbridgeable gulf yawned. Hutterites shared, too, the evangelical Anabaptists' belief in the redemptive value of suffering, regarding suffering as the inevitable lot of true Christians on earth. Like their master, they must be ''as a lamb led to the slaughtering-block'' (in the words of the Hutterite leader Peter Walbot, written *ca.* 1577). Instead of seeking revenge for injuries done them, Christians must ever exemplify outgoing love. Therefore Hutterites condemned participation in war, and they refused military service. In fact, their witness for peace was more radical than that of the Anabaptist Mennonite mainstream, for Hutterites, unlike the latter, consistently refused to pay war taxes or to perform any kind of labour they believed to be connected with the prosecution of war.

In the *Account of Our Religion, Doctrine and Faith (Rechenschafft unserer Religion, Leer und Glaubens)*, which the intellectual leader of mid-century Hutteritism, Peter Riedemann, composed in 1540-41, we find a detailed exposition of his community's opposition to war taxation. When Christ told his followers to render unto Caesar the things that were Caesar's, ''he spoke not of taxation for the shedding of blood''. Therefore, Riedemann continues, ''where taxes are demanded for the special purpose of going to war, massacring and shedding blood, we give nothing. This we do neither out of malice nor obstinacy but in the fear of God, that we make not ourselves partakers of other men's sins''. Riedemann obviously regards all warfare as essentially aggressive, destructive rather than constructive in character, and different in its aims and methods from the enforcement of domestic order. The waging of war by the state he brands as ''wanton wickedness''. Neither Christ, nor St. Paul in his epistle to the Romans, had intended to justify support of this, while enjoining the payment of ordinary taxes for the upkeep of the magistrates even if the latter should use part of the money wrongly. ''We . . . give it not for their wrong use, but for their appointed office. But because wars and the destruction of nations are more against their office than with it, nothing is ordained them for this purpose, and we can give nothing for this for the sake of the office, since it is not appointed.''

Threat of Turkish invasion appeared in Moravia (not for the first time) at the end of the 1570's, and with it demands from the authorities for extraordinary taxation for the purpose of resisting the enemy. Thus, the Hutterites were now faced with putting their principles into practice; for it seems as if over the previous decade they had experienced little trouble in regard to this issue. In 1579-80 on their refusing payment of a special war levy, cattle, sheep, horses, and other property were seized from the *Brüderhofe* to meet this demand. In 1584 and again in 1589 when similar demands were made, the same procedure ensued on refusal. The brethren joyfully accepted the spoiling of their goods. For had not Paul the apostle said in his epistle to the Hebrews (X, 34) that for this they would receive in heaven ''a better and an enduring substance''? Therefore, it was preferable to suffer in this way ''rather than do what would be a stain, spot and burden to our consciences''.

From 1596 on, special war taxation became an annual affair: war with the Turks had begun again three years earlier. In 1595, in expectation of the testing time which awaited them, the elders of the community had resolved as follows: ''If something is taken away from us by force, for instance, taxation by the authorities, one should not resist them with improper words. Or if the soldiers take something away from us or press hard upon us with wicked words, then nobody should be caught in talking back to them which might cause them to do harm to the *Gemein* (community). In this every earnest Christian should be very careful." The elders told the governor (Landeshauptmann) of Moravia, Fridrich of Žerotin, that they conscientiously objected either to making contributions of money to the war against the Turks or to allowing their horses and waggons to be used for military purposes, because such aid would signify a willing participation on their part "in the shedding of blood". A little later they wrote to the Emperor Rudolf II in further explanation of their stand. Fear of God, they told him had motivated their disobedience. Žerotin, moreover, was one of the Hutterites' warmest friends among the Moravian nobility: yet they had preferred to risk his displeasure and the possibility of expulsion from his lands rather than compromise on this issue.

The Hutterites manifested an equally uncompromising spirit in regard to war work. We have just seen that whereas they had no scruples concerning their obligation to perform whatever corvées might be required of them if these were unconnected with war, they were not prepared to act as teamsters with the army, even at the risk of antagonizing a powerful protector. An even more heroic witness had been shown in 1539 after some 90 members had been arrested by order of Ferdinand I and sent as galley slaves to the Mediterranean fleet. There they refused orders to row — and despite floggings they persisted in this refusal, explaining that their disobedience resulted from the warlike character of such labour. For the fleet, they said, was organized to fight "against the Turks and other enemies (and) for use in plundering and war; . . . therefore they were as little willing at sea as they were on land to commit wrong or to sin against God in heaven".

In the same way Hutterites forbade their members to manufacture weapons of war. Riedemann has a section on this in his Rechenschafft entitled "Concerning the Making of Swords". Pointing to Christ's commandment to beat swords into ploughshares and to eschew revenge, he goes on: "Now, since Christians must not use and practice such vengeance, neither can they make the weapons by which such vengeance and destruction may be practised by others . . . Therefore, we make neither swords, spears, muskets nor any such weapons. What, however, is made for the benefit and daily use of man, such as bread knives, axes, hoes and the like, we both can and do make . . . If they should ever be used to harm another, we do not share the harmer's guilt, so let him bear the judgment himself." This policy was consistently carried out by the communities throughout the subsequent decades. We find Hutterite craftsmen famous throughout Moravia and even beyond its frontiers for their axes, pruning-hsears, bread-knives, and such instruments, the primary purpose of which was for domestic use. But they refused absolutely to have anything to do with the manufacture of guns, swords, pikes, daggers, etc.

Outsiders, even the Hutterites' enemies, testified to the high moral standards of these simple German peasants and to the consistency with which they lived out their religion. This, however did not prevent the expulsion of the Hutterites from Moravia in 1622, a consequence of the Protestant defeat at the Battle of the White Mountain in Bohemia two years earlier. It was not, in fact, surprising that the Hutterites now had to go: all who were unwilling to accept Catholicism were forced into exile, including proud noble families like the Žerotins.

For the next 140 years the Hutterite brotherhood became centered in Habsburg-ruled Slovakia. Even though a limited measure of religious freedom continued to exist in this area and the noble landowners welcomed religious dissidents who brought them economic profit, the Hutterites, like other Protestants, were subjected to increasing pressure from the Jesuits and the other forces of the Counter-Reformation. To compound their difficulties, they also suffered not infrequently from the depredations of Turkish raiders based on the occupied central and southern parts of the Hungarian kingdom: in many *Brüderhofe* men, women, and children were slaughtered or carried off into slavery. Their chronicles for this period continually lament the misfortunes which befell the brethren from the various soldieries — by no means only Turkish — who rampaged at intervals through the land.

The Turkish menace disappeared at the end of the seventeenth century: religious intolerance remained. It reached a climax in the reign of Maria Theresa (1740-80). Prompted by her Jesuit advisers the queen and her officials, by confiscating Hutterite devotional books, by suppressing their services or worship, by seizing their children and educating them in the Catholic faith, and by the forcible conversion of all but the most determined adults, succeeded by the 1760's in making the further existence of independent communities impossible. In Slovakia the sect was altogether suppressed, though after their forcible conversion to Catholicism its members were permitted for several generations to continue their communal way of life. (They were henceforward known as the *Habaner,* a nickname given them by the Slovak peasants.) In Transylvania, however, where a solitary *Brüderhof* had existed since 1621, the Hutterites remained intact. There the accession to the Hutterite faith in 1756 of a group of Lutheran migrants from Carinthia had instilled new life into the dwindling sect. But it felt insecure now under Habsburg rule; and so in 1767 the whole group fled across the mountainous frontier into Wallachia, moving on three years later to Ukraine, where a Russian nobleman, Count Rumiantsev, had offered them a haven on his estate at Vishenka.

Despite a modest revival of the *Brüderhofe* in the middle of the seventeenth century under the able leadership of the miller Andreas Ehrenpreis, who proved a worthy successor to Hutter, Riedemann, and Walbot in the preceding century, the period from 1622 onwards had been one of decline in most respects: size, economic development, cultural level, and spiritual vitality. This need not surprise us in view of the successive blows dealt the Hutterite brotherhood either by its rulers or by invaders from outside. During the Thirty Years' War the communities continued to refuse payment of war taxes "as our forefathers had also refused to do" (to quote the words of their *Klein-Geschichtsbuch*). As of old, various items of property were confiscated, and to this the brethren meekly submitted in consonance with their belief in nonresistance.

In 1633, however, an incident had occurred which shook the brotherhood to its foundations: at Sobotište members of the local *Brüderhof* offered violent resistance when servants of a local nobleman Ferenc Nagy-Michaly, attempted to requisition some of their horses. True, it was not a very serious affair. The men of the community had seized the nearest lethal instrument, whether it were ax, pitchfork, or stick, and driven Nagy-Michaly's people off. No one was killed or even seriously injured: a bruised limb or two and some cuts was all the damage that was done. The outbreak of violence took place at a time when the farm manager had just died and the elder of the community was laid up in bed, and there was no one present with sufficient authority to control the situation. It happened, moreover, when nerves were already strained as a result of the incidence of sporadic acts of violence at the community's expense: now these nerves had simply snapped. Although there are indications that in areas where the brethren had recently suffered assault a few members had gone around armed at least with nonlethal weapons, this does not really appear to have portended a wholesale abandonment of nonviolence even among those who participated in the mêlée. Yet the leaders of the brotherhood were profoundly shocked. For one thing, it threatened to have serious repercussions, since a member of the nobility was involved: several brethren who had taken part in the fray had been arrested and were threatened with deportation for forced labour at a fortress on the Turkish frontier. Moreover, even though Nagy-Michaly was eventually placated after the community had paid a large fine in compensation for the injuries done to his servants, the moral stain remained. For the first time in the history of the brotherhood, violence had been used. Only a stern warning, thought the leaders, would bring home the gravity of this to all members.

At a "great assembly" of church leaders, held at Levar on 28 November of the same year, an ordinance was passed dealing with the subject of nonresistance. Its author was almost certainly Andreas Ehrenpreis. The conduct of the Sobotiště brethren was inexcusable, it stated. The brethren who, "in their eagerness to preserve the property of the *Gemein*", had recently acted with violence, "rashly out of human weakness", were called upon to repent. Those who should transgress this ordinance in future, whether by open violence or by "cursing and slandering and (anything) which could provoke anger", were threatened with the ban.

The ordinance seems to have had its effect. At any rate, we do not hear again of any violent outbreaks of this kind among the Hutterites in the period prior to their settlement in Russia.

On the Rumiantsev estates in Russia the Hutterites enjoyed freedom from military service as one of the conditions of their settlement contract. When in 1787 a special war tax was imposed by Catherine II, the Hutterites, while they rejected direct payment, finally agreed to a proposal of the count's agent that the community should give the count a fixed annual sum, out of which the latter would forward the monies owing to the government in the way of special taxation. The Hutterites knew that if the contribution demanded by the government did not reach its coffers somehow they faced the possibility of expulsion from the country. On the other hand, the count did not relish the idea of losing such excellent tenants and was anxious to find some way out of the dilemma. A new contract was drawn up immediately incorporating the proposal agreed upon. The arrangement, it would seem, was to some extent a face-saving device; the brethren could not have failed to be aware that included in the new impost was the war tax, the payment of which they had declared to be contrary to their consciences. It is difficult to imagine sixteenth-century Hutterites agreeing to a solution of this sort. Perhaps their descendants were made of weaker stuff than they were or, more likely, the tragic experiences of the two preceding centuries led the Hutterites at this juncture to value the advantages of a secure resting-place for their continued existence as a people above the merits accruing to each individual from a rigid adherence to the letter of the religious discipline.

Nine years later, when a new Rumiantsev owner took over the estate at Vishenka, he proceeded to double the amount of the yearly tribute. This brought home to the Hutterites the precariousness of their situation. They stalled at first — but finally paid up. "The community", wrote their chronicler, "had reservations about contributing such money, because it was known now that it had been raised by the young count instead of the recruitment, and they could not give aid to war in good conscience. After many discussions it was finally agreed to pay the required sum, but only for a short time . . . until our matter should be decided upon by the Emperor''. The Emperor Paul, who had just succeeded to his mother's throne, continued, as she had done, to look with favour on groups like the Hutterites and the Mennonites (who, like the Hutterites, had recently arrived in Russia). His *Gnadenbrief* of September 1800, issued to the former and promising them and their descendants, among other things, freedom of worship and exemption from all military duties on payment of a general land tax to the state, parallelled the guarantees given simultaneously to the Mennonite community in Ukraine. These privileges were confirmed by Alexander I on his accession the next year. In 1802 the Hutterites left Vishenka to settle on near-by crown lands. For government purposes, henceforward Hutterites and Mennonites were classed together. Thus the nineteenth century opened a new chapter in the history of the Hutterites.

Note

I have discussed the Hutterite attitude to war on a broader background in my book *Pacifism in Europe in 1914* (copyright (c) 1972 by Princeton University Press). I would like to thank Princeton University Press for permission to include excerpts (from pp. 234-246) in the present study. This study represents not research in depth, but an attempt at synthesis.

The Hutterites were excellent record-keepers, and their chronicles provide rich source materials for a study of this kind. Of these chronicles, there are three major collections available in modern scholarly editions: *Die Geschichts — Bücher der Wiedertäufer in Oesterreich-Ungarn,* ed. Josef Beck (Vienna, 1883), a mosaic of shorter items arranged chronologically; *Geschicht-Buch der Hutterischen Brüder,* ed. Rudolf Wolkan (Macleod, Alta, and Vienna, 1923), known usually as "Das grosse Geschichtsbuch"; *Das Klein-Geschichtsbuch der Hutterischen Brüder,* ed. A.J.F. Zieglschmid, (Philadelphia, 1947), written by elder Johannes Waldner between 1793 and 1802, to which the editor has appended a bibliography of the Hutterite movement. Zieglschmid also published an orthographically exact replica of the manuscript "Grosse Geschichtsbuch", which was compiled by successive annalists between ca. 1565 and 1665: *Die älteste Chronik der Hutterischen Brüder* (Ithaca, N.Y., 1943). All these volumes contain some material on Hutterite nonresistant principles and practice. For the Hutterite view of war, as for every other aspect of their ideology, Peter Riedemann's *Rechenschafft* is essential. With every page studded with Biblical quotations or paraphrases, the treatise is marked by the clarity, cogency, and force with which the author sustains his arguments and by the graphic character imparted by the occasional example taken from daily life. Since there is a static quality about Hutterite doctrine, Riedemann's exposition holds for most of the subsequent history of the group. (H:s book was written in 1540-41 but not published until 1565). I have used the translation made by Kathleen E. Hasenberg: *Account of our Religion, Doctrine and Faith* (London, 1950). František Hrubý published in his study, "Die Wiedertäufer in Mahren". pt. 2. *Archiv für Reformationsgeschichte,* vol. XXX (1933), on pages 185-196, an account of the taxes imposed on the Hutterites between 1570 and 1620, in which he gives frequent citations from the original sources. The Hutterite ordinance of 1633 on nonresistance has been translated and published by the leading authority on the Hutterites, Robert Friedmann, who has written extensively on their history and thought. It originally appeared in the *Mennonite Quarterly Review*, vol. XXV, no. 2 (April 1951), and was reprinted in his *Hutterite Studies* (Goshen, Ind., 1961).

General information on the history of Hutterite nonresistance is given, among other places, in John Horsch, *The Hutterian Brethren 1528-1931* (Goshen, Indiana, 1931), and Victor John Peters, "A History of the Hutterian Brethren 1428-1958" (Ph.D. dissertation, University of Göttingen, 1960). Peters is also the author of an excellent introduction to the twentieth-century *Brüderhofe* in the New World: *All Things Common: The Hutterian Way of Life* (Minneapolis, 1965). Data concerning the large literature on the Hutterites is to be found in Hans J. Hillerbrand, *A Bibliography of Anabaptism 1520-1630* (Elkhart, Indiana, 1962; German-language edition, Gütersloh, 1962), esp. pt. I (3), and current publications are usually listed annually in the April issue of *Mennonite Life,* published at North Newton, Kansas. For the background of Moravian Anabaptism, see the recent study by a scholar of Czech origin, J.K. Zeman, *The Anabaptists and the Czech Brethren in Moravia 1526-1628* (The Hague, 1969), as well as his supplementary *Historical Topography of Moravian Anabaptism* (Goshen, 1967), originally published in three separate issues of the *Mennonite Quarterly Review*, vols. XL and XLI (1966-67).

Marianka Sasha Fousek

ON SECULAR AUTHORITY AND MILITARY SERVICE
AMONG THE BOHEMIAN BRETHREN
IN THE 16TH AND EARLY 17TH CENTURIES

The social ethos of the *Unitas fratrum* changed drastically when the Brethren decided to give up their principles and way of life which they inherited primarily from Peter Chelčický and their founding father, Gregory the Tailor. The revolution was formally completed in 1495, when the authority of the older writings, especially those of Br. Gregory, was formally rejected by *Unitas'* official leadership.(1) The about-face was both theological and sociological, or at least had profound sociological consequences. The older Brethren had rejected from their midst secular power ('the power of the sword') and trade as totally unbecoming for a Christian. There were other trades which had been banned as well, and country-life had been seen as just about the only safe way to salvation. City-life had been thought of as not only more corrupt and tempting, but as also involving civic responsibilities which the Brethren had thought to be forbidden to Christians, who must avoid both the oath and magisterial powers — primarily those of passing verdicts which deprived others of life, property or exposed them to cruel punishments. The older *Unitas* has thus also naturally barred its doors to the nobility.(2) Now, however cautiously, the doors were opened to the more dangerous professions in the cities, to civic responsibilities and even to the nobles.

While all this was a revolution, it was a cautious one; the *Unitas* did not exactly encourage its members to enter into work and positions which it still and for a long time to come (and some practically throughout its history) considered dangerous to salvation, nor did the Brethren make it easy for nobles and others in power to enter their ranks and to live in their communion. Moreover, we need to keep in mind that a group of Brethren — the ''Minor Party'' — seceded from the greater *Unitas* in protest over the betrayal of *Unitas'* original principles.

In spite of all the caution and warnings against the temptations and corruptions of the paths of life newly opened to the Brethren, the *Unitas* soon became an essentially *urban* phenomenon, living in cities belonging to its noble patrons. Of the aristocracy it was primarily the *barons* who entered the *Unitas* — at least until 1530.

In our pursuit of the development of *Unitas'* social ethos in the era of the 16th century, we shall concentrate on its directions to its members in secular authority and on how they pictured them. A treatment of the entire social ethos of the Brethren would unfortunately take much more space than we have at our disposal. But something of the general flavor of the Brethren's life, and attitudes toward life in the world and in the Christian community should come through even in this limited investigation.

It is an irresistible temptation to see certain striking analogies between the development of the *Unitas* and the early Christian Church in this sphere. While at the time of Origen, e.g., Christians were accused of social irresponsibility for their refusal to serve as magistrates or defend the Empire, and Origen could not conceive of Christians 'bearing the sword' for the defense of internal or external peace, Athanasius and Ambrose in the next century praised brave soldiers in war, and Emperor Theodosius II allowed only Christians in the Army (416 A.D.). The Bohemian Brethren never became a majority church, of course, and so they never faced the same problem as the Church in the 4th or 5th century. Also, in general, they maintained a much more cautious attitude toward the sword in Christian hands (especially in the matter of going to war) and kept warning their nobility of the precariousness of their position before God. The one exception, as we shall see, at least in the 16th century, will be Benedict *(Beneš)* Bavoryňský, writing in the early 1530's.

The *Unitas* did not encourage its members to write in their own name or on their own initiative. Even when an individual wished to write on his own he was almost required to receive a sort of *imprimatur* or *nihil obstat* from the governing Select Council *(Úzká rada)* of the *Unitas*. Thus, almost all of the writings directed to those in power are in the form of official "decrees," or "directives" issued by the *Unitas'* governing Council or the general conventions, or synods, of the entire *Unitas*. These synods gradually became composed entirely of clergy. Participation of lay delegates at synods became a complete exception and then disappeared altogether (we know of lay participation at synods in 1490, in 1500 and 1534, the last date being apparently the last occasion; it was at this synod that the baptism of converts from other Churches was abolished); this otherwise regrettable feature saved at least the *Czech* branch of the *Unitas* from coming under too great an influence of its aristocratic members. (In Poland the *Unitas* unfortunately lost is character as a Church of the commoners, becoming almost choked by its noble benefactors.) Most of the directives concerning secular authority certainly 'mince no words' in a deference to the high-born.

The earliest decrees concerning the acceptability of the noble and rich in the *Unitas* — as long as they are willing to subject themselves to the discipline of the *Unitas* — date from the 1490's naturally. The one recorded in the official collection of *Unitas' Decrees* justifies its new policies along the following lines: There is no discrimination (of status) before God. Actually, even the poorest and lowest men can be luxury-prone, and proud, and there are rich who can be humble. Besides, the Church on earth is not perfect, being a net which catches all sorts of fish; the apostles had both rich and poor among their converts. We cannot exclude the high-born or the rich, as long as they will accept our discipline, since Christ *accepted sinners. (sic.)* The keeping of money and the carrying out of trade can be done well or ill; all we can do is to give instruction and warning, and leave the rest to God and to the conscience of the person concerned. As the Lord Jesus said, ''Do not judge, etc.,'' for ''we know only imperfectly.'' As there are no explicit Scriptural passages about many things, we need to ''commit ourselves'' and our future — after a careful seeking of God's will — ''to the faithful Creator'' in the hope that he will not let us err in our decisions in an irreparable way.(3)

Then there is the decree concerning nobles which is apparently a rephrasing of principles from Augustine's *De civitate Dei* (V. 24) and which we find in the 4th volume of *Unitas'* archives *Acta (Akty)* under the title ''The Convenient Cloak prepared by Luke and his Brethren for the Sake of the Nobles'' — evidently dubbed so and originally preserved by the Minor Party. ''We consider those nobles happy who remember they are men and pay no attention to flattery, etc., are slow to exercise vengeance and never exercise it except to govern and protect the commonweal, forgive easily — not to forgive injustice but in the hope of restoring and correcting the offender — and if they have to judge someone severely balance it by mercy, gentleness and benevolence.''(4) This, too, apparently dates from the 1490's. In many ways, these thoughts pervade all of the later decrees and directives of the *Unitas* addressed to the nobles.

In spite of the laudatory style of the above decree it is clear that *Unitas'* acceptance of magistrates into its membership was far from joyful welcome; public offices and functions remain considered dangerous to the soul. So the 1499 Decree confirms the earlier decision that the *Unitas* accepts "secular authority" in its midst, that is, "those lords or officials, councilmen or mayors who have their position for worthy reasons and *cannot get away from them.* "(5) *(italics ours)* Would-be officials are told not to run after secular offices;(6) Brethren are forbidden to bring suits against each other before secular courts; even when their adversary is not a member of the *Unitas* they are to be extremly hesitant before going to a secular court, especially if the case does not affect one's livelihood or arises from a desire for vengeance or might endanger someone's life (capital cases).(7) Mayors and councilors are to avoid being the cause of any accused person's death;(8) no Brother is to hire himself out as a lawyer; if he is to defend anyone before a secular court he must consult the Seniors of the *Unitas,* and he may not defend anyone whose cause is not just.(9) Brethren are even warned not to volunteer to serve as witnesses before secular courts; even if they are certain of a case and the case is just, they and their counselors (from among the Brethren) must beware lest their witness will not cause a greater evil and thus go against *God's* justice.(10) The Brethren are especially warned against military service, especially if the war is unjust. But *no* Brother is to serve as a *mercenary* soldier; if he is required to provide military service, he is to pay an outsider (i.e., not a Brother) to perform it if at all possible. If a Brother cannot avoid being a soldier he is to avoid actual warfare if at all possible. "For either he himself will be killed in his sins or kill someone else in his sins, or do great injury to others by taking their property or burning it . . . Wars are against the natural law, the Old Law (Testament) and the New."(11)

Those who are in secular authority are to know that they are called to a work, namely to be servants of the people. The high-born are not to exalt themselves above men but know that they are equals by nature and servants by their character (condition); they are to use their authority for the benefits of their subjects.(12) Their actual service consists in governing, judging and disciplining so that the subjects might earn their living in peace and not harm one another.(13)

Since an important part of the nobility's responsibilities were their judicial functions, these early decrees, as well as many of the later directives to the nobility, set out to describe what the *Unitas* expected of its members in their function as judges in secular court. (Cases among Brethren were not to be judged there but before *Unitas'* own "Judges," or local lay Elders, whose main function was to reconcile plaintiffs and defendants and bring the guilty to voluntary reparation and repentance, on the pain of church discipline in case of obduracy.) The directives to the nobility concerning justice are both 'philosophical' and concrete, giving definite guidance and yet leaving much to the judge's own spiritual discernment. Customary and positive secular laws receive scant attention mostly to the effect that the nobility should not take advantage of them but pay attention to God's justice instead.(14) The judges, while they should not be ''respecters of persons,'' need to take into account the circumstances, occasion, and causes of the offence, as well as the condition (state) of the accused. The goal of the punishment is to be the correction of the accused or of others. Punishments may be by means of verbal embarrassment (private or public), without anger, by the taking away of honor, of property or even by corporal punishment and by taking away of life. When fines are to be imposed or property taken away the judge must consider whether this can lead to correction or whether he is not motivated by his own avarice. The judges should not fine or take away property from the ignorant or the weak or where it would work against the common good, or to avenge themselves or the ordinances of their ancestors. Likewise with all other types of punishments the judge must consider whether the desired end will be achieved by the severe punishment, whether a lighter punishment might not work better, and whether the offence really calls for such a heavy punishment, such as demotions from office, expulsion from the community or guild, torture, prison or death. In all of the punishments it is necessary to avoid cruelty, anger, revenge and hatred, but rather judge with mercy and ''turn the laws to the present advantage of the subjects.'' Moreover, secular power is not to be wielded in the interest of things spiritual.(15)

The last of these early directives reminds the nobles not to think of the subjects as ''theirs,'' but as God's people and Christians, entrusted to them for government, preservation and defense. They are to lighten the unjust burdens which had been imposed on their subjects previously and not allow any such new ones. They are to have mercy on the needy and help them make a living. Finally, they are not to exact cruel taxes or corvee labor just because these may be in their rights.(16)

The poor, on the other hand, are admonished by the same series of decrees, to consider their state as safer for salvation than that of the rich; to be patient, not envy the rich and not make claims on their property (literally: not make rights for themselves in receiving). They should serve the rich faithfully but without flatteries. They should bear their wants with patience, knowing that the future life in heaven is full of delights and without any wants.(17) The *Unitas* certainly did not train or incite peasant or proletarian rebels or uprisings! It is not surprising that the aristocracy was eager to have the Brethren as their subjects and protected such reliable and diligent subjects as much as they could from the king's fury. The Brethren's churches flourished on the estates and in the cities of the gentry and feudal lords who gave them their protection. It is a small *wonder* that under such conditions *Unitas'* spiritiual leaders in Bohemia and Moravia were by and large consistent in their demands that the noble members of the *Unitas* must submit themselves to its directives and discipline.

We have dealt in some detail with the directives from the first years of *Unitas'* accepting the higher classes into its membership — they all apparently date from the end of the 15th century — to show with what seriousness the *Unitas* undertook its newly accepted task of taking spiritual charge of classes it previously considered beyond the reach of ordinary means of grace, what high expectations it had of its converts in positions of tempting authority, and how true it stayed to these basic guidelines in most of the many directives to the nobility which were to follow in the next century. The tone has been set.

II.

The next period which furnishes us with admonitions to and a picture of the nobles in the *Unitas* is 1510, a year marked by pastoral encyclicals from *Unitas'* Seniors (bishops and lay officers) calling the Brethren to repentance in view of the widespread persecution which hit the *Unitas*, especially its Bohemian part, after the "St. James Mandate of 1508" (an edict directed against the *Unitas)* became the law of the land of Bohemia. The Brethren always interpreted catastrophes as a chastening rod of God calling them to self-examination and repentance. The picture which the "Letter of the Senior Brethren to the Churches" paints of the life of *Unitas'* rich and powerful members is not a pretty one.

> "The few who are high born have brought into the *Unitas* wordly dignities, as if they were some gods and as if they deserved to receive more from their noble birth than one receives from spiritual rebirth. And they do not know that they are more miserable than the commoners and stand in greater danger and lead others to greater danger . . . rarely does one find one who has really given up his pride (of birth)." The nobleman insists on the privileges of his rank, oppressing his subjects "and when the pastor sees it . . . and says anything he is told: you don't understand or you are getting involved in secular matters." This way he covers up the fact of his undisciplined servants, the luxury of his court, and his inability to do good to the poor. "The avaricious lord takes away people's meadows to make fishponds for himself . . . and forces people to work at them, . . . spoiling the good air (apparently by creating marshy areas) and bringing sicknesses on people . . . "(18)

The Pastoral exhorts the powerful to repent of their inordinate use of power, of their pride, flattery, mercilessness, indifference, covetousness, and all that goes against God's law, "no matter what the laws of the land say (entitle them to)."(19)

Wordly (showy or improper) and rich clothing is also severely attacked, not only on the part of the rich but also on the part of the poor who buy such clothes for their wives and children on an instalment plan (!). "If someone doesn't want to put on Christ, he will lose his part in Him, because he lacks His spirit of humility." "Those . . . who do not want to abide by this (ruling) will have no part in Christ or with us." "Repent all of you whose clothing . . . does not show that you are Brethren and that you do not belong to the world!"(20) The spirit of medieval piety is indeed at war with the spirit of the new Renaissance fashions within the ranks of the *Unitas.*

It is not until the (temporary) victory of Lutheran influence in the *Unitas* that Bp. John Augusta in 1535 is able to encourage joy in the good gifts of God *among which he sees also worldly goods* which the earlier Brethren would have seen as vanities: "It is a great foolishness," he writes, "when a man judges someone to be dissolute and without the fear of God just because he enjoys wordly honor, a nice house, . . . a fine skirt or fur coat, a beautiful wife, or because he is cheerful, or in a good mood, likes to laugh, likes to sing."(21) However, the new-found freedom vis-a-vis the world did not last long in the *Unitas;* a return to some of the older discipline in the mid-16th century occurred as a reaction to the license which many Brethren mistook for freedom.

III.

From the Lutheran-oriented period come to us two documents which deal with the duties of the nobility. The first is the Brethren's classical Confession of Faith of 1536 and the second one is the afore-mentioned writing of Benedict Bavoryňský. The brief *Confession* doesn't have much to say about the nobility; characteristically for the *Unitas,* in contrast to the other Churches, it restricts the role of the nobility to oversight and protection in *worldly* matters. Its later editions speak about the duties of nobility in more explicit terms and give it a certain measure of responsibility for the guarding of God's claims and the defense of the Church; yet even then the freedom of conscience is stressed, and the responsibility of subjects is treated very briefly. Its edition of 1564, published again by Comenius in exile, makes the point that those in secular authority are subject not only to the kings but also to all his appointees, as long as such obedience does not lead against

God.(22) This is the only place where I discovered a reference to the nobility's duties toward their king and his representatives. While the Brethren always stressed the hierarchical system of (fallen) human society, it is strange that none of their exhortations to their nobles seem to enjoin obedience to the king. They did require obedience even to evil superiors when they addressed themselves to the common people! The Bohemian Brethren who rebelled against their kings at the start of the Schmalkald War and the Thirty Years' War were evidently not trained in docility toward the royal establishment by their Church. It must be said, however, that the Brethren who were leaders in the Schmalkald conspiracy had not consulted *Unitas'* Seniors and that their leading bishop, Br. John Augusta, thought them fools for engaging in a venture which he considered doomed.

It is in *Unitas'* Senior Benedict Bavorynský's work "On True Religion" *(Kniha o pravem náboženství křeslanském)* that we meet with the full impact of Luther's appreciation of secular authority on the *Unitas*. The work, published post-humously in 1543, shows Luther's high concept of a Christian's life-work as his calling from God (in Bavorynský's language, echoing James 1:26, his "true religion") and Luther's stress on the God-given task of the secular arm in Christendom no less than among the unbelievers. (Bavorynský himself was from a baronial family and studied at Wittenberg.) Gone, for the moment, are the Brethren's scruples about the office of the secular power, even when harsh judgments have to be meted out. Gone is now the Brethren's discouragement of participation in war. (The Turkish danger and *Unitas'* so-called 'Turkish Book' of 1530, encouraging the Brethren to fight and not spare the Turks, need to be kept in mind.) The Brethren's lords are encouraged to learn the arts of war (against the Turks) and the common Brethren are to accompany them or to defend their towns in concord with their fellow-citizens. Bendict B. has no illusion about the actual conduct of the gentry. He does not idealize the lords. He paints a grim picture of lords and officials robbing and oppressing people by exorbitant taxes and corvees.(23) But this does not diminish his enthusiasm for the work of government, for as he says, their work is for the good of the multitude and so it is a "true religion" and ranks next to that of those who serve in matters pertaining to salvation.(24) He even sees secular power as bearing the image and likeness of God (!), who is merciful and loving to the *just* and who is an angry avenger of unrighteousness.(25) It is hard to see how Benedict could have learned that from Luther, with his Gospel for sinners. Bavorynský does not mention the government's representing only the "left hand" of God in the language of Luther. As true servants of this kind of God, Benedict exhorts the lords to "wreak vengeance" — how un-Brotherly could he get? — on the ungodly, adulterers, drunks, etc.(26) While Benedict gives some useful advice to the lords how to reform the government of their estates — how they should be protectors of widows and orphans and how they should enquire whether their officials do not mistreat them or exploit them,(27) he sees no hindrance to salvation for those who carry out their governmental responsibilities. It is therefore with some relief that one finds that this overestimate of the role of nobility was not maintained in the next documents of the *Unitas,* much as a greater appreciation of the role of secular authority may have been needed.

As historical background it is also useful to remember that in 1530 the *Unitas* received into its membership twelve feudal lords by the rite of (re-) baptism. Hitherto *Unitas'* gentry had consisted primarily only of the members of the (lower) baronial estate, even though the *Unitas* had enjoyed the favor of some of the higher lords already for some time. This influx of powerful lords into the *Unitas* did not keep the Seniors from forbidding the gentry in 1534 its taking away city trades, such as the sale of beer, from burghers. The gentry is subject to *Unitas'* judgments (and judicial-disciplinary procedures) just as any other Brethren.(28)

IV.

In 1546 came another of those great turning points in *Unitas* history: a deliberate return to its pre-Lutheran, domestic heritage.(29) The following year saw the disastrous defeat of the Schmalkald League. The Brethren, whose Bohemian nobility played a heavy part in the conspiracy against the King, were hit hard. The *Unitas* was outlawed in Bohemia; severe persecutions and confiscations of property followed. Many Brethren were forced to recant, or go into exile. The turmoil led to a self-examination on *Unitas'* part. After gathering the necessary information on the state of its members, the *Unitas* published in 1553 an "Admonition to all the Faithful"(30) to correct their ways by radical repentance. The Admonition is generally known as the "Correction," *Náprava.*(31) The nobility and all the Brethren in positions of secular authority receive in it what amounts to an ultimatum "if they wished to be saved." *Unitas'* older emphases re-appear here and a somber picture of the social conditions and of the class conflicts between Brethren who are "lords" and subjects is drawn. The exaltation of the secular offices disappears completely. The official directives from this period to the nobility share — in an increasing degree — the critical and demanding, or rather commanding, tone of the ''Correction'' and its concern that the nobles stand in great peril of their salvation.

The necessity to issue such an abundance of critical directives to its nobles within so short a time — two in the early 1550's and an expanded one in 1563 (31) — is a testimony to the disappointment of the *Unitas* with its noble members.(32) The directives stress the social responsibility of the nobles and other officials; they are seen first of all as agents of God's protection of and mercifulness to his people, and only in the second place as agents for the correction of the wicked. Those in authority are to take care of the material well-being of their subjects, avoid their exploitation, flee pride, avarice, and the desire to extend their own property; above all they are to show compassion, instead of anger, toward their people.

After 1563 no further official attempt to issue new directives to the Brethren's nobility is in evidence. Perhaps it was felt that enough had been written, and that further writings would prove equally fruitless. While there is a great scarcity of documents about the *Unitas* from the last quarter of the 16th century and the beginning of the 17th, it is quite evident that the general tenor of *Unitas* 'life, the distinction between the Brethren and the rest of society, as well as the number of Brethren all were on the decline. The attractiveness of the *Unitas fratrum* was evidently disappearing.(33) The Brethren were heading toward some sort of Union with the ''Evangelicals,'' (the Protestant Neo-Utraquists, who formed the majority of the nation). as well as trying to hold on to what was theirs. Further, the Bohemian Brethren depended completely on their nobles in the negotiations for religious freedom in this period. The influence of the ''magisterial'' Reformation movements from abroad was steadily increasing. All this would lead the *Unitas* to a greater acceptance and tolerance of the position and conduct of their nobles.

The Brethren's last document which deals with the role and responsibilities of those in positions of secular authority — Matthew Konečný's early-17th century *Book on Christian Duties (Kniha o povinnostech křestanských)* — while exhorting superiors to be just, humble and merciful, accepts the feudal and bourgeois forms of life without any embarrassment or sense of tension, enjoining a severe strictness toward subordinates at fault. The *Unitas* seems to have come to terms with the secular social order on which it had looked so long with anxiety and misgiving. However, even then it refused to accept the authority of secular magistrates in spiritual matters. At least in Bohemia and Moravia (but not in Poland) it remained faithful to its ancient principle of the separation of secular and spiritual authorities to the bitter end.(34)

By then, though, the end of the *Unitas* in its native land, and the end of Cezech independence were only a few years away. The Brethren, or at least large numbers of them, had lost their sense of their ecclesiastical *raison d'être*, and thus their *élan vital.* The *Unitas*, just as Czech independence, seem to have died more from inner causes than from an external defeat by the Habsburgs. The erosion of the *Unitas* in Poland in the 17th century, where so many Brethren found refuge after the Schmalkald War in the mid-16th century and after the fiasco of the Battle on the White Mountain in 1620, confirms such a conclusion. The Brethren's exile in the mid-16th century was followed by a vigorous life in Poland (and eventually at home); the second exile ended with Unitas' dissolution within one generation, for all practical purposes. The submissiveness of its Polish branch to its noble patrons, and the progressive calvinization of both the *Unitas* and of the Polish nobles go a long way to explain their fate.

NOTES

1. *Dekrety Jednoty bratrské,* Gindely, Ant., ed., Prague, 1865, p. 2.

2. See Peter Brock's excellent *(The) Political and Social Doctrines of the Unity of the Czech Brethren in the 15th and early 16th centuries,* The Hague, 1957.

3. *Dekrety,* pp. 64-6.

4. *Akty* IV, 62.

5. *Dekrety,* p. 87.

6. *Ibid.,* p. 92; cf. *Zprávy kněžské* 214a.

7. *Ibid.,* pp. 94-5; cf. *Zprávy* 216a.

8. *Ibid.,* p. 95; cf. *Zprávy* 216a.

9. *Ibid.,* p. 96.

10. *Lec. cit.;* cf. *Zprávy* 217a and b.

11. *Ibid.,* p. 97; cf. *Zprávy* 218a.

12. *Ibid.,* p. 90.

13. *Ibid.,* p. 91.

14. e.g., *Dekrety,* p. 92.

15. *Loc. cit.*

16. *Ibid.,* p. 99.

17. *Ibid.,* p. 100.

18. As cited and paraphrased in Říčan, R., *Dějiny Jednoty bratrské,* Prague, 1957, p. 109.

19. "The Senior Brethren . . . to the Churches," *(Bratřie starši . . . .)* C 1b and 2a, in *Spis o mnohém a rozličném pokušeni,* 1510 (see *Knihopis* 5032).

20. *Ibid.,* C 2a, b and 4a-6a.

21. From "A Sermon about the Marital Estate . . . by John Augusta . . . A.D. 1535" *Kázdni o stavu manželském . . . .),* cited in Cisařová-Kolářová, Anna, *Žena v Jednotě bratrské,* Prague, 1942, p. 85.

22. *Vyznáni viry Jednoty Bratři českých,* Komenský, J. A., ed., 1662, Prague, 1935, article XVI.

23. Bavoryňský z Bavoryně a Vlčiho Pole, Beneš, *Kniha tato jest o pravém náboženstvf křesťanském,* (Prague University Library 54B 94), *f.* 25b.

24. *Ibid.,* H 1b.

25. *Ibid.,* 24b.

26. *Loc. cit.*

27. *Ibid.,* 25b.

28. *Dekrety,* p. 149.

29. See *ibid.,* p. 164.

30. *Napomenuti stálé všem věrným.*

31. In addition to the *Correction,* there are the *Directives to the Noble and Powerful (Zpráva urozených mocných),* written at the latest in the early 1550's, now kept at Stuttgart (Sign. Th. F4. 434) and the *Instruction and Directive to those who have been given the Power of Secular Government (Naučeni a zpráva lidem v moci k zprávé světa postavených),* expanded revision of the former *Directive,* now at the Breslau City Library (8K 1640). Typescript copies were made available to the present author (as in the case of the other primary sources cited which have not received a modern edition). Limitations of space make an adequate presentation of their contents impossible in this brief survey.

32. See the 1563 complaint of *Unitas'* Seniors from Bohemia, Moravia, and Poland concerning the growing decline of moral and ecclesiastical discipline in the *Unitas,* especially among its gentry. The Brethren's gentry are pitied here rather than censured, "because it is impossible for them to flee everything in the secular offices and court services, and not become contaminated in the course of time; and therefore *they are to be pitied, and be borne with more than others (italics* ours) . . . ." *Dekrety,* pp. 216-17.

33. For some of the evidence see Marianka S. Fousek, "Spiritual Direction and Discipline: Key to the Flowering and Decay of the *Unitas fratrum* in the 16th and early-17th centuries," *Archive for Reformation History* 62/2, 1971.

34. For the history of the Polish branch of the *Unitas* see Bidlo, Jaroslav, *Jednota bratrská v prvnim vyhnanstvi,* I-IV, Prague, 1900-32; Jos. Th. Mueller, *Geschichte der Boehmischen Brüder,* III, Herrnhut, 1931; Rud. Říčan, *Jednota bratrská,* Prague 1956, chpts. XII and XIX (German transl.: *Die Böhmischen Brüder,* Union Verlag, Berlin, 1961); *idem. Dějiny Jednoty bratrské,* Prague, 1957, chpts. XVI, XIX and XXIII. — The loss of *Unitas'* spiritual and moral vigor, about which the exiled bishop Comenius anguished, may, however, be the most important factor in the extinction of the *Unitas.* See Fousek, *op. cit.* The loss of its traditional distinctness from the "Magisterial" Churches and of its spiritual-moral fiber, and appeal, may all be deeply interconnected.

Béla K. Király

PROTESTANTISM IN HUNGARY
BETWEEN THE REVOLUTION AND THE AUSGLEICH

The evolution of Protestantism in Hungary between the Revolution of 1848-49 and the *Ausgleich* of 1867 offers an outstanding example of Eastern European religious dissent, particularly in its lay rather than theological aspects. Indeed, the constitutional and political questions raised completely outshine the religious issues. The Concordat of 1855 and the Protestant Patent of 1859(1) together precipitated the most militant and widespread movement of defiance in Hungary since Világos, a crisis that showed just how wide the gap had become between Habsburg autocracy and Hungarian liberalism.

Political matter though it was, however, the patent crisis was also an integral part of the Protestants' long struggle to secure their traditional rights. The whole history of Hungarian Protestantism revolves around the clash between the Counter-Reformation policies of the Habsburgs and the Protestants' tenacity in pressing for guarantees of their freedom of conscience and their ecclesiastical and educational autonomy. Over the long term the Protestants were successful in their aims, but their victory was never complete; the Habsburgs went down to defeat but were never routed. This stalemate filled the relationship between the Protestant church and the Catholic state with ambiguities.

Paradoxically, the Protestants' first and most substantial victory in Hungary coincided with the peak of militant Counter-Reformation in the Habsburg lands. It came at the same moment as Czech and Austro-German Protestantism was defeated. The basic elements of the Hungarians' victory were embodied in the Treaty of Vienna of 1606 between the Habsburg dynasty, the Hungarian estates and the state of Transylvania. The treaty confirmed the constitutional rights and religious freedoms of the Hungarian estates. Its provisions were enacted by the Hungarian diet of 1608 and promulgated as the law of the land by the Habsburg king. Subsequent treaties endorsed them several times more.(2)

Why was Hungarian Protestantism given such amazing freedom at the height of the Counter-Reformation? The key was Transylvania, a strong, civilized, well-administered state that enjoyed greater religious tolerance than anywhere else in Europe in the early decades of the seventeenth century. Transylvania under the protection of the Ottoman Empire was beyond the reach of Habsburg military power; the easternmost regions of Bohemia, German Austria and Royal Hungary, on the other hand, were within the military potential of Transylvania. The Protestants' liberties were simply the result of Habsburg realpolitik.

Following the long war of liberation that concluded with the Treaty of Karlovic in 1699, Transylvania lost Ottoman protection and fell within the military sphere of the Habsburgs, putting an end for good to Transylvania's capacity to safeguard the Hungarian Protestants' rights. Now the Habsburg Counter-Reformation began to clamp down on Hungary in earnest. The Habsburg kings issued a series of decrees, all of them contrary to Hungary's constitution, regulating the Protestants.(3) They restricted their rights to public worship, made them subject to visitation by Catholic bishops, obliged them to celebrate Catholic holidays. But the greatest blow of all was the *decretalis* oath. The prerequisite for public office, it invoked the Virgin Mary and the saints of the Roman church, and thus effectively excluded any Protestant believer from accepting any official position.

This winter of Protestant discontent lasted a century. Then Joseph II's Protestant Patent and the laws enacted by the diet of 1790-91 lifted all political restrictions on the Protestants and reestablished their ecclesiastical and educational autonomy on the pattern of the laws and treaties of the early seventeenth century.(4) The survival of Protestantism was no longer at stake. But the laws of 1790-91 contained two reservations. All churches were put under the supervision of the king and he was invited to propose permanent solutions to all outstanding questions. These reservations were the basis of the Habsburg attempt in 1859 to impose a solution.

Finally Act XX of 1848 proclaimed the complete equality of all the "received churches."(5) The Unitarian church was now included among the received churches, whose budgets were to be subsidized by the state, whose members were to be free to attend each other's schools, and which were to be entitled to appoint their own chaplains to army units.(6) After Világos, however, the Habsburg autocracy declared the act null and void — and, indeed, suspended the whole constitution.

Protestant Policies under General Haynau and Archduke Albrecht

The Habsburgs considered the Protestants of Hungary rebels to a man and they were even more severely persecuted than Hungary's Roman Catholics. At every level of government Czech and Austro-German officials replaced Hungarian officials. These agents "served to hold down and act as spies, often in the most despicable fashion," says Joseph Redlich.(7)

The first important measure against the Protestants was General Haynau's Open Order of February 10, 1850. Though only a provisional order, it suppressed the activities of all church officials. All superintendents were replaced by administrators appointed by the commander in chief. Each Protestant church district was administered by a committee consisting of the commander in chief's appointee and carefully selected ecclesiastical and lay trustees. Even then, meetings of these committees of men handpicked for their loyalty to the dynasty were permitted to take place only in the presence of state commissioners. Haynau announced his appointments of administrators for the most important church districts immediately, selecting mostly ethnic Germans and Slovaks.(8) All Protestant rights guaranteed by laws and treaties signed by the Habsburgs over the centuries were suspended by Haynau's order.

In a sense Haynau's Open Order was laudable, for it said what it meant and meant what it said. It was couched in the language of autocracy and repression; there was no subterfuge. It was superseded in 1854(9) by new regulations issued by Archduke Albrecht, the governor-general. Lacking the straightforwardness of General Haynau's Open Order, the new regulations were a much more typical Habsburg measure. They spoke of a return to legality, to the status quo ante according to the laws of 1790-91, but they bespoke the same aim as before, repression. Limited church assemblies were now allowed, but police surveillance was as strict as ever.(10)

Both these directives dealt only with the administration of the Protestant churches, but the Protestants also had much influence in the educational system. This, too, had to be curbed. It was brought under provisional control by the *Entwurf* of 1849. These regulations were made permanent by a rescript issued on December 16, 1854, by Vienna's Minister of Cults, Count Leo Thun,(11) a Czech statesman of proven Habsburg loyalty. German was made a set language in all gymnasia, and the higher the grade, the more courses were required to be taught in it. Only teachers capable of giving their courses in German were to be hired, and only gymnasia that met these requirements could be licensed. Thun showed great resourcefulness in harassing and circumscribing the Protestant schools of Hungary, according to the contemporary historian Berzeviczy.(12) One such harassment was an 1854 ban on Protestant schools accepting Catholic pupils, despite the fact that Catholic schools could take anyone. In 1857 Jewish students were forbidden to enroll in Protestant schools.(13)

Of the schools that adopted the Thun system 24 were Hungarian, three were Slovak, one was Slovak-Hungarian, six were Serbo-Croat and two were Rumanian. Forty-five Hungarian, one Serbo-Croat and two Rumanian gymansia lost their public licenses because they did not comply with the new regulations.(14) Most of the Hungarian schools that were forced to close were Protestant. The Habsburgs, who paraded so long as the civilizers of East Central Europe, closed down twice as many Hungarian schools as they licensed. Moreoever, the closure of a quarter of the non-Hungarian schools lent weight to the general impression that the Rumanians, Serbs and Croats were receiving as a reward for their loyalty to the Habsburgs in 1848-49 precisely the same treatment as was being used as a punishment for the Hungarians for rising in revolt. Despite the harassments, however the Protestant primary and secondary schools retained their leading position in Hungary. The Protestants' tradition of organizing and maintaining their own schools without aid or interference from the government paid them handsome dividends. Under the Bach government, there was one primary school for every 809 Protestants in Hungary, the best ratio for any religious denomination. By contrast, there were 2,860 Greek Orthodox inhabitants for every primary school of their denomination,(15) the worst ratio.

The Protestant Patent of 1859

Archduke Albrecht's decree of 1854 temporarily regulating Protestant church administration pledged eventual reestablishment of the legal situation created by the diet of 1790-91. One year later a draft proposal for a permanent settlement was presented to a select group of Protestant leaders.(16) They rejected it. The proposal covered four main areas.

An *Oberkonsistorium* or *Oberkirchenrat* was to be set up on the pattern of the Prussian Lutheran Supreme Church Council. Even Catholics could be council members, who were to be appointed by the crown for life.(17) This council was to be the highest source of church superintendence, administration and judicature.(18)

State supervision of the schools was to be continued on the basis of the regulations of 1854. Secondary schools and teacher-training colleges were to lose the last vestiges of their autonomy and become fully state-supervised.

Contrary to long-standing tradition, all meetings of church officials were to be closed to the public. Presiding officers were to be held responsible for seeing that there were no discussions or resolutions on matters that were outside the meetings' specific areas of interest or infringed the law — and the law, naturally, included all unlawful imperial rescripts. Resolutions and even minutes of meetings were not valid without ministerial approval. Nor were appointments or elections of teachers and ministers. The election of superintendents and district presbyters was subject to imperial consent.

The fourth area included in the proposed patent would indeed have restored the legal conditions that were set up in 1790-91, but they were secondary matters. The authority of the Protestant church judiciary was to be reestablished over Protestant marriages. The rights of Hungary's Protestants were to be extended to the Protestants of Croatia and the Military Frontier Zones.(19) The superintendencies were to receive annual state subsidies.

The provisions of the draft wiped out the Protestant churches' centuries-old traditions of self-government. Rather than a return to legality, it amounted to making an extraordinary situation permanent. The patent would arrogate to the state rights that did not belong to it but instead were the sole prerogatives of the church councils, which under the constitution were the supreme legislative organs of the Protestant churches. The Habsburg state, which was Roman Catholic by nature, a fact that had been reinforced by the Concordat, would have a say in all Protestant affairs, great and small. The fact that Catholics could sit in the *Oberkirchenrat* simply and gratuitously underlined the point.

Immediately after the draft was published in 1855, first the Protestant leaders, then the Protestant masses, then gradually the Catholic hierarchy and finally the vast majority of the Hungarian nation united in militant opposition to it. In 1858-59, concurrently with the international crisis into which Austrian diplomacy had dragged the empire, a critical situation developed in Hungary, a situation in which discontent with the draft patent was a major element.(20)

Delegations visited the Viennese authorities. Petitions flooded into the Court. Meetings, both legal and illegal, protested against the provisions of the patent. Articles published in Hungary and abroad reflected the national mood and the general determination to reject the patent if it were promulgated. Amidst such turmoil and in the wake of

Solferino (June 24), Villafranca (July 12) and Francis Joseph's noted Laxenburg Manifesto (July 15), Count Thun on September 1, 1859, issued the Imperial Protestant Patent. The following day his own executive order was published. They fell like a bombshell.(21)

It is very hard to understand how at that particular moment of history Thun could so seriously misinterpret the climate of opinion in the monarchy. How could he have failed to comprehend that resistance to the patent had united the Hungarians as never before(22) and that the Habsburg state just did not have the coercive force to deal with the situation? Redlich speaks of the patent adding ''a piece of most combustible fuel to the flames.'' Hugo Hantsch characterizes the upheaval as ''die Unverlasslichkeit der Ungarn.''(23) Macartney says that the fact that the patent was in the nature ''of an octroi violated the autonomy which both churches felt to be essential to their existence.''(24) In a modern Marxist interpretation Lajos Lukács claims: ''Specific political illiteracy and a complete misunderstanding of the real power relations were essential for the Austrian regime to have done what it did in promulgating the Protestant Patent.'' Marxists make strange bedfellows with nineteenth-century aristocrats, but practically the same view was put forward by the contemporary liberal Hungarian statesman, Baron Zsigmond Kemény: ''But God only knows what will happen if the government makes another blunder in its analysis of the situation in some other area like the one Count Thun has committed in the matter of religion.''(25)

''A thousand years of Hungarian history should have made it clear to anyone knowing the country that it accepted permanent arrangements of its state or church affairs only when it made them of its own free will. In 1859 members of every church rallied to the cause of the Protestants' rights, firm in the conviction that they were fighting for Hungary's constitutional political rights.''(26) A few months before the crisis had come to a head, Széchenyi, whose loyalty to the Habsburgs was above question, had expressed much the same idea in his dramatic essay, *Blick*.(27) In this tragic final warning, he had cautioned against the *faux pas* of the Bach regime. ''Your Excellency,'' Széchenyi wrote to Bach, ''men will even put up with tyranny if some high intellect is expressed through it. But when tyranny includes duplicity and hypocrisy as well as being bloody and inexplicably cruel, then every drop of decent men's blood bursts in bitterest revolt.'' Thus not only were radicals, nationalist extremists and bigots in an uproar in 1859, but even the moderates' patience had been tested beyond endurance by the Bach government. Széchenyi's suicide on April 7, 1860, was a fateful portent.

Mass Action, Students, and Liberal and Conservative Attitudes

However well stocked a tinderbox, something has to kindle it. The spark was supplied by a particularly shortsighted provision of the patent. Thun banned all the activities of the existing district authorities of the church, yet they alone had the administrative personnel to implement the patent. Thun ordered the patent to be put into effect by the leaderships of the new districts into which it had arbitrarily reorganized the Hungarian Protestant churches, but they had no staffs to do the job. The patent, in short, had a major obstacle built in to its own realization. What happened was that the old, traditional district leaderships simply ignored the order and continued with their regular day-to-day business. Their refusal to act on the patent turned passive resistance into a movement of open defiance. In an attempt to force a solution, scores of church leaders were arrested and jailed, but many were paroled and threw themselves back into the struggle with even greater determination. Defiance rapidly became nationwide.

For the first time since 1849, March 15, 1860, was openly celebrated as the anniversary of the Revolution of 1848. The students of the University of Pest took the lead with a public commemorative demonstration. As Kossuth described the event on the basis of eyewitnesses' letters: "A clash occurred and as a result of the stupidity and the brutal orders of Prottman, the Czech Chief of Police of Pest, the police fired into the crowd. Fifteen persons were wounded, Géza Forinyák fatally."(28) Now the movement even had a martyr, something that always makes movements more militant and more radical. So it was in Hungary in the spring of 1860. A requiem mass was celebrated in memory of Count Lajos Batthyány, the revolutionary prime minister who was sentenced to death during the Habsburg terror of 1849. On several occasions state commissioners dispatched to break up public meetings were so afraid of an outbreak of violence that they merely announced the government's ban and then hurried away, leaving the meeting to continue without more ado.(29)

A massive campaign was begun to collect signatures for petitions both in favor and against the patent. In all, 39,610 signatures were collected in support of it and 2,684,033 in opposition to it. Most of the signatures for the patent came from Lutherans, that is, mostly from Slovak and German parishes.(30)

The movement of defiance did not, however, run exclusively along ethnic lines. The police commissioner of Nagyvárad, for instance, reported on December 21, 1859: "Catholics and Protestants, liberals and arch-conservatives, and, what needs more careful watching, all the nationalities of Hungary — Hungarians, Slavs, Rumanians, Serbs, Germans and Jews — are all opposed to the government."(31)

Unquestionably, the main political force behind the movement was liberal nationalism, but rather unexpectedly the most conservative aristocracy also contributed its share. After the Laxenburg Manifesto they had hoped for a return to the situation that had obtained before 1848 when the aristocracy had been preeminent. When Vienna showed that it was not interested in enlisting their aid, they reacted by throwing their weight behind the movement of defiance, both for their own political ends and in the hope of stopping it from becoming too extreme. A conservative pro-Habsburg aristocrat, Ede Zsedényi, took the lead at a mass protest in Késmárk on September 27-29. Other members of the aristocracy were on the platform at meetings in Sopron (October 5-6), Debrecen (October 8), Pest (December 15), and at the second rally in Debrecen (January 11, 1860) which was attended by delegates from all over the country. Zsedényi and several other conservative noblemen were jailed, but when there was no sign of the crisis abating, Vienna began to consider working with the aristocracy to try to bring it to an end. The device it chose was to have the controlled press give wide publicity to the imprisonment of Zsedényi and his peers in order to make them martyrs in the eyes of the public. Then, if the government had to collaborate with them, it could be assured that they enjoyed the highest prestige possible among the Hungarians.(32)

Though liberal nationalism was the main inspiration of the movement of defiance, Hungary's liberal leaders and Ferenc Deák in particular stood aside from it. Deák still pursued a policy of passive resistance, though there had been a more vigorous element in the long-range objectives he published in 1858 in the daily, *Pesti Napló:*

> The paramount goal will be to keep alive in the nation an awareness of and an ardor for our constitutional freedoms, so that, should the opportune moment arise, by the stroke of a pen we can restore the Hungarian constitution and within twenty-four hours be in possession of our free, constitutional state; if, on the other hand, an appreciation of these subline principles should be lost to the people, their true constitutional liberties could never be returned to them either through good faith or by a ruler's grace.(33)

Deak's passive tactics were still being followed at the time of the patent crisis. Thus *Pesti Napló* said on December 6, 1859:

> Our devotion is greater than ever to our historic rights and to the nationhood that the blood of our forefathers defended. We have always had the capacity for hope but at the same time we have also learned the art . . . of waiting. With our backs straight and strong, with clear awareness of our might, with manly vigor and with patience, we stand upon the firm foundation of our historic rights.

Deák and *Pesti Napló* were both convinced at the time that Hungary could wait out the Habsburgs. Kossuth attacked their attitude fiercely. He called for active resistance, and day by day the difference between him and Deák became more acute. The fact was, however, that the situation was out of Deák's control and Kossuth from exile was in no position to take a lead.

The Leaders of the Movement of Defiance

The fame of those who stood up against Habsburg autocracy spread far and fast, especially those who showed organization skill, but from among their names two in particular warrant mention: one a future politician, the other a Calvinist minister and distinguished historian.

The first was Kálmán Tisza, who was to become Prime Minister of Hungary at the end of the Deák era. At this time he was only 29 years old and a minor official of the Calvinist church. He wrote an article(35) condemning the patent and the Habsburg claim to have the right to regulate the affairs of the Protestant churches. Since the dynasty did not have that right, he told his countrymen, they should not turn their backs without a struggle on the many laws that had been passed through the centuries guaranteeing Protestant rights. Tisza went to meetings, gave speeches, and became an indefatigable movement organizer. He was arrested and persecuted for his pains, but went on undeterred. As a result he quickly gained national renown, which he was to turn to good account later in his life.

A more attractive and influential man than he was Imre Revesz, a Calvinist minister who became the movement's ideologist. Between 1856 and 1859 he published several pamphlets, the basic arguments of which were always the same. He drafted two major documents for his church, a "Petition of the Hungarian Reformed Church, Trans-Tisza District," dated October 8, 1859, and the *Tájékoztatás* (Orientation), approved on January 28, 1860, and published by the Trans-Tisza District on March 1, 1860. A high-ranking Protestant delegation had taken the petition to Vienna, but since the delegation had been appointed before the patent was promulgated, once it had come into effect, it theoretically made the delegation illegal and therefore neither Francis Joseph nor his government would receive it.(36)

The decision to draft the *Tájékoztatás* was taken immediately after this rebuff. The delegation had been alarmed to hear that Thun was going to issue an order to have all ministers read the patent from the pulpit on two consecutive Sundays. Fearful that the more naive members of the clergy might do just that, the delegates had the *Tájékoztatás* prepared at once. The church authorities gladly endorsed it and helped to have it distributed throughout the country.

Its purpose was to show the Protestant parish ministry why Thun's order to read the patent should be ignored. It put forward both moral and legal argument that the defiance would be in accord with the law and the constitution, which Thun's order violated. It stressed that:

Ministers did not proclaim secular laws; they preached the Gospel.

Under the laws of 1791, the Protestant churches were subject only to their own church council, not to any other authority.

The Protestant hierarchy had forbidden the whole parochial clergy to publish the patent, so individual ministers were not at liberty to do so on their own.

Specific canons and the whole spirit of church law militated against ministers acting independently of their superintendents.

Were a minister to announce the patent, he would forswear his oath to observe canons and obey his ecclesiastical superiors, violating the very essence of the *presbyteriale regimen.*

He should be aware that all other ministers and church districts were abstaining from helping to implement the patent.

Finally the *Tájékoztatás* urged all ministers to disregard the patent's ban on meetings and hold them whenever they felt there was a need.(37)

Tájékoztatás was probably the most outspoken and influential document of the whole movement of defiance. Only a handful of ministers, mostly German and Slovak Lutherans, obeyed Thun's order and read the patent in church. On April 2, 1860, George Popa, the Rumanian prosecutor for Nagyvarad District Court, searched Révész's home and demanded the original copy of *Tájékoztatás.* Révész refused to surrender it to him, but told him that if he would give him a printed copy of it he would sign it in acknowledgment of his authorship. The prosecutor did as Révész bid and Révész signed it, fully aware that he was putting his name to his own arrest warrant. Proceedings against Révész were begun, but he was still free on bail when on May 15, 1860, the patent was revoked and all charges brought in connection with it were quashed.(38) This final triumph was achieved not only as a result of the strength of the domestic opposition to the patent. The struggle was also waged far beyond the borders of the Habsburg empire.

Exile Activities and the Press War

Hungary's exiles, especially Kossuth, took full advantage of the patent crisis to strike out at Francis Joseph's autocratic regime. Their main effort was to try to use the Western press itself rather than use their own publications to try to sway Western public opinion.

Kossuth's own attitude to what was happening he summed up as follows:

> Even if the Austrian government has learned nothing else from the bitter history of the past ten years, it might have learned one thing: that there is no weapon in the arsenal of its power that could force the Hungarian Protestants to give up their right to autonomy in their churches and their schools, and to consent to the state's right to *supervise* being replaced by a right to *command*. (Kossuth's emphases)(39)

Referring specifically to the patent, Kossuth, to whom the dramatic turn of phrase came easily, wrote: "As the tocsin rouses the warrior from his sleep, so has this attempt by the government roused Hungary's Protestants from the paralysis into which the public's spirits have sunk in mourning for ten years' terrorism."(40)

Kossuth was at pains to inform the West of what was happening in Hungary. It was no lone effort, however; he was simply the heart of exile activities. His greatest ally and the greatest fillip to the cause he represented was the Hungarian exile press bureau in Brussels, headed by Baron Miklós Jósika, a liberal Transylvanian nobleman,(41) which scored a remarkable record of achievement in a very short space of time.(42)

Kossuth stressed that the Habsburgs' efforts to force Hungary's Protestants into submission was part of a wider canvas of dynastic despotism, so that the basic issue was not one simply of religious freedom but one of political liberty and national independence too. He spelled this out clearly in a letter to the citizens of Glasgow in which he sought to enlist their support to keep the general public informed.(43) This letter to such a Protestant stronghold as Scotland produced a mass rally of support, which was attended by many local and national dignitaries, including at least five Members of Parliament.(44) A resolution passed at the Glasgow rally was subsequently widely reprinted in the British press. It strongly endorsed the Hungarian movement of defiance and stated that the Glaswegians were watching with "admiration and sympathy" as the Hungarians "resist the interference of tyranny, which attacks their freedom of conscience and the legal rights of their ecclesiastic and church autonomy." It praised Hungary's Roman Catholics for their aid to the Protestants and acclaimed the Hungarians' struggle for national independence.(45)

The Habsburgs were not laggard in attempting to give their side of the picture. With the entire Austrian press in their service, their main argument was the *Verwirkungs-Theorie,* the assertion that the

Hungarians had forfeited all their constitutional rights as a result of the Revolution of 1848-49. Any rights they now enjoyed were granted by the grace of the Habsburgs.(46) Ever since the time of Leopold II (1790-92) the Austrian press and the mouthpieces the Habsburgs subsidized in various German states had maintained a screen of hostile publicity against the Hungarians. In all that time Western public opinion had seen life in Hungary through a distorting mirror. All dispatches reaching the West had an anti-Hungarian bias, a bias that even colored supposedly scholarly works simply because objective accounts of Hungarian affairs were not available. During the patent crisis, however, the exiles finally broke through this barrier and the West at last was treated to both sides of events. A war was thus waged between the press inside Hungary and that outside.

Inside Hungary the *Evangelisches Wochenblatt,* edited by the Slovak Hornyánsky and subsidized by Thun, claimed that the patent introduced nothing fundamentally new and the little that was new was to the benefit of the poor. It likewise asserted that ministerial endorsement of newly elected teachers and ministers was necessary to prevent "suspicious persons" from gaining influence.(47) It repeated these and similar claims in a pamphlet it published. To counter it, Imre Révész and Károly Kerkápolyi published their own pamphlet defending freedom of conscience and the autonomy of the churches.(48)

An interesting sidelight on the pamphleteering was thrown by a series of simplified broadsheets couched in the form of correspondence between fictitious persons explaining the essence of the issues in everyday language that could be understood by the common folk. The main argument of one pro-Thun broadsheet, for example, was: "It would be dangerous to argue or struggle against the Almighty, against superiors accepted by God."(49)

The two most cogent antipatent pamphlets,(50) most of which had to be published abroad, were written by Baron Gábor Prónay and Mór Ballagi. Both emphasized the indivisibility of the struggle against the patent and Hungary's constitutional rights. Victory in the fight for Protestant rights would help the cause of constitutional freedom, they said, but Protestants should strive to preserve their own ecclesiastical administration not for political reasons but because the foundation of it was the Gospel. Believers had a sacred duty to resist any attack on that foundation. As such an attack, the patent had to be opposed by all means. "Hungary with Austria," Ballagi wrote, "forms a formidable great power. Hungary could thus be the foundation of the monarchy. Hungary in opposition to Austria has shown itself to be a powerful state in the recent past (in 1849), when it alone mauled Austria."

Hungarians were not revolutionaries. he concluded, but, aware of their strength, they were demanding their rights.

Many German Protestants misunderstood the patent issue. They were told that the patent was a monarch's act of generosity, much more liberal than the church constitutions in many German Protestant states. From the point of view of the forms, there was a certain truth in that interpretation, but not in essence. It failed to take into account the historical evolution of Hungarian Protestantism, the relationship of the Protestant churches to the Habsburg state, and the internal organization of Hungary's Protestant churches, all of which were markedly different from those of any of the German Protestant states. For centuries the Hungarian Protestant churches had had to rely on their resources to survive and they had had to do so against the overwhelming odds of an oppressive Catholic Habsburg state and the rich and powerful Roman church. The German Protestant churches, on the other hand, had been allies of the state and their development had been interdependent with that of the states, a fact that had made them more bureaucratic than their Hungarian counterparts. The Hungarian Protestant churches were subject to an alien ruler, the German churches were not. The Hungarian Protestants had had to face the Counter-Reformational zeal of Catholic monarchs; the German Protestants had been ruled by coreligionists. The Hungarian Protestant churches had evolved along presbyterial lines, the German, mostly along consistorial lines.

These distinctions were rarely perceived at the time of the patent crisis. Most German Protestants and most of the German press labored under fundamental misunderstandings and supported the Habsburgs rather than their coreligionists. The Swiss Calvinists and their press, by contrast, clearly appreciated the situation. They grasped the difference between a free church in a free state and a subject church under an absolute ruler. On January 1, 1860, *Zeitstimmen* commented:

> Who could blame the Hungarian Protestants for rejecting the free church constitution offered by the Habsburgs? It is true that this constitution is more liberal than that of any Protestant church in any state. However, the Hungarians say: 'We do not accept even the freest constitution from the hands of an absolutist regime, as an act of imperial grace. What the absolutist regime gives today, tomorrow, if it so pleases, it can take away. On the basis of old laws and contracts, we have the right to administer our own affairs.' They are right! They are speaking like men! The Hungarian Protestants' actions cannot be understood by foreigners, because they believe they stem from political grievances. Naturally, they are inspired by political considerations, but the sources of them are the same as the sources of their religious considerations. Political and denominational autonomy on the one hand confronts bureaucratic absolutism on the other.(51)

This must be counted as the most perceptive and most lucidly and succinctly stated contemporary foreign interpretation of the patent crisis of 1860.

Repeal of the Protestant Patent, May 15, 1860

The movement of defiance was not a total victory for the Hungarians. Some parishes, mostly Lutheran, that is, Slovak and German, accepted the patent. By March 31, 1860, 226 Lutheran parishes had accepted it and 345 had rejected it. The Reformed Church of Hungary, whose members were ethnic Hungarians,(52) virtually unanimously rejected it. Out of some 2,000 Reformed parishes, only one percent acceded to the patent. This degree of success was due to the encouragement of determined leaders, the support of the conservative aristocracy and non-Protestant priests and laymen — including the Roman Catholic prelature, the inspiration of the press war, and the solidarity displayed at meetings of clergy and laity abroad. Vienna simply could not stand up against the pressure of so many resolutions, delegations and petitions. (53)

Vienna had also been embarrassed by certain diplomatic demarches. Soon after the patent was promulgated, Lord Westmoreland, a Secretary of the British Embassy in Vienna, visited Buda and Pest, where he consulted with Protestant leaders, including Kálmán Tisza. As a result of their exchange of views, Imre Révész drafted a memorandum on the issue, which was passed through Tisza to Lord Loftus, the British ambassador, when he himself visited the Hungarian capital on November 10, 1859. The memorandum was then published in the *Edinburgh Review*. According to the *Kreuzzeitung* of Berlin, in the wake of British inquiries the Habsburg government had to circulate apologetic explanations of the patent among the chancelleries of Europe. Kálmán Tisza attributed the patent's repeal mostly to British intercession.(54)

Others ascribed it to the influence on Francis Joseph of General Lajos Benedek, who was appointed to succeed Archduke Albrecht as Governor General of Hungary in April 1860.(55) However much he contributed to revocation of the patent, this was only part of the story. The fact that Benedek, a Hungarian and a Protestant, was appointed Governor General was indicative of the changing climate. Benedek was the only general who had acquitted himself with honor in the Habsburg military humiliation in northern Italy in 1859. That the only man considered an effective general had to be spared for political duties in Hungary rather than charged with the reorganization the Habsburg army sorely needed in 1860, dramatized the pressing necessity of pacifying Hungary by concessions instead of using greater force. What was to culminate in the *Ausgleich* of 1867 began with the appointment of Benedek in April and, even more so, with the repeal of the Protestant Patent on May 15, 1860, even before it had been really implemented.(56) The patent that was to have imposed a lasting settlement endured only eight and a half months. In comparison, Maria Theresa's *Urbarium*, issued as a temporary measure, lasted sixty years. The sudden rescinding of the Protestant Patent, considered in conjunction with the fate of the October Diploma, the Olmütz Constitution and similar permanent legislation, would seem to suggest that the Habsburgs' temporary measures were often more durable than their permanent ones.

NOTES

1. The Concordat was concluded on August 18, 1855, Emperor Francis Joseph's twenty-fifth birthday. It was promulgated in the Habsburg lands in the form of an imperial patent on November 5, 1855. The Hungarian version was published in *Pesti Napló* in the issues of November 14 and 15. A modern Hungarian Marxist interpretation of it states: "The spirit of the fifteenth century rather than the nineteenth issued from the Concordat, which surpassed anything in the recent past for groveling before the church." Aladár Mód, *400 év küzdelem az önálló Magyarországért* (The 400-Year Struggle for an Independent Hungary) (Budapest: Szikra, 1954; 7th expanded ed.), 262.

The protestant Patent, as it was commonly known in Hungary, was properly entired: *Kaiserliches Patent vom 1. September 1859, betreffend die innere Verfassung, die Schul- und Unterrichts-Angelengenheiten und die staatsrechtliche Stellung der evangelischen Kirche beider Bekenntnisse in der Königreich Ungarn, Croatien und Slavonien, in der Wojwodschaft Serbien mit dem Temeser Banate und in der Militärgrenze.* Wien: Aus des k. k. Hof- und Staatsdruckerei, 1859. Published in the *Reich-Gesetz Blatt*, 1859, nos. 10 and 13. The imperial patent was followed a day later by an executive order of Count Leo Thun, Minister of Cults. The official Hungarian version of both was published in *Protestáns Egyházi és Iskolai Lap* (Protestant Ecclesiastic and Scholastic Journal), 1859, nos. 38-41.

2. The Treaty of Nikolsburg (modern Mikulov) of 1621, the Second Treaty of Vienna of 1624, the Treaty of Pozsony (modern Bratislava) of 1626 and the Treaty of Linz of 1645 — all guaranteed the estates' religious freedom, and the autonomy of the Protestant churches and schools. Béla K. Király, *Hungary in the Late Eighteenth Century: The Decline of Enlightened Despotism* (New York: Columbia University Press, 1969), 114-117. The most comprehensive history of Protestantism in Hungary is contained in the works of Imre Révész, whose classic is *A magyarországi protestantizmus története* (The History of Protestantism in Hungary) (Budapest: Magyar Történelmi Társulat, 1927).

3. *Explanatio leopoldina* in 1691 and *Carolina resolutio* in 1731 most notably. See Király, *op. cit.*, 117-122.

4. Act XXVI, 1791, guaranteed to the Protestant churches of Hungary freedom of worship, exemption from regulation by royal decrees, restoration of the authority of the diet, elimination of all violations of their freedom of worship, repeal of all laws passed since 1647 restricting Protestants' freedom, an end to supervision by the Roman Catholic prelature, complete autonomy for the two recognized Protestant churches, the right to open schools at all levels, equal rights with Catholics to hold state offices, full authority over Protestant marriages, security for their properties, and sanctions against all violators of their rights. A few restrictions favoring Roman Catholics endured: mixed marriages had to be performed by Catholic priests and all matters connected with such marriages remained under the authority of Rome. "Despite the latter, Act XXVI of 1791 became the cornerstone of the Protestant churches' constitutional position in Hungary in modern times" (Révész, *op. cit.*, 50). *Corpus juris hungarici: 1740-1835 évi törvényczikkek* (The Corpus of Hungarian Law: Acts of the Years 1740-1835) (Budapest: Franklin-Társulat, 1901), 168-177; Henrik Marczali, *Az 1790 91-diki országgyűlés* (The Diet of 1790 91), 2 vols. (Budapest: Magyar Tudományos Akadémia, 1907), II, 221-288.

5. "Received churches" were established churches, those protected under the constitution and the law. For Act XX, 1848, see Géza Ballagi, "Az 1848. XX. t. cz. a történelem világánál" (Act XX of 1848 from an Historical Viewpoint), *Protestáns Szemle* (Protestant Review), XV (1903), 36 et seq.; Mihály Zsilinszky, *Az 1848-iki vallásügyi törvényczik története* (A History of the Ecclesiastical Affairs Act of 1848) (Budapest: Luthertársaság, 1938).

6. *1847 8-ik évi országgyűlési törvényczikkek* (Acts of the Diet of 1847 8) (Pozony (Bratislava), 1848); *Corpus juris hungarici: 1836-1868 évi törvényczikkek* (Corpus of Hungarian Law: Acts of the Years 1836-1868) (Budapest: Franklin-Társulat, 1896), 243-244; Zsilinszky, *op. cit.;* Ballagi, *op. cit.,* 36 ff; Erzsébet Andics, "Az egyházi reakció 1848-49-ben" (The Reaction of the Church in 1848-49) in Aladár Mód et al., *Forradalom és Szabadságharc 1848-1849* (Revolution and the War of Independence 1848-1849) (Budapest: Szikra, 1948), 315-413.

7. *Emperor Francis Joseph of Austria: A Biography* (Hamden, Conn.: Archon Books, 1965), 238.

8. Among them were Leopold Wohlmuth, Jan Chalupka and Samuel Reisz. Albert Berzeviczy, *Az abszolutizmus kora Magyarországon, 1849-1865* (The Age of Absolutism in Hungary, 1849-1865), 2 vols. (Budapest: Franklin-Társulat, 1922), I, 156.

9. The order thus outlived Haynau, who was dismissed in 1851 and replaced by Archduke Albrecht, who was appointed Governor General of Hungary.

10. Révész, *op. cit.,* 60.

11. Count Leo Thun und Hochenstein (1811-1888), Governor General of Bohemia, Minister of Cults (1849-1860), head of the Czech Federalist Party, member of the Bohemian *Landtag.* "Count Leo Thun was one of those Czech statesmen whom Francis Joseph used in suppressing the Hungarians." Géza Ballagi, "A protestáns pátens és a sajtó" (The Protestant Patent and the Press), *Protestáns Szemle,* IV (1892), 5.

12. *Op. cit.,* II, 140.

13. *Ibid.,* II, 140.

14. *Ibid.*, II, 71.

15. In Royal Hungary, Croatia and the Banat there were 4,538 Roman Catholic primary schools, 1,786 Calvinist, 926 Lutheran, 478 Greek Catholic, 434 Greek Orthodox, and 150 Jewish. Attendance by pupils not above school-leaving age in elementary schools was 61.3% in Hungary, 60.3% in the Banat, and 29% in Croatia. *Ibid.*, I, 70. Members of the Greek Orthodox church in Hungary, who were mostly ethnic Serbs and Rumanians, were still faring worse than any other group half a century later. In 1910 Hungary's 2,900,000 Rumanian inhabitants had 2,300 elementary schools in which Rumanian was the language of instruction. The situation, nevertheless, was better than in the Kingdom of Rumania where there were at that time 4,458 elementary schools for the country's seven million inhabitants. Had the Hungarian ratio applied, the Kingdom of Rumania would have had to have some 5,550 elementary schools. Symptomatic of educational standards was the fact that 59% of Rumania's military recruits were literate, 20.3% of Serbia's were, and 70% of the Rumanian recruits in Hungary were. Paul Teleki, *The Evolution of Hungary and Its Place in European History* (New York: The Macmillan Co., 1923), 158, 160.

16. Two versions of the draft exist. One is *Törvényterv a két evangélikus hitfelekezet egyházi ügyeinek képviseletét és igazgatását Magyarország, a szerb vajdaság, és a temesi bánságban illetőleg* (Draft Law on Representation and Administration of the Affairs of the Two Churches of the Evangelical Faith in Hungary, the Serbian Voivodina, and the Banat of Timis) (Pest: Emich Gusztáv, 1856). The other version was translated into German under the supervision of Pál Apostol, the Calvinist Superintendent of the Cis-Tisza, and published by the press of the College of Sárospatak in 1856. The draft contained 58 paragraphs. The main ground for its rejection was that only the Protestant Church Councils had the authority to introduce changes of such substance.

17. Emperor Francis I had wished to set up such an *Oberkirchenrat* but circumstances had prevented him from doing so. Ever since Count Thun had become Minister of Cults, one of his main ambitions was to impose such a body on the Hungarian Protestant churches. Révész, *op. cit.*, 60-61.

18. György Bartók, *A református egyházak presbiteriális szervezete* (The Presbyterial Organization of the Reformed Churches) (Kolozsvár (Cluj): Gáman János, 1904), 135.

19. In the Military Frontier Zones, administered from Vienna by the *Hofkriegsrat,* the Counter-Reformation had been carried through as rigorously as it had in the Bohemian and Alpine provinces of the empire. In Croatia, on the other hand, anti-Protestant legislation was not Habsburg-inspired but in-digenous. Since the beginning of the seventeenth century Croatian diets had repeatedly declared that only the Roman Catholic religion was recognized in Croatia and that heretics (Protestants) were to be expelled. Such laws had been promulgated by King Rudolf (1576-1608) and King Matthias II (1608-1619) at exactly the same time as Hungary was enacting the Protestants' freedoms. Ferdo Sišić (ed.), *Monumenta spectantia historiam Slavorum meridionalium* (Zagreb: Yugoslav Academy, 1917), XLI, pp. xxii and 603, quoted in Francis H. Eterovich and Christopher Spalatin (eds.), *Croatia: Land, People, Culture,* 2 vols. (Toronto: University of Toronto Press, 1969), I, 206. In 1848 the Hungarian legislature, and Kossuth especially, advised the Croatian diet to grant equal rights to the Protestants but the Croats refused, so that, in principle, even in 1848 Protestants were banned from settling in Croatia. *Ibid.,* II, 39.

20. C. A. Macartney, *The Habsburg Empire, 1790-1918* (New York: The Macmillan Co., 1969), 492-494. An excellent, concise summary is also in Ferenc Pulszky, *Életem és korom* (My Life and My Times), 2 vols. (Budapest: Szépirodalmi Könyvkiadó, 1958), II, 215-217.

21. Macartney, *op. cit.*, 496-497.

22. Ballagi, "A protestáns pátens ...," *loc. cit.*, 10.

23. Redlich, *op. cit.*, p. 288. Hantsch, *Die Geschichte Österreichs*, 2 vols. (Graz: Verlag Styria, 1968), II, 356.

24. Macartney, *op. cit.*, 500.

25. Lukács, *Magyar függetlenségi és alkotmányos mozgalmak, 1848-1867* (Hungarian Independence and Constitutional Movements, 1848-1867) (Budapest: Művelt Nép, 1955), 191. Letter of Baron Zsigmond Kemény to Miksa Falk dated November 17, 1859. Dávid Angyal (ed.), *Falk Miksa és Kecskeméthy Aurél elkobzott levelezése* (The Confiscated Correspondence of Miksa Falk and Aurél Kecskeméthy) in the series "Fontes Historiae Hungaricae Aevi Recentioris" (Budapest: A Pesti Lloyd Társaság, 1925), 462.

26. Sándor Márki and Gusztáv Beksics, *A modern Magyarország, 1848-1896* (Modern Hungary, 1848-1896) (Budapest: Atheneum, 1898) Vol. X, 526.

27. Count István Széchényi, *Ein Blick auf den anonymen 'Rückblick'* in *Gr. Széchenyi István Döblingi irodalmi hagyatéka Blick és kisebb Döblingi iratok* (The Döbling Literary Papers Left by Count István Széchenyi, Blick and Minor Döbling Papers) in the series "Fontes Historiae Hungaricae Aevi Recentioris" (Budapest: Magyar Történelmi Társulat, 1925). Hungarian version in M. Papp, *Magyar Remekírók* (Hungarian Classics) (Budapest, 1907), Vol. XVII: "Selected Works of Count Széchenyi." For a diplomat's view, see Lord Augustus William Frederick Spencer Loftus, *The Diplomatic Reminiscences of Lord Augustus Loftus, 1837-1862*, 2 vols. (London: Cassel & Co., 1892), II, 149-157.

28. Lajos Kossuth, *Irataim az emigráciôbôl* (My Papers in Exile) (Budapest: Atheneum, 1881), II, 71. "The funeral of the law student Géza Forinyák on April 4, 1860, became a demonstration that rallied more than a third of the inhabitants of Pest and Buda." György Szabad, *Forradalom és Kiegyezés válaszútján, 1860-61* (At the Crossroads of Revolution and Compromise, 1860-61) (Budapest: Akadémiai Kiadó, 1967), 27. On the earlier occasion, "the university students of Pest held a huge demonstration on December 16, 1859. They gathered en masse, demanding that the Police Commissioner release a student. A great many people supported them. About 15,000 people crowded into the market place." *Archives of the Asboth Family, 1849-1866: Data on the History of Movements against the Autocratic Regime* (Pest: Ráth Mór, 1871), 149.

29. Ballagi, "A protestáns pátens ...," *loc. cit.*, 21.

30. *Ibid.*, 27.

31. Lukács, *op. cit.*, 195.

32. *Ibid.*, 191-195. The scheme of the government and the conservatives misled no one. People well remembered the earlier treacherous behavior of men like Zsedényi. "Zsedényi, the chairman of the Protestant Lutheran meeting in Késmárk, was the president of the Pecsovics (nickname for the pro-Habsburg) party in 1848, and after 1848 he was a leading supporter of the Austrian tyranny. Yet he himself is now under arrest together with 129 other persons of

that ilk." *Archives of the Asboth Family, . . .*, 149. László Szőgyény, such a loyal servant of the Habsburgs that he was appointed to the *Reichsrat*, wrote: "He (Zsedényi) will leave prison with greater popularity and fame than he could ever have hoped for." Szabad, *op. cit.*, 12.

33. Manó Kónyi (ed.), *Deák Ferencz beszédei, 1842-1861* (The Speeches of Ferenc Deák, 1842-1861), 3 vols. (Budapest: Franklin, 1903), II, 396.

34. Kossuth, *op. cit.*, II, 72, n. 3.

35. Full text is in *Protestáns Egyházi és Iskolai Lap* (Protestant Ecclesiastic and Scholastic Journal), 1859, no. 40. See also Ballagi, "A protestáns pátens . . .," *loc. cit.*, pp. 16-26; Szabad, *op. cit.*, 13.

36. Ballagi, "A protestáns pátens . . .," *loc. cit.*, 36.

37. *Ibid.*, 34. Thun's ministerial rescript of January 10 ordered all Protestant parishes to comply with the patent by March 31, 1860. Szabad, *op. cit.*, 13.

38. Ballagi, "A protestáns pátens . . .," *loc. cit.*, p. 34.

39. Kossuth, *op. cit.*, II, 68.

40. *Ibid.*, II, 69.

41. Baron Miklós Jósika (1794-1865), liberal statesman, Supreme Court justice, one of Hungary's most fertile writers of historical novels. After Világos, he became Kossuth's trusted associate in exile. The other members of the Hungarian exile press bureau in Brussels were Ede Horn, János Ludvigh and Frigyes Szarvady. A vivid description of the bureau, which began its activities on November 1, 1859, is in Kossuth, *op. cit.*, II, 81 ff.

42. János Ludvigh, a member of the bureau, wrote three weeks after it began functioning: "As far as our press activities are concerned, I can now state that they are a success beyond anything we anticipated. The following newspapers have already published articles about us or by us: *The Times, Daily News, Standard, Morning Herald, Patrie, Débats, Courrier de Dimanche, Revue Contemporaine, Indépendance, Kölnische, Observateur, Journal de Belgique, Nord*, etc. Our cause, in the proper sense of the word, has become an issue of the day . . . . Since November 1, when our enterprise began, more than 30 articles have been published, several of them long and substantial. In addition to these, ten or twelve other newspapers excerpted parts of the articles." Letter of János Ludvigh to Count László Teleki, dated November 22, 1859, published in Kossuth, *op. cit.*, II, 84. Even the Russian émigré press used some of the bureau's articles. Szabad, *op. cit.*, 25. See also Ballagi, "A protestáns pátens . . .," *loc. cit.*, 49. A treasurehouse of information about the exile press activities at that time is Tolnai Gábor (ed.), *Tanárky Gyula Naplója, 1849-1866* (The Diary of Gyula Tanárky, 1848-1866) (Budapest: Szépirodalmi Könyvkiado, 1961).

43. Kossuth, *op. cit.*, II, 128.

44. Lord Shaftesbury from the House of Lords, and Messrs. Buchanan, Dalgleish, Crum, Kinnard and others from the House of Commons. Kossuth, *op. cit.*, II, 128.

45. *Ibid.*, II, 129.

46. Ballagi, "A protestáns pátens . . .," *loc. cit.*, 49.

47. *Ibid.*, 139.

48. Károly Kerkápolyi, *Protestáns egyház-alkotmány tekintettel történeti fejlődésre* (The Protestant Church Constitution with Regard to Historical Development) (Pápa: College of the Reformed Church, 1860).

49. János Szeberényi, *A császár-király és a reformáta vallás, vegyis*

Boldoghǎzy Istvǎn R . . . falusi jegyző és fia közötti levelezés az 1859-ki szept. 1-
én kelt cs. kir nyílt parancsra (The Emperor-King and the Reformed Church, or
the Correspondence of Istvǎn Boldoghǎzy, village notary of R . . ., with His Son
about the Imperial-Royal Public Order Dated September 1, 1859) (Pest:
Wodianer, 1859).

50. Baron Gǎbor Prónay, *Das k.-k. Patent vom 1. September 1859 als
Mystification des Protestantismus in Ungarn* (Hamburg: Hoffmann und
Campe, 1860); and Mor Ballagi, *Protestantenfrage in Ungarn und die Politik
Oesterreichs,* 2 vols. (Hamburg: Hoffmann und Campe, 1860).

51. *Zeitstimmen aus der reformierten Kirche der Schweiz,* 1860, I, 3. The
commentary was written by the editor in chief, Lang, himself.

52. Ethnographers claim that in Hungary Calvinism was restricted virtually
exclusively to ethnic Hungarians. Oszkǎr Jǎszi composed a definition of the so-
called Calvinist key, a concept first advanced by Martin V. Schwartner in
Statistik des Königreiches Ungarn (Ofen (Buda): 1809). According to the
definition: "Since we consider the Calvinist population to be typical,
representative **Hungarian**, a population that has absorbed no other by im-
migration or assimilation and that has therefore increased only by natural
growth, the percental growth of the Calvinist population may be taken once for
all as the *natural rate of growth of the whole Hungarian population.*" (Jǎszi's
italics) Oszkǎr Jǎszi, *A nemzeti államok kialakulása és a nemzetiségi kérdés*
(The Evolution of Nation States and of the Nationality Problem) (Budapest:
Grill Kǎrolym 1912), 380-381. A measure of the accuracy of Jǎszi's thesis is
provided by the 1910 census, the last taken in Hungary as its borders existed
before World War I. The data for Transylvania show the degree of correlation
between nationality and faith:

Roman Catholics)			
Calvinists)	906,000:	918,000	Hungarians
Unitarians)			
Jews)			
Lutherans)	229,000:	234,000	Saxons
Uniates)			
Greek Orthodox)	1,542,000:	1,526,000	Rumanians
			and Gypsies

Paul Teleki, *The Evolution of Hungary and Its Place in Uropean History* (New
York: The Macmillan Co., 1923), 218.

53. Pǎl Kǎrmǎn, "Néhǎny adat a protestǎns pátens történetéhez" (A Few
Data on the History of the Protestant Patent), *Protestáns Szemle,* V (1893),
132; Lukács, *op. cit.,* 194.

54. Kǎlmǎn Révész, "A pátens visszavonásának körülményei" (The Circumstances of the Revocation of the Protestant Patent), *Protestáns Szemle,*
XV, 535-536. See also Mǎrki and Beksics, *op. cit.,* X, 528-530.

55. Pǎl Török, a senior Protestant lay leader, in his report to the annual
council of his district in 1881, said of Benedek: "It was he who gained his

Imperial and Royal Majesty's consent to repealing the validity of the notorious patent . . . . Later perhaps I shall be able to say more." Jenő Szoványi, "A pátens visszavonásának körülményei" (The Circumstances of the Revocation of the Protestant Patent), *Protestáns Szemle*, XV (1903), 469; Szabad, *op. cit.*, 25.

56. Szabad, *op. cit.*, 32.

PART II

HASIDIC-MITNAGGEDIC POLEMICS IN THE JEWISH COMMUNITIES OF EAST CENTRAL EUROPE

Mordecai L. Wilensky

THE HOSTILE PHASE *

Polish Hasidism, whose Founder was Rabbi Israel Ba'al Shem Tov (BESHT),(1) encountered strong opposition on the part of the organized Jewish community as early as the second half of the eighteenth century. The conflict between the Hasidim and Mitnaggedim was confined at first to the Jewish community and manifested itself in the imposition of bans and sanctions, libelous writings, and economic and social deprivation. As the conflict continued, each of the opposing camps resorted to bringing the issue before the non-Jewish authorities.(2)

As long as these groups operated in Podolia and the Ukraine, backward provinces in terms of Torah Learning, they aroused no organized opposition. Soon the center of the movement moved northward to Volhynia, and the emissaries of R. Dov Baer, the Maggid of Mezeritch,(3) successor to the Besht, began preaching their teacher's doctrine in White Russia, Polesie, and even tried to penetrate Vilna, the center and stronghold of Lithuanian Torah study, it was then that organized war against the new movement began. The heads of the Vilna community, led by Gaon R. Elijah,(4) began their overt war against Beshtian Hasidism in 1772, and continued their aggressive opposition to the movement up to the beginning of the 19th century.

Three waves of controversy arose during the forty years of the dispute. The first was in 1772; the second in 1781; and the third began in 1796 and extended into the early 19th century. All three originated in Vilna, each starting with the imposition of bans and sanctions on the new sect.(5)

* * * * * * * * * * * * * * * *

The polemical literature between the Hasidim and the Mitnaggedim both printed and manuscript, is scattered. In referring to this literature, much of which is otherwise inaccessible, I have cited my two volume collection: *Haisidim U-Mitnaggedim* (Jerusalem Mossad Bialik, 1970). Referring to my book will also allow the reader to use the introductory and explanatory material which, of necessity, I have shortened in this article. References to the book are indicated simply by volume number and page (I,p. .; II, p. .).

Each of the three phases of the conflict had a specific cause. The first ban, in the spring of 1772, was decreed after the Hasidim succeeded in infiltrating Vilna and in establishing their own prayer house (minyan). The second ban was imposed in 1781, one year after the appearance of the first Hasidic book *"Toledot Yaakov Yosef"*,(6) a commentary on the Pentateuch. This book by R. Jacob Joseph of Pulnoye, an ardent disciple of the Besht, forced severe criticisms against contemporary Rabbis and communal leaders, and in turn aroused Vilna's Mitnaggedim from their relative inaction. The appearance in print of the book *"Tanya"*(7) by R. Shneor Zalman of Liozne(8) (henceforth Rashaz), head of Russia's Hasidim; and the growth of the Hasidic movement caused the third phase of hostility.(9)

As has already been mentioned, during the third altercation, the site of the conflict moved beyond the confines of the Jewish community. Each side brought his claim before the Russian government which had only recently annexed large parts of Poland. As a result of the two enemy camps having resorted to the Russian civil authorities, the government used this opportunity to reduce communal authority.(10) It should be noted that the most graceless intervention of the Russian government in the conflict was in Vilna at the end of the last decade of the 18th century.(11)

Contrary to accepted scholarly opinion, it was not the Mitnaggedim, but the Hasidim who first turned to the Russian government who, incidently, included some of the wealthy members of the Jewish community.(12)

In 1798, a strongly written complaint was submitted to the government by the Vilna Hasidim. This complaint claimed that the community *(Kahal)* was persecuting them, and included slanderous information about the organization of the *Kahal*.(13) While there is no justification for this act of slandering, it should be noted that it did result from extended insufferable persecution by Vilna's Mitnaggedim, which became particularly acute after the death of the Gaon. Patience to endure any more had failed. As a result of their complaint, the government allowed the Hassidim to pray in their own Minyanim and the authority of the community was further decreased.(14)

The Vilna *Kahal* did not sit idle either and turned to the government with slander about the Hasidim. As a result, Rashaz was imprisoned in St. Petersburg at the end of 1798. His second imprisonment came in November 1800, as a result of information provided by the zealous Mitnagged Avigdor ben Hayyim, the Rabbi of Pinsk.

The Russian government's position favoring the Hasidim, which was expressed both by the exoneration of Rashaz and by the promulgation of the "Statute of 1804" by Alexander I,(15) in which the Hasidim were given legitimate status was one of the causes of the abatement of the conflict between the two hostile camps. Although the dispute continued for many more years and its traces are discernible throughout the 19th century, by the first decade of the 19th century, both sides had reached a point of peaceful coexistence in Vilna, and the rest of the communities of White Russia and Lithuania soon followed in their footsteps.(16)

Much has been written about the course taken by the dispute, I would prefer to concentrate on specific accusations made by the Mittnaggedim against the Hasidim, deal with ideological, economic, and social causes of the conflict, and to consider the reactions of the Hasidic camp to Mitnaggedic charges.

The Mittnaggedic literature, available to us from the period of conflict includes, mainly: a) declarations of sanctions, miscellaneous writings by individuals and communal authorities; b) essays. Most of the essays were written during the 1790's by two zealous opponents of Hasidism: R. David, the Maggid of Makov(17) and R. Israel Loebel of Slutzk, Maggid in various Lithuanian and White-Russian communities.(18) Their essays(19) include criticisms against the new sect and its leaders.

There is a paucity of written reaction on the part of the Hasidim to the conflict. Presumably, the reason for this is that few of their number had the literary ability to express their reactions in writing. The primary Hasidic spokesman was Rashaz, who from 1772 to the abatement of the controversy continually attempted to reconcile between the two camps.

In his letters, he turned to his adversaries, at times pleadingly and at times resolutely, in order to make them see their error and stop their war with the Hasidim.(20) Initially, he wrote letters to his followers, in which he prevailed upon them not to antagonize the Mitnaggedim, not to insult those who studied Torah, and to be sure to respect the Gaon of Vilna.(21)

Aside from Rashaz, others who attempted to actively defend the movement in its difficult days were R. Samuel (Shmelka) Horowitz(22) of Galicia, later Rabbi of Nicholsburg, and to some extent R. Elimelech of Lizensk(23) and Rabbi Menachem Mendel of Vitebsk in his letters from Safed,(24) following his emigration to Palestine in 1777.

Despite the fact that the amount of the polemical Mitnaggedic literature is far greater than that of the Hasidim, one cannot assert the same regarding its quality. Written reaction on the part of the Hasidim is more restrained and its writers avoided being dragged into using the harsh and provocative language found in Mitnaggedic writings, including those that were penned by the Gaon of Vilna. The Hasidic authors and especially Rashaz concentrated on the heart of the matter and did not write on petty things as did many of the Mitnaggedic writers.

The overwhelming majority of arguments and accusations on the Hasidim by the Mitnaggedim throughout the conflict, were expressed already in the very beginning of the controversy. The first anti-Hasidic writings of 1772 were collected in the pamphlet — *Z'mir Aritzim Ve-Harevot Tzurim* (The Song of the Terrible Ones and Knives of Flint).(25) This pamphlet, published in 1772 includes the first bans imposed on the Hasidim and voices most of the objections made, during the entire conflict, against the new sect, except the one about the "elevation of strange thoughts" during prayer.(26) The accusations against the Hasidim can be summarized: as separation by the Hasidim from the established prayer houses and founding their own private *minyanim*, in which they introduced changes in liturgy, changes in the set times of prayer according to the *Halakha*, changes in the methods of prayer. Changes in ritual slaughter *(shehitah)*, using boned knives. Neglect of Torah Study and disrespect for Torah scholars. Bizarre actions. Suspicion of sabbatianism. Much merrymaking and partying. Greediness of Hasidic *Zaddikim* (Hasidic Masters) causing waste of Jewish money. Miracle-working by Hasidic *Zaddikim*. Other accusations like: change of dress, a great deal of pipe smoking, etc.

I will deal only with the accusations: changes in prayer; changes in ritual slaughter; bizarre actions; suspicion of sabbatianism. I shall end with the accusation that most hurt the Lithuanian and White Russian Mitnaggedim, that the new sect was causing neglect of Torah Study and disrespect for Torah Scholars.

PRAYER

The Mitnaggedim opposed Hasidic prayer on several different grounds: the change in the liturgy from Ashkenazic to Sephardic, or, more precisely, to Lurianic rite; the separation of the Hasidim from the established prayer houses, and their establishing of special houses of worship; lack of precision regarding *halakhically* defined times of prayer; new modes of prayer, such as praying aloud, strange motions and gestures; elevation of strange thoughts during prayer.

We may assume that the Besht and his circle prayed in the Lurianic rite.(27) It was, however, the Besht's successor, R. Dov Baer of Mezeritch, who provided the ideological basis for this. In brief, his reasoning was that when the people of Israel were in their own land and the Temple existed, each of the tribes would pray using its own rite and would direct its prayers to its own particular gate in the Temple. With the destruction of the Temple and the subsequent lengthy dispersion of the Jewish people, a Jew no longer knew from which tribe he came.

Therefore, R. Yitzhak Luria (Ari — the famous Kabbalist who lived in Safed, 16th century) arranged a version of the prayers, known as the Lurianic rite, which included the versions of all twelve tribes.(28)

Hasidic prayer in the Lurianic rite is an important topic which has been widely discussed. It was most recently treated in Dr. Louis Jacob's book, *Hasidic Prayer.*(29) Here, we will consider only the debate on the change in prayer as it is seen in the polemics of the two opposing camps. The Mitnaggedim were not opposed to the Lurianic rite as a matter of principle. For example, the community of Brody in Galicia, although it forbade changes in the prayer rite in its decree against the Hasidim in 1772, did permit local Kabbalists to pray according to the Lurianic rite.(30)

Opposition to the change in rite resulted largely from the new sect's audacity in abrogating a custom which had existed for generations. R. Abraham Katzenellenbogen, rabbi of Brest-Litowsk, in his letter to R. Levi Yitzhak of Berditchev, protested the impertinence of ''Defiling the prayers of all our true and God-fearing brethren, the Children of Israel.''(31) He maintained that the great minds of the Jewish people in recent generations also knew this form of prayer and still ''. . . chose the Ashkenazic rite, and it never entered the mind of any of them to change anything''.(32) The Mitnaggedim also saw this change in the rite as an attempt on the part of members of the new sect to throw off the authority of the community and to compete with it. Likewise, Mitnaggedim saw the overt change as a kind of presumptuousness on the part of Hasidim with regard to the rest of the community which prayed in the Ashkenazic rite. In the anti-Hasidic ordinances of Leshnov, a town near Brody, this was emphasized: ''. . . haughtiness had rooted itself in their hearts making them change the prayer rite''.(33)

This is the source of the harsh language in the Mitnaggedic proclamations emanating from Vilna and Brody (1772); the proclamations of Grodno and Slutzk (1781); the decisions of Minsk (1797) et al. In the proclamations issued in Crakow in 1785, it was even stated that one who prayed according to a different rite ''would be excommunicated and banished and (. . .) would be dishonorably buried''.(34)

Opposition to the changed version also stemmed from the fact that it drew the Hasidim away from established synagogues, leading them to establish separate *minyanim.* In addition to the fact that this meant that the Hasidim were separating themselves from the community and denying its authority, there was also an economic consideration.

Separation of the Hasidim obviously reduced the number of people praying in the established synagogues and consequently reduced revenues We find mention of this in the decisions of the Vilna *Kahal* against the Hasidim in the late 1790's.(35) It should be noted that in the generation preceding the growth of Hasidism, the organized community opposed the establishment of separate places of worship for craftsmen. One source of this opposition, too, was economic.

These, then, are the reasons for the community's opposition to separate prayer houses for the sect from 1772 on. They even resorted to the imposition of sanctions. In the ban of Vilna in 1797, the sanctions are specified: it was forbidden to appoint Hasidim to office in the community or its organizations. A *"Rodeph Ne'elam"* or Secret prosecutor was appointed to implement this. Vilna Mitnaggedim were not above threatening to expel the Hasidim from the community.(36) Although we know of no instance in which they actually carried out this threat, we do know that one of Vilna's Hasidim, in whose courtyard a Hasidic *minyan* met, was publicly flogged.(37)

The Mitnaggedim saw the Hasidic lack of precision with regard to the established times of prayer as a violation of *Halakha*, (Jewish Law). We find criticsm of this custom even before 1772.(38) This charge is found throughout the writings and sanctions of the Mitnaggedim. In its proclamation of 1781, the community of Slutzk claims that the Hasidim allowed the *Shahrit*, the morning prayer, to continue "until midday".(39) In *Z'mir Aritzim*, R. David of Makov accuses the Hasidim of Koznitz and Lublin of praying *Minhah*, the afternoon prayer, after the stars have already appeared.(40) R. Hayyim of Volozhyn in his *Nefesh ha-Hayyim* criticizes this new custom, whereby "(. . .) they have almost forgotten the time for the afternoon prayers which was determined by the rabbis of blessed memory".(41) In his book *Sefer Viku'ah*,(42) R. Israel Loebel maintains the Hasidim "tell stories and gossip and obscenities among themselves before prayer and consequently are late in beginning to pray".(43)

In answer to this the Hasidim argued that the most important aspect of prayer is intention *(Kavvanah)*, and that it is impossible to call up in oneself the proper intention at a specific time. Intention requires preparation. This preparation for prayer is so integral a part of prayer itself that one is rewarded for it too. He who hires someone to chop down trees for him, must also pay the woodsman for the time he spends honing his ax.(44) Preparation for prayer falls within the category of honing one's ax. R. Hayyim of Volozhyn is strongly opposed to this justification and sees this as a "stratagem of the evil inclination" which is liable to bring about "the destruction of the entire Torah".(45)

Because not every Hasid could arouse in himself the proper intention, despite delaying prayer for a long while, in some courts the Hasidim would be advised to transfer their thoughts to the Rebbe. The Hassid should intend only that his prayer correspond to his Rebbe's and that his prayer rise wherever the Rebbe wanted it to, because the Rebbe knows all the thoughts of his followers. We know about this transference of thoughts to the Rebbe, *Mesirat Mahshavah la Rebbe*, as it was practised in the court of R. Hayyim Haykel, the Zaddik of Amdur, from evidence taken before the Vilna rabbinical court.(46) In one of his letters, R. David of Makov notes the Gaon of Vilna saw this "Total idolatry"(47)

Hasidism saw the matter of "transference of thoughts to the Rebbe" in a different light. The purpose was that the Rebbe, in his great wisdom direct the conscious thoughts of the supplicant and raise them to their source (God), even if the individual himself did not know how to do this.

It must be noted that, after the severe criticism of the Hasidic imprecision regarding the times of prayer, some Hasidic Masters began to recite the morning *Shema* at its appointed time. In the nineteenth century, there were even those in the Hasidic camp who protested the inordinately late times of prayer.

The Mitnaggedic polemical literature is also replete with criticism and mockery of the new customs of prayer introduced by the Hasidim — praying aloud, strange movements and gesticulations during prayer. The Mitnaggedim view these customs, not only as trespassing against the words of the Sages and deviation from tradition, but also as an arrogant attempt on the part of the new group to impress the masses, "to show themselves more sanctified and purified before God than any other Jew".(48)

As to praying aloud, the Hasidim were said to "roar like lions while praying".(49) The Mitnaggedim also saw this as a deviation from the Sages who said that "He who raises his voice in his prayers shows himself to be a man of little faith".(50) It is said of Hannah, the mother of the prophet Samuel, that when she prayed, "only her lips move, but her voice could not be heard".(51) The Hasidim, however, not only "show their voices as if they were torches, but also go mad and behave boisterously in their movements."(52)

R. Samuel Horowitz's defense of the Hasidim, that even R. Akiba moved about while praying ". . . a man would leave him in one corner and find him later in another"(53), was met with the Mitnaggedic reply that R. Akiba behaved that way only when he prayed in private, but never during public prayer.(54) To R. Horowitz's argument that even King David danced about before the Lord,(55) R. Israel Loebel answers that this was a unique event in David's life. The Hasidim dance and gyrate all the time. Loebel adds that even R. Yitzhak Luzia, whose prayer rite the Hasidim adopted, forbade movement during prayer. Why do the Hasidim pay no attention to his words?(56)

A rational explanation for gesticulations during prayer may be found in writings attributed to the Besht.(57) A man who is drowning in a river grimaces in order to draw the attention of those onshore so that they will come to save him. He is not to be laughed at, because he is fighting for his life. Similarly, a Hasid while praying is fighting for his soul against the forces of evil trying to drown him in a sea of impurity. Thus, he grimaces. The Hasidim also found support for movement in prayer in the erotic section included in *Tzavaat HaRibash* (The ethical will of the Besht).(58)

The literature of the conflict also includes an accusation against the doctrine of "elevation of strange thoughts" during prayer. In other words, how would a Hasid react if a strange thought entered his mind while he was praying? Would he suppress it or try to elevate its source in God? The basis of this doctrine is in the Lurianic theory of *Shevirat hakeylim*, the breaking of the vessels, which was adopted by Sabbatianism and infiltrated Hasidism. Because of limitations of space, I will not discuss it here. It should be said that this doctrine is attacked only in R. David of Makov's writings,(59) and that there were those who objected to it in the Hasidic camp as well.(60)

At the end of this discussion of the controversy over prayer, it can be stated that it was not prayer aloud, nor gesticulations during prayer, nor even changes in liturgy and in the set times of prayer, which aroused the fury of the Mitnaggedim to the degree that they waged war against the Hasidim. The essence of the conflict over prayer resulted from a difference in approach to the concept of prayer, its value and importance. The Mitnaggedim opposed Hasidic elevation of prayer to the highest level of Jewish values.(61) This, the Mitnaggedim opposed in principle; hence their strong reaction.

In support of this assumption, I will close with Rashaz's reaction to the Mitnaggedic war against Hasidic prayer. We find Rashaz's reaction in a letter written to one of the moderate Mitnaggedim in Shklov, and deals with the matter of prayer. The letter is included in my book(62) and because of its importance, I have included part of it as translated by L. Jacobs.(63)

Rashaz opens by saying that the Mitnaggedic war against Hasidic prayer is "a decree of apostasy against prayer". Indeed, the text of the prayers and the three fixed daily services, Rashaz says, are of rabbinic origin; but those who say that prayer itself is of rabbinic origin "have never seen the light . . . The concept of prayer and its essential idea belong to the very foundation of the Torah, namely to know the Lord, to recognize His greatness and His glory with a serene mind, and through contemplation, to have these fixed firmly in the mind. A man must reflect on this theme until the contemplative sould is awakened to live the Lord's name, to cleave to Him and to His Torah and greatly to desire His commandments . . . . .''

Rashaz deduces from this that the whole Mitnaggedic approach to prayer is different from the Hasidic one, for Mitnaggedim see prayer as a rabbinic ordinance. For this reason, they have no right to criticize the Hasidic methods of prayer. They certainly cannot force the Hasidim to pray ''hurriedly and without any bodily movements or raising of the voice . . . Anyone who has drawn near to God and has once tasted the fragrance of prayer, knows and appreciates that without prayer, no man can lift hand or foot to serve God in truth, rather than as the commands of men who learn by rote''. These words are among the finest and most profound uttered during the lengthy conflict between the two camps over prayer.

SHEHITAH

Haisidim practiced ritual slaughter, shehitah, with sharply honed knives, the Mitnaggedim opposed it vehemently.

The practice of Shehitah with finely honed knives had its inception in the early period of Hasidism. Already in 1772, the first Mitnaggedic proclamations and bans included the charge that the new sect had introduced this custom. The Hasidim adopted the sharply honed knife ''on the basis that only from a finely ground cutting edge could every indentation be honed away.''(64)

There were various opinions about who in fact ordained the use of these sharply honed knives, but it was Rashaz who provided the legal basis:(65) According to Halakha, the knife used for ritual slaughter must be both sharp and smooth, but Rashaz explained that when knives were made very sharp they were not smooth. He did add that there were some skilled shohetim who could sharpen a knife that it would be both sharp and smooth, but such expertise was most rare. Furthermore, unlike the finely honed knives, sharpening unhoned knives required a great deal of time which was frequently unavailable to the shohet; therefore the Hasidim favor the finely honed knives.

The Mitnaggedim bitterly attacked this change in ritual slaughter. ''They argued that finely ground blades were liable to becomed nicked upon first contact with the skin of the creature about to be slaughtered, and thus cause the animal to become nebelah.''(66)

It should be pointed out that the prohibition against Hasidic *shehitah* had no support in Jewish Law. Consequently, in all the bans promulgated against the Hasidim by the Vilna community, this charge is absent. In the proclamations issued in Lithuanian Grodno and Pinsk too, we do not find this prohibition. R. Israel Loebel never once mentioned this Hasidic practice in his polemical essays against the Hasidim, and R. David of Makov only noted the practice in passing. From one of Rashaz's letters, we know that R. Hayyim of Volozhyn recalled that the Gaon of Vilna admitted that Hasidic *shehitah* did not violate Jewish law. If he, the Gaon, prohibited it, it was only as a means of fencing off the next sect.(67)

In this matter, not all the rabbis or lay leaders, even from Lithuania and White Russia, agreed with the Gaon. Rabbi Katzenellenbogen of Brest-Litowsk, the anti-Hasidic zealot who made no bones about his feelings: "It is well-known that I always have hated and persecuted these sectarians"(68), complains that the Vilna community did not include in its published bans the prohibition against the Hasidic *shehitah*.(69) The Lithuanian community of Slutzk also included this prohibition in its proclamation of 1781 against the Hasidim.(70) The ordinances of the Shklov community in White Russia, issued in 1787, contained a special section against the Hasidic *shehitah* — "What their *shohetim* kill may not be eaten, it is carrion, the dishes they use are polluted and forbidden . . ."(71) Similar action was taken in Minsk in 1797.(72) The Brody community, Galicia, already in 1772 prohibited the ritual slaughter by honed knives: "They make for themselves honed *shehitah* knives *("geshleefeene")*, not called for in the entire Talmud and the rabbinical authorities. Meat slaughtered by these honed knives are *nebelah* and *terefah*.(73)

This strong language is especially surprising in view of the fact, mentioned above, that the Hasidic *shehitah* does not contravene Jewish law. Thus we may suppose that the *Halakhic* aspect did not account for this strong opposition and that there were other factors with regard to Hasidic *shehitah* which irritated the Mitnaggedim.

It may be assumed that the origin of opposition to Hasidic *shehitah* was rooted in the fear that separate *shehitah* might not be carried out properly in outlying regions lacking a high level of Jewish learning, e.g. Podolia and the Ukraine, where the first Hasidic groups were organized. This explains why R. Samuel Horowitz in his letter to the Brody community stressed that Hasidim were careful to use God-fearing *shohetim*.(74) Possibly the fear of Sabbatianism contributed to the earliest rabbinic and communal opposition to Hasidic *shehitah*. In Podolia, the birthplace of Hasidism, Sabbatian cells still existed. Nor can it be mere chance that the first ban on Hasidic ritual slaughter was issued in Brody, in 1772, only sixteen years after that community had excommunicated those suspected of Sabbatian tendencies from serving as *shohetim*.(75)

Even after these fears were largely dissipated, other factors led to continued opposition to Hasidic ritual slaughter. The fact that Hasidim separated themselves from the community and refused to eat animals slaughtered in the Ashkenazic manner, the norm for generations, and the refusal of Hasidic *shohetim* to accept the authority of the community, undermined the establishment. The *Kahal* viewed the Hasidic action not merely as a rebellion against its authority, but also as a kind of arrogance and pretension just as it had viewed other new customs of the Hasidim ''in boasting before the masses to indicate that they are especially careful in fulfilling the *mitzvot*'' (the Commandments).(76)

R. Katzenellenbogen offered another reason for his opposition to the Hasidic practice. He declares that the fined honed knife could become too easily dented when cutting the skin and thus lead to the sale and consumption of meat which had become unkosher through improper slaughtering. He was aware that Hasidic *shohetim* did reinspect their knives after slaughtering and, if they found that the knives had been damaged, making the *shehita* improper, they would declare the animal unfit for Jewish use. Still the Rabbi from Brisk disparages this, asking, ''Why should they waste Jewish money for no reason?''(77)

One of the sources of opposition to the new practice was due to the fact that Hasidic *shohetim* often served as propagandists for the new movement. A Hasidic *shohet* after he had established himself in a certain settlement began to organize a Hasidic group in that place.(78)

Another factor, and apparently not the least important in the strong opposition of the communal leaders to the Hasidic *Shehitah* was the economic one. *Shehitah,* through the *korobka* tax, provided a significant part of the budget of the Jewish community. Thus, communal leaders saw separate *shehitah* as a grave danger to the balancing of the communal budget. Even the Vilna community, which also received a significant percentage of its revenues from the tax on *Shehitah,* joined the battle against Hasidic ritual slaughter after the death of the Gaon.(79) Fiscal considerations were one of the determining factors in the conflict concerning ritual slaughter, it was also fiscal considerations which led to the working out of a modus vivendi with Hasidic *shehitah* in many communities, when Hasidism had become well entrenched at the beginning of the nineteenth century.

In concluding my deliberations about *shehitah,* I want to discuss its relationship to the belief in the transmigration of souls (metempsychosis). Kabbalistic literature discussed the transmigration of souls, especially of sinners, into inanimate, vegetable and animal forms. It was indicated that souls which have become animals, can be purified and restored by undergoing ritual slaughter and then being consumed by a *Zaddik.* With this belief, a special importance would attach itself to the knife used in ritual slaughter, for any imperfection was liable to hinder the soul's restoration.(80)

The polemical literature between the Hasidim and Mitnaggedim includes s document which discusses the relationship between metempsychosis and the Hasidic *shehitah.*(81) *Shever Posh'im* by R. David of Makov contains testimony taken at a Mitnaggedic court in 1774, and the following account is recorded: The local *Shohet* slaughtered a cow and declared it kosher despite the fact that according to *Halakha,* it was forbidden to slaughter it. The *shohet* apologized, explaining that he had the approval for his action from the local Hasidic *Maggid.* When the communal supervisor of *shohetim* told the *Maggid* that his cow's flesh was unkosher according to Jewish law, the *Maggid* responded, "If I said it, it must be kosher. There must be a soul in this cow and God wants Jews to eat this cow's meat and restore its soul."(82)

Although the incident did not refer to *shehitah* with a finely honed knife, there is nevertheless great significance in the story. First, the communal *shohet* consulted the Hasidic *Maggid* before he slaughtered the cow. More important, is the reason adduced by the *Maggid,* a reason associated with the belief in transmigration of souls. We note, too, the bitter communal opposition to the *shohet's* act and the interesting response of the communal supervisor of the *shohetim* to the *Maggid:* "I do not deal in mysteries."

One may even find a hint of the connection between Hasidic *shehitah* and the belief in metempsychosis preserved in *Shivchei Ha-Besht* in the story about a certain *shohet* who was discharged by the *Besht.* When the *shohet* protested to the *Besht,* that it was forbidden to eat meat which he had inadvertently rendered unkosher in the act of *shehitah,* the *Besht* replied: "But this cow has requested that I eat of her."(83)

BIZARRE PRACTICES

The charge that the Hasidim introduced bizarre and disgusting practices, which deviated from the traditional Jewish framework, is mentioned in all the polemical literature under consideration. The charge was leveled at a variety of odd activities.

In one of the documents issued in 1772 in Vilna, there is testimony before the communal court, investigating the new sect, about one Hasid who was accused of homosexual behavior.(84) R. David of Makov alludes to the goings-on in the *Zaddik* of Amdur's court: "They all gather at night and sleep together in a loft, and who knows what disgusting things are done there."(85) The author mentions other strange acts in R. Hayyim Haykel's court at Amdur and provides the ostensible reason for them — the elimination of sadness.(86)

There were other odd doings as well. R. Katzenellenbogen feels that R. Levi Yitzhak of Berditchev's tendency to repeat the *Tetragrammaton* two or three times during prayer is "something strange and frightening". He also asks him why "before reciting the *Shema,* he throws off his shoes."(87) R. Israel Loebel in his *Sefer Viku'ah* would use the word *af(-* even, anger) deemed uncomplimentary, since it was the first word to issue from the snake, from Pharoah's chief baker, and from Haman.(88) According to Habad tradition,(89) Rashaz was questioned during his second imprisonment in St. Petersburg about his use of *af.* The questioning resulted from R. Avigdor's treacherous accusation to the government that both the Besht and Rashaz used the word *af* in their prayers, entreating the Almight to raindown His *af,* His anger, on the non-Jewish rulers.(90

The Hasidic bizarre activity most often singled out for criticism by the Mitnaggedim was their somersaulting. By 1772, the Vilna communal leaders were complaining that the Hasidim "are a topsy-turvy generation who do somersaults before the ark of God's covenant . . . . . . their heads are downward and their feet are in the air." And the Vilna Mitnaggedim ask caustically: "Has one ever heard of or seen such license as this?"(91) R. David of Makov bitterly attacks this custom which he saw with his own eyes.(92) The Gaon of Vilna views this practice as idolatry, "their somersaults are fitting for Peor" (a pagan Deity).(93)

It has to be noted that only certain circles within the new movement, especially those guided by R. Abraham of Kalisk, White Russia, and R. Hayyim Haykel of Amdur, introduced the custom of somersaulting. Rabbi Abraham of Kalisk was the student of the *Maggid* of Mezeritch and went to Palestine in 1777 with R. Menachem Mendel of Vitebsk, whom he replaced as the head of the Hasidic community in Palestine after the latter's death in 1788. We know from reliable sources that when R. Abraham was in Russia, he and his followers used to practice somersaults. The *Maggid* of Mezeritch was displeased by R. Abraham's behavior and rebuked him. Rashaz, in one of his letters to him, reminds him of the sins of his youth, among them the somersaults in the streets of Kalisk.(94)

As noted before, R. Hayyim Haykel of Amdur, also a student of the *Maggid* of Mezeritch, was the target of much of the Mitnaggedic criticism because of the strange activities of his court. There, too, somersaults were customary. As we learn from testimony taken in 1772, the Amdurites would somersault in the prayer house and in the street, reciting: "For the sake of God and for the sake of the rebbe." The evidence also records the reason given for such behavior. "When a man is afflicted by pride, he must turn himself over."(95)

Though Rashaz opposed this practice, he too was criticized by R. Israel Loebel for his behaving, while dancing, like one of the common folk.(96) A Habad source tells us, approvingly of course, that when Rashaz had reached a peak of enthusiasm in prayer, "he would roll on the ground almost without consciousness."(97)

Dr. Louis Jacobs, in his *Hasidic Prayer*,(98) has pointed out that somersaults were the custom of the Shaker sect which began in England in the second half of the eighteenth century and moved over to America. We may safety assume that the Hasidic leaders neither knew of nor were influenced by the English group. Jacobs rightly ascribes these phenomena to the *Zeitgeist*.

More relevant is the mention in the polemical literature of other Christian sects and their practices. R. David of Makov criticizes the manner in which the Hasidic Zaddikim would offer "Torah teachings" without preparation during the traditional third meal of the Sabbath, and adds that the tendency to offer teachings without preparations applies as well to Mennonites and Quakers. He discusses the patterns of worship of these groups in detail.(99) Rabbi David was acquainted with the Mennonites since many of them had settled on the border of Poland and Prussia at the beginning of the eighteenth century. By means of this comparison, the author seeks to show that Hasidic mystical practices draw upon non-Jewish sources. Even when the *Maggid* of Makov admits that the Hasidim possess good qualities, such as the practice of deeds of loving kindness, he points out that these qualities are also found among the adherents of these Christian sects and in the Masonic order. Every new sect which wants to catch souls in its net, our Mitnaggedic author comments, emphasizes the attribute of loving kindness.(100)

SUSPICION OF SABBATIANISM

I need not stress that the belief in Sabbatai Zevi and in the teachings of Nathan of Gaza did not come to an end with the supposed messiah's conversion to Islam nor even with his death. We know today from the research of Gershom Scholem and others that many Jews, among them great Torah scholars, kept faith with the Sabbatian heresy in its different manifestations throughout the eighteenth century, the era of growth of Beshtian Hasidism. Moreover, precisely at the time of Hasidism's rise, Polish Jewry was traumatized by its experiences with Jacob Frank and its followers, their bitter disputation at Kaminetz, and the resulting burning of the Talmud.(101)

Thus, we can understand why the Jewish establishment was suspicious of any new movement which arose in its midst and which introduced deviations from the tried and true path. And no one would dispute the contention that Hasidism was a deviation from the norm. It is therefore, clear why the Mitnaggedic camp was particularly sensitive to Hasidism which had originated in Podolia, the Ukraine, and Galicia, regions where Sabbatian cells still functioned underground. There is no doubt that some of the bizarre customs of various Hasidic groups helped to strengthen these suspicions.

We are not concerned here with an examination of the penetration of Sabbatian thought into Hasidism or with the ways in which the Sabbatian underground influenced, directly or surreptitiously, the proto-Hasidic groups or the first students of the *Besht*. In dealing with Sabbatianism and Hasidism, my aim is to examine the Mitnaggedic fears that the new movement was poisoned by Sabbatianism — complete heresy to Mitnaggedim — and to cite the ways in which these fears were reflected in the polemics.

The arch-Mitngaggedic writers, R. David of Makov and R. Israel Loebel, emphasize the link between Sabbatianism and the new Hasidic sect, but they generally speak in hints and allusions. They include Hasidism among the heretical sects which have arisen during Jewish history, and their aim was to bring destruction to the Jewish people. R. David of Makov warns that the Hasidim will, like Sabbatai Zevi, bring tragedy to the Jewish people.(102) R. Israel Loebel, in scoffing at the wonders performed by the Hasidic Zaddikim, notes that Sabbatai Zevi performed similar wonders; the analogy is, of course, clear.(103) An anti-Hasidic pamphlet by R. Aaron Auerbach, included in R. David Makov's *Shever Posh'im*, states that "the tyrants of our generation" the new ones, i.e., the Hasidim, "act more outrageously toward us than all the earlier rebels"; among these rebels he lists Sabbatai Zevi and Jacob Frank.(104) R. David himself seems to go beyond analogy when describing the machinations of the court of the Amdur Rabbi. He has heard, he tells us, that "once on the night of Ti'sha B'Av the Hasidim were speaking obscenities, and singing songs of passion and idolatrous hymns all night."(105) The insinuation is transparently clear. The *Maggid* of Makov also introduces the Vilna Gaon's opinion of the Hasidim: ". . . Their insides are full of heresy (absorbed) from the Sabbatian sect."(106)

The Brody community's proclamation against the Hasidim in 1772, included in the pamphlet *Z'mir Aritzim VeHarevot Tzurim*, also expressed the suspicion that the new sect would bring both disaster on the Polish Jewish community and the public desecration of God's name, as the Frankists did. The Brody leaders feel that the current threat is more dangerous since the Council of the Four Lands has been disbanded, and thus there was no leadership to step into the breach.(107) The editor of the pamphlet, notes that he has received information from Vilna that when the Hasidim pray, they ''shout out'' certain words which, when their letters are reversed according to the proper codes,(108) spell out the name of Sabbatai Zevi. According to the Vilna Gaon, ''this is a great *Kelipa*'' (evil spirit).(109)

As far as can be determined, only one in the Mitnaggedic camp, R. Avigdor ben Hayyim, the rabbi of Pinsk, explicitly accuses the Hasidim of being Sabbatians and Frankists. The Hasidim of Pinsk had been instrumental in removing R. Avigdor from his rabbinic post and the rabbi had sued for reinstatement in the municipal courts of Pinsk, but had lost the case. His prior ideological opposition was thus joined to his personal pique, instead of remaining a mere adversary of the Hasidim, he became an informer. In the spring of 1800, he submitted written accusations about the Hasidim to Czar Paul and these resulted in R. Shneor Zalman's second imprisonment in St. Petersburg.(110)

In his accusations, to which he attached selections from *Tzavaat Ha-Ribash*, he unfolds the tale of Sabbatai Zevi in Turkey and the Jacob Frank chapter in Poland. Sabbatai Zevi rebelled against the Sultan, and Frank and his followers were charged by the Polish government with being plotters. They, the Frankists, were expelled from the Jewish community, and thereupon, became Catholics. Three of their group, however, Israel of Medziboz, Berel of Mezeritch, and Jacob of Pulnoye(111) managed to evade punishment and established for their own aims this new group, the sect of Hasidim. In short, the members of the new sect are continuing the traditions of Sabbatai Zevi and Jacob Frank, both rebels against governmental authority. And, indeed, in his charge brought against R. Shneur Zalman, R. Avigdor calls the Hasidim *''Sabbatai Zevinikes''*.(112)

R. Shneor Zalman's response to most of R. Avigdor's charges, among them the Sabbatian charge, has not been preserved, but in one of his letters to his followers, we do have his response to the charge of Sabbatianism. Rashaz tells them not to be troubled by it. On the contrary, the accusation of Sabbatianism makes him happy since it is exaggerated and extreme that it will not be believed and will lead people to refuse to believe all other charges leveled by the Mitnaggedim at the Hasidim.

As far as I know, this is the only extant Hasidic reaction to this grave accusation in the polemical literature.

NEGLECT OF TORAH STUDY AND
DISRESPECT OF TORAH SCHOLARS

In discussing the role of prayer in the conflict, I said that it was not the new and strange ways of prayer, nor even the changes in liturgy, which angered the Mitnaggedim enough to impose sanctions against the Hasidim. The wrath of the Mitnaggedim on the issue of Hasidic prayer resulted from their execessive emphasis on the value of prayer and its importance in the range of Jewish values. This is closely tied to the last accusation, which we will examine now, — that the new sect caused neglect of Torah study and disrespect for Torah scholars.

The Mitnaggedim, particularly those from Lithuania, were enraged by the attitude of the new movement to the primary importance of the study of Talmud and Codes of Law *(Poskim)*, which had been unquestioned for many generations. The viewpoint of the Lithuanian Mitnaggedim was that a Jew is required to study Talmud, Codes of Law, and their commentaries diligently, and that anyone who wavered from this road struck at the very heart of Judaism and committed heresy.

In the light of the Mitnaggedic view, then, this argument was well-founded. The Mitnaggedim knew of the saying attributed to the Besht: "The *Neshama* (Soul) told the Rav(Besht) that the reason why the supernal matters were revealed to him was not because he had studied many Talmudic tractates and Codes of Law, but because he recited his prayers with great concentration."(113) In his book *Toledot Yaakov Yosef*, R. Jacob Jeseph of Pulnoye censured study: "One should not habituate oneself to constant diligence of Torah Study, but should also become involved with other human beings."(114) Persistent study of Torah, the ideal of the Gaon and his followers, had reduced importance in Hasidic ideology. R. Jacob Joseph also voiced severe opposition to the swarms of Yeshivah students: "The more they weary their feet in going to Yeshivah to study, the more you add to the rebellion to go away and turn from God."(115)

The Mitnaggedim were of the opinion that the study of Torah was of high merit even it if was not done for its own sake, and event a person who studied Torah not for its own sake, would ultimately grow to do so for its own sake. The Besht and his followers placed all the emphasis on intention *(Kavvanah)*, not only in prayer, but also in the study of Talmud and Poskim.

In his book *Nefesh Ha-Hayyim*, R. Hayyim of Volozhyn voices
strong opposition to the approach which emphasizes the intention
exclusive'y: "If a man pursues Torah even not for its own sake,
although he has not yet reached the true high level of holiness, it is
forbidden to belittle him, even in one's own mind."(116)

The Mitnaggedim thought that this "New Torah" they, the Besht's
followers, were practicing was likely to influence the common people
who would base their mode of behavior on this and neglect Torah Study.
This neglect would bring in its wake disrespect for those who studied
Torah. When the leader of the Vilna Hasidim, Meir ben Rafael, was
summoned by a special committee to account for his membership in the
Hasidic sect, he was asked, "Why did he ridicule, insult, and belittle
scholars and students of Torah?"(117)

Thus, the leaders of the Mitnaggedim realized that the new sect was
making changes in the traditional hierarchy of Jewish values, — a
hierarchy in which the highest level was Torah learning.

Here is hidden the explanation of why the Mitnaggedim fought
relentlessly against the Hasidim: floggings, prohibition of marriage
with the sectarians, economic sanctions and more. According to
Mitnaggedic sources, the Goan was not satisfied with the punishment
dealt the leaders of the Hasidim in Vilna in 1772. In his opinion the
punishment was too mild: "Had the decision been mine, I would have
done to them as the prophet Elijah did to the prophets of Ba'al."(118)
In his letter against the Hasidim, written the day after Yom Kippur,
1796, he writes: "No man should pity them and none should treat
them mercifully."(119)

In all Mitnaggedic writings, from 1772 on, the argument that the
Hasidim are fostering neglect of Torah study and denigrating scholars is
raised repeatedly. This accusation is often associated with the additional
fact that instead of engaging in Torah Study, the Hasidim waste their
time with numerous parties and celebrations. In a letter from Vilna, at
the beginning of the conflict, the Hasidim are accused of saying:
"Heaven forbid that they spend their days in Torah Study . . . and God
forbid that they be sad. There should always be laughter and
gaiety."(120) "And they despise those who study the holy Torah and
always (spend) the days in laughter and fun and joyous
dissipation."(121) In the above mentioned letter to R. Levi Yitzhak of
Berditchev, R. Katzenellenbogen voiced strong opposition to the
members of the sect "who had despised the Oral Law and who think of
the Talmud commentators as nothing and are contemptuous of
them."(122)

In court testimony in 1774, it was said that in a Hasidic Prayer House on the night of Shemini Atzeret, the Hasidim "made fun of one rabbi who was a great Torah scholar" and the Hasidic *Maggid* stood upon the table and mocked a rabbi "who was not a member of their sect."(123)

The writings of the Mitnaggedic authors R. David of Makov and R. Israel Loebel are full of sharp criticisms of neglect of Torah Study and the humiliation of its students in the Hasidic camp. I shall present but a few examples. In *Shever Posh'im* David of Makov quotes the words of a Hasid to a Mitnagged: "I will give you good advice. Do not spend your time (studying) Gemera and Tosefot for that is unnecessary study. We have a Torah given to us by the divine man Israel Ba'al Shem (Tov)"(124) Elsewhere in the same essay, he cites a Hasid, Leib Cohen, who declared publicly: "I wish to do your will, Master of the Universe, but what can I do with your Torah in my gut, the Gemara is weighing on my gut; because of the Gemara I have learned I cannot fulfill the will of the Creator."(125)

In his letter to R. Shlomo Lipshitz, Rabbi of Warsaw, the aforementioned zealous Maggid of Makov, states that the Hasidim "despise God's Torah . . . by calling the study of Gemara a mere *Kelipa.'*(126) In his ethical will to his sons he says: "They (the Hasidim) make an abomination of Torah study and of those engaged in it."(127) In one of his essays, he also cites a Hasidic rite in which a Torah scholar is humiliated after death.(128)

In *Sefer Viku'ach*, R. Israel Loebel complains of the new sect that precipitated a decline in Torah study, Leobel declares that the Hasidic Zaddikim are ignorant boors. No-one, says Loebel, has ever heard of a rabbi who was not learned in Torah "and you choose an illiterate for your rabbi."(129) This is not really surprising, Loebel continues, considering that the Besht, the sect's founder, whom he calls "the instigator" was himself an ignorant boor.(130)

The previsouly quoted statement, attributed to the Besht, that his soul told him that the reason why the supernal matters were revealed to him was not because he studied Gemara and Poskim . . ., totally infuriated Loebel: "If he is telling the truth and the soul told him that, then it lies, and if the soul does not lie but did not tell him this, then he (the Besht) is a liar."(131)

Loebel complains bitterly that in Hasidic Houses of Study only Hasidic books are studied ". . . but not our holy Torah, both written and oral."(132) Such accusations are made not by the most zealous Mitnaggedim alone. R. Hayyim of Volozhyn, a moderate Mitnagged, also complains about the deterioration of Talmud study among the Hasidim and testifies that he himself saw that in most Hasidic Houses "There is not even one complete set of the Talmud."(133)

Comments in the writings of R. David of Makov and R. Israel Loebel indicate that they were occasionally asked why they made the target of their attacks the Hasidim, rather than the *Maskilim,* who openly opposed traditional Judaism and lured the young generation away from the study of Gemara and other rabbinic literature. R. David wishes them "a plaugue on both their houses."(134) Loebel makes the distinction that the Maskilim are known to have overthrown the Torah and have declared themselves to be free-thinkers, unlike the Hasidim who misrepresent themselves as faithful to Torah and *mitzvot* and are consequently more dangerous.(135) In his German anti-Hasidic essay,(136) he repeats this and maintains that the hatred of the Hasidim for the Mitnaggedim is also greater than the hatred of the Maskilim for faithful Jews.(137)

Hasidic authors recognized the severity of the accusation that they neglected Torah and therefore attempted to refute it. R. Samuel (Shmelka) Horowitz maintains repeatedly that there is no basis for this Mitnaggedic claim that the Hasidim threw off the yoke of Torah and said that the opposite was, in fact, true, that ". . . they drank of the waters of Torah both written and oral."(138) In a letter in the late 1780's to the community of Mohilev on the Dnieper,(139) Rashaz complains bitterly over the Mitnaggedim in Mohilev and Shklov who segregate the Hasidim from the Jewish community and call them ". . . those who belittle the words of the sages." He said that if an individual were found who "could be numbered among the belittlers," he should be punished, but it was wrong to accuse the entire body of the Hasidim. By believing in this way, the Mitnaggedim were lending a hand to the anti-Semites who also generalized from the crime of an individual Jew and ascribed it to all Jews. This was also similar to the ". . . intellectuals who had recently arisen" i.e. the Maskilim, "who lend a hand to the evil doers of the nations of the world."(140)

In his conscience Rashaz knew that there was some truth to the Mitnaggedic complaint that the Hasidim belittled Torah students and for this reason, he demanded that his followers put an end to their disgraceful habit. In one of his letters to them, he strictly warns the younger Hasidim who habitually ". . . heap insult and disgrace upon Torah scholars that if they persist, they will become estranged from him."(141) In a letter to R. Abraham of Kalisk in Tiberias, written at the beginning of the nineteenth century, (142) in which he retrospectively describes the beginnings of the conflict, Rashaz notes that even the *Maggid* of Mezeritch spoke sharply to R. Abraham of Kalisk, for disrespecting scholars and belittling them. According to Rashaz, this was the determining factor in the Mitnaggedic imposition of sanctions upon the Hasidim in 1772.

It may be assumed that the vitriolic attack on the Hasidim by the Mitnaggedim regarding the neglect of Torah Study was the cause of the change of attitude in the Hasidic camp to the traditional study of Torah. This change was one of the factors leading to the reconciliation of the two opposing camps. But this phase of dialogue and reconciliation will be treated by Prof. Norman Lamm.

NOTES

1. ca. 1700-1760.
2. Even during the lifetime of the Besht, criticism was voiced against the first Hasidic groups, which he headed, although his name was not explicitly mentioned. See G. Scholem's articles in *Tarbitz*, Jerusalem 1949, 228-240; *Zion*, Jerusalem 1955, 73, 81.
3. ca. 1710-1772.
4. 1720-1797.
5. At the head of the signatories of the decrees imposing these sanctions appeared the name of the *Gaon* of Vilna, a name revered in Lithuania, White Russia, throughout Poland and beyond.
6. Koretz 1780.
7. Slavita 1796; see I, 188, note 20.
8. He settled in Liady after he left Liozne.
9. This last controversy also had an additional cause: rumors spread by the Hasidim that the *Gaon* of Vilna had ended his opposition to them, see my article in *Bitzaron*, New York 1968, 143-148.
10. *De jure* autonomous institutions of Polish Jewry no longer existed. The Council of Four Lands and the Council of Lithuania, had been dissolved by the end of the Polish rule (1764), but the real power of Lithuanian Jewish communities had not yet faded. Regional committees, which met at intervals in order to pursue common goals, were also troublesome in the eyes of the government. These facts may explain why Lithuanian Jewry was able to succeed for a while in halting the infiltration of the new sect into its borders, and why, in the final analysis Lithuania never turned into "Terra Hasidiana."
11. As a result of this intervention the communal organization was taken over by the Hasidic minority in Mitnaggedic Vilna on February 6, 1799. (I, 216-218).
12. I, 210-229.
13. It is noteworthy that this complaint was registered with the approval of Rashaz and later he regretted it. Later appeals of the Hasidim to the Russian authorities, accompanied by slander, were made without Rashaz's knowledge. In fact, he protested vehemently after he became aware of it. I, 313.
14. I, 212.
15. paragraph 53; I, 295.
16. In my recently published document concerning the controversy in the early 19th century, there is reflected the situation during the abetement of the controversy, see *Hagut 3*, Jerusalem 1974, 112-119.

17. Congress Poland; he was a native of Lithuania, see II, 50.

18. II, 253-254.

19. II, 57-180; 189-250; 266-342.

20. I. 161-167; 198-203.

21. I, 296-312; See also D.Z. Hillmann. *Iggerot Ba'al Ha-Tanya,* Jerusalem 1953. 48-49.

22. I, 85-88.

23. I, 169-176.

24. I, 90-97.

25. This title is based on *Isaiah* 25:5 and *Joshua* 5:2. The word "Z'mir" is ambiguous; it may mean song, referring to the custom of the new sect, attacked by the Mitnaggedim, to sing, merrymaking, and partying; it may also mean pruning hook, as a parallel to "Knives of Flint."

26. This last accusation is dealt only by R. David of Makov.

27. *Shivhei Ha-Besht,* 13a (Zolkiev edition, 1850).

28. *Maggid Devazav Le-Yaakov* 16a (Lemberg edition 1796); It must be noted that not all the Masters of Hasidism agreed with the *Maggid* of Mezeritch's reasoning. R. Elimelech of Lizensk preferred the Lurianic rite but did not deny the validity of the accepted Ashkenazic rite, see *Iggereth Ha-Kodesh,* I, 171-172.

29. New York, 1973.

30. I, 47.

31. I, 128.

32. I, 124.

33. I, 67

34. I, 139.

35. I, 208-209; 227-229.

36. I, 205-206.

37. I, 211; In the literature of the conflict we find no direct Hasidic reaction to the complaint of establishing separate prayer houses. Justification for separate *minyanim* appears in a book by R. Aaron of Karlin II -- a book which first appeared in 1875. There he says: "(. . .) it is better to pray with few men where the spirit of friendship rests among them, then to pray in a large congregation with people whose hearts are elsewhere." He relies on a responsum of R. David ben Zimra, a sixteenth century scholar, which discusses separation from an established synagogue. See A. Wertheim, *Halakhot Ve-Halikhot Ba-Hasidut,* Jerusalem 1960. 71: See also Jacobs, ibid., 43-44.

38. See above, note 2.

39. I, 118.

40. II, 214.

41. II, 348.

42. Warsaw 1797.

43. II, 273.

44. This illustration which justifies the delay of prayer, was reputedly offered by R. Mendel Morgenstern, the nineteenth century Rebbe of Kotzk. See *Amud Ha-Emet,* 82.

45. II, 347.

46. *Shever Posh'im,* 58; II, 149-150.

47. David of Makov adds that *"Mesizat Mahshvah la-Rebbe",* transference of thought to the Rebbe, was also practised in the court of R. Israel Hofstein, the Zaddik of Koznitz, II, 236.

48. I, 125.
49. II, 192.
50. *Berakhot,* Babyl. Talmud, 24b.
51. I, *Sam.* 1:13.
52. I, 62, 125; II, 87.
53. *Berakhot,* 31a.
54. I, 87, 125.
55. II *Sam.* 6:16.
56. II, 302-303.
57. *Keter Shem Tov,* I, 27a (Lemberg edition 1857).
58. (Crakow edition 1896), 14.
59. II, 146-147; 153-154; 157-160; 245-246.
60. The topic is treated by Joseph Weiss in his articles in *Zion,* 1951, 46-106; *Journal of Jewish Studies,* vol. 9, 1958, 163-192; by Tishbi-Dan in *Encyclopedia Hebraica,* Vol. 17; L. Jacbos, ibid, 104-120.
61. See N. Lamm, *Torah Lishma,* Jerusalem, 1972, chapters: 3, 4, 5; on the preference of Torah study over prayer, see ibid., 126-127.
62. I, 299-301.
63. Ibid., 18; 58.
64. See J. Berman, *Shehitah,* New York, 1941, 78.
65. See responsum 7, appendix to Rashaz's *Shulhan Arukh,* Vol. 5, Juzefov, 1875.
66. carrion; see J. Berman, *op. cit.*
67. I, 311.
68. I, 130.
69. I, 117.
70. I, 120.
71. I, 151-152.
72. I, 193.
73. I, 46; 48; see also the letter of R. Meshulam Igra to the Lwow community in 1794, I, 178.
74. I, 86.
75. See I. Halperin, *Pinkas Vaad Arba Aratzot,* Jerusalem 1945, 417.
76. It should be noted that Rashaz in his responsum (see note 65) stated: The use of honed knives by the Haisdic *shohetim* should not be taken to reflect upon the kashrut of meat slaughtered by shohetim who used the unhoned knife. Furthermore, in a letter to his followers in Vilna, Rashaz advised them that while participating at a religious feast together with other members of the community (Mitnaggedim) "God forbid that they should separate from them and thereby, imply that they were eaters of unkosher food. He himself did not avoid using utensils which had been in contact with meat slaughtered by the Ashkenazic method even if they had been used that very day." I, 312 .
77. I, 126-127.
78. See R. Mahler, *Ha-Hasidut Ve Ha-Haskalah,* 1961, 176.
79. *Korobka* "basket-tax," imposed on consumption items, mainly on kosher meat. I, 310-311; as early as 1773, R. Horowitz in his letter to the Brody community, alluded to the role of non-halakhic considerations in the community's struggle against Hasidic ritual slaughtering, I, 86 .
80. See Ch. Chmeruk's article: *The Social Significance of the Hasidic Shehitah* (Hebrew), *Zion* 1955, 58.

81. Ibid., 62-64. Shmeruk knew this document, but only cited it in passing, ibid., 64, note 71.

82. II, 138-139.

83. 15b-16a (Zolkiev edition, 1850)

84. I, 65; see also 41; 43.

85. II, 174; R. Moshe Satanov's *Mishmeret Ha-Kodesh* (1746), which includes criticism of the first Hasidic groups, also speaks of this base act. See G. Scholem's article in *Tarbitz* 1949, 232.

86. I, 162-163.

87. I, 126.

88. See *Genesis* 3 : 1; *Esther* 5 : 12 and *Midrash Megillat Esther*, 9.

89. *Ha-Tamim*, Warsaw 1935, 56.

90. II, 293.

91. I, 39-40.

92. II, 172.

93. I, 40; See *Num*. 25 : 3.

94. I, 40.

95. II, 140.

96. II, 293.

97. H.M. Hielman, *Bet Rabbi*, Berditchev 1903, 178-179; see also 31.

98. 56.

99. II, 166-167.

100. II, 169.

101. M. Balaban, *Le Toledot Ha Tnuah Ha-Frankit*, Tel Aviv 1935, Vol. 2, 181-192.

102. II, 180.

103. II, 321.

104. II, 104.

105. II, 174.

106. II, 179.

107. I, 46.

108. Aleph-Taf-Beth-Shin.

109 II, 178.

110. R. Avigdor's written charges have been published by S. Dubnow, along with other documents in this episode in *Jevreyskaya Starina*, 1910, 90-109, 253-281.

111. R. Avigdor's names for the three pillars of Hasidism: R. Israel Baal Shem Tov; R. Dov Baer, the Maggid of Mezeritch; R. Jacob Joseph.

112. *Jevreyskaya Starina*, 266.

113. *Tzavaat Ha-Ribash*, 8.

114. *Vayyetze*, (Warsaw edition 1881), 28.

115. *Vayyechi*, Ibid., 39.

116. II, 346.

117. I, 223; When asked why he had joined the Hasidic sect, he answered: "In our community (Vilna), he saw no truth and there (in Liozne, the home town of Rashaz) he saw the truth.", ibid.

118. I, 66.

119. I, 189.

120. I, 38.

121. I. 41.

122. I, 128.
123. II, 140.
124. II, 157.
125. II, 145.
126. evil spirit; II, 235.
127. II, 244.
128. II, 155.
129. II, 320.
130. II, 290.
131. II, 307.
132. II, 309-310.
133. R. Hayyim of Volozhyn does not mention the Hasidim explicitly, but there is no doubt that he was referring to them, see N. Lamm, *Torah Lishma*, 222.
134. II, 226.
135. II, 286.
136. *Glaubwürdige Nachrichten von einer neuen und zahlreichen Sekte unter den Juden in Polen und Lithauen, die sich Chassidim nennt, und ihren die Menscheit empörenden Grundsätzen und Lehren,* Frankfurt on the Oder, 1797; this essay was reprinted in *Sulamith,* I, 1807, 308-333.
137. II, 332; Despite these comments, it may be assumed that the advent of the Maskilim was a factor in reconciliation between the two camps.
138. I, 85.
139. I, 161-167.
140. I, 165.
141. I, 309; See also his letter published by D.Z. Hillmann, *Iggerot Ba'al HaTanya,* 213-214.
142. I, 40.

Norman Lamm

THE PHASE OF DIALOGUE AND RECONCILIATION

The end of the phase of hostility between the Hasidim and the Mitnaggedim, and the beginning of genuine dialogue between them, was occasioned by a multiplicity of causes, ranging from the political and economic to the historical and psychological. However, in order to isolate, insofar as it is possible to do so, the basic mechanism of reconciliation that made possible the existence of vigorous dissent within a pattern of "tolerance," I shall restrict myself to the realm of ideas and the interplay of religious values and theological concepts. By thus limiting the scope of this inquiry, we can perhaps sharpen the focus on what I think marks the beginning of the reconciliation which ultimately assured that Hasidism would remain within the fold of Traditional Judaism, and whereby the Mitnaggedim, although they continued to reject the foundations of Hasidism, accepted the Hasidim as authentically traditional Jews, thereby implying, indirectly, their acceptance of Hasidism as a legitimate variant of Judiasm.

We shall concentrate on one individual on the Mitnaggedic side, R. Hayyim of Volozhin (1749-1821), and, as a foil to his work, *Nefesh ha-Hayyim*, the works of R. Shneur Zalman of Ladi (1745-1813). R. Shneur Zalman, one of the youngest of the disciples of R. Dov Ber (the Maggid of Mezeritch) who was successor to the Besht, was the founder of the HaBaD school, the most cogent and profound intellectual formulation of Hasidism. R. Hayyim was the most distinguished student of R. Elijah, the Gaon of Vilna, spiritual leader of the Mitnaggedim, and he was the founder of the well-known Talmudic academy, the Yeshivah of Volozhin in Lithuania.

The period on which we shall concentrate is, approximately, the first two decades of the nineteenth century. The Gaon died in the Fall of 1797, and that is the approximate date of the publication of *Likkutei*

Amarim by R. Shneur Zalman. In 1800, R. Shneur Zalman was released from his imprisonment in St. Petersburg, determined to effect a reconciliation. During the decade that followed we know that R. Hayyim had a number of encounters with important Hasidim, including R. Levi Yitzhak of Berditchev. R. Hayyim died in 1821.

I

Eliezer Zevi Zweifel was the first of the Maskillim to take an unbiased and sympathetic view of the Hasidic movement.(1) Zweifel recognized R. Hayyim as a genuine moderate, although he overstates the case when he asserts that R. Hayyim secretly accepted all basic Hasidic doctrines but simply endeavored to restrain the Hasidim from being rash in spelling out their implications in practice.(2)

R. Hayyim's moderation — possibly the expression of the influence upon him by his earliest teacher, R. Raphael of Hamburg — is what kept him, in an atmosphere of polemical passions and hostility, from signing the various bans and excommunications against the Hasidic movement.(3) This negative act becomes far more meaningful when one considers the incredible awe and reverence of R. Hayyim for his teacher, the Gaon of Vilna.(4) Moreover, R. Hayyim deeply loved and respected his younger brother, R. Zalman, and the latter signed the anti-Hasidic proclamation in Vilna in 1781,(5) along with the Gaon.

R. Hayyim, as I have elsewhere attempted to show,(6) was not at all interested in the social and communal aspects of the controversy. In none of his writings does he ever refer to the Hasidim as a *kat*, sect, which was the popular term used by the Mitnaggedic writers for the movement, and which clearly was pejorative, implying that Hasidism was guilty of schismatism. R. Hayyim confronted the Hasidim solely on ideational grounds. His personal relations with them were apparently free from any animus, and he permitted Hasidic young men to study at his Yeshivah.(6) I take it as significant for R. Hayyim's role in healing the breach, that he used as his anonymous foil not many of the radicals in the Hasidic movement — who would certainly have been easier and more vulnerable victims for polemical vitriol — but the far more cerebral, intellectual and, at least outwardly, more moderate HaBaD school of R. Shneur Zalman. Buber has referred to R. Shneur Zalman's system as an attempt to synthesize Rabbinism with Hasidism;(7) Scholem considers it an attempt at synthesizing the Hasidism of the Maggid of Mezeritsch with Kabbalism.(8) Both are right. And this shared common ground of Talmudic Judiasm and Lurianic Kabbalah is the bridge on which the dialogue was conducted and the reconciliation effected.

It is my belief, which I have endeavored to document elsewhere, that the *Nefesh ha-Hayyim* of R. Hayyim was a response to R. Shneur Zalman's opening to the Rabbinic world; it was the first and most significant gesture of the Mitnaggedim to the Hasidim. It narrowed the gap and sharpened the issues; it made the differences clearer and stripped them of their excessive emotional impact. True dialogue was now possible.(9)

What motivated R. Hayyim in undertaking this first Mitnaggedic effort at dialogue with Hasidism? Three answers commend themselves. First, there were his theological views *per se*, about which more will be said shortly. Second, he possessed an essentially irenic personality.(10) Third, he was aware of changed circumstances — a *sina qua non* for enlightened communal leadership. The moderates had triumphed over the radicals (such as R. Abraham of Kalisk and R. Hayyim Heikel of Amdor) in the Hasidic movement. Moreover, and perhaps more important, the Hasidim were no longer an embattled sect struggling for recognition, but were rapidly becoming the majority.(11) One cannot lightly — and even for serious polemical reasons — read a or the major part of the Jewish community out of the patrimony of Israel.

Of crucial importance is R. Hayyim's technique of dialogue and reconciliation — how he went about making tolerance and dissent compatible. This technique consisted of accepting the theological structures, modes, and even vocabulary of Hasidism, especially that of R. Shneur Zalman, but so reformulating them that the basic Mitnaggedic position is salvaged and elucidated. Thus, he not only establishes his minimal position while yielding on what he feels is not absolutely necessary to safeguard his main concern — the integrity of Halakhah and the primacy of the study of Torah — but also arranges a framework for the dialogue, and for both dissent and understanding. In this, R. Hayyim undertakes a remarkable departure from his great teacher, the Gaon of Vilna. R. Hayyim learned from the Gaon the virtue of intellectual independence — and he used it, thus arriving at a different orientation in the controversy with the Hasidim. Expressed colloquially, the approach of the Gaon was that of "No, never!," while that of R. Hayyim was, "Yes, but."

We shall now trace the use of this technique by R. Hayyim in a number of key issues, dividing them into two of the main themes of Hasidism: the religious value of *devekut* — the ecstatic-contemplative communion with God, and the metaphysical principle of divine immanence. Under *devekut* we shall include prayer, the study of Torah, and the *Musar* literature. Under immanence, we shall discuss the Lurianic doctrine of *Zimzum* and the question of immanence and transcendence.

II

Devekut has a long and colorful history in Judaism. Scholars like Scholem and Weiss(12) have written perceptively about it. What is most significant in the Hasidic treatment of *devekut* may be summarized as:

a) It interpreted it primarily as a rhapsodic, ecstatic experience, rather than one of a serene *elevatio mentis ad deum.*

b) It made of it the ethos of *hoi polloi,* not only the privilege of a mystical elite.

c) It placed it at the beginning rather than at the climax of the spiritual quest and religious life.

This democratization of *devekut* carried with it a number of dangers; emotional intoxication, in the history of religion, always threatens to overwhelm normative structures and sanctified patterns of conduct. Specifically in Judaism, this visionary abandon jeapordizes the strict rules of the Halakhah on the performance of the commandments, and leads to the notion that intention is more important than deed, and ultimately to the idea that intention alone, without the deed, suffices. Further, since the study of Torah, classically considered the most important commandment, requires the full concentration of intellectual powers and focus of attention, *devekut* compromises it and denies it its fundamental cognitive and conceptual character.

R. Hayyim's general strategy is directed towards these two elements. Thus he seeks: a) to keep *devekut* under control; and b), to separate it from one's intellectual exertions whilst engaged in study. Interestingly, R. Hayyim does not engage in a frontal attack on Hasidic *devekut* as such. He is only opposed to its abuse. Indeed, he uses the term *devekut* interchangeably with יְרְאָה, "fear" — word that clearly implies normative piety. Furthermore, he uses the term *devekut* sometimes in its classical, pre-Hasidic sense. and sometimes in the characteristically Hasidic way — from which we may infer that he does not deny legitimacy to, or fundamentally disapprove of, Hasidic *devekut.*

Devekut, in its peculiarly Hasidic character, applies most prominently during the performance of the commandments incumbent upon the Jew, and especially during prayer which is the most obviously "spiritual" of all the observances. It is here that *devekut,* with its potential for explosive pneumatic anarchy, poses a threat to the normative structure of prayer so carefully elaborated by the Halakhah.

One of the earliest manifestations of this latent antinomian aspect of *devekut* was the indifference of some Hasidim to the strict time limitations imposed by the Halakhah on the three daily services and upon the recitation of the *Shema.* A *devekut*-orientation to prayer tends to ignore such artificial stricutres; the spirit, after all, cannot be summoned up on schedule. One of the earliest mentions of this Hasidic deviation already appeared in print during the life-time of the founder, the Besht by the anti-Sabbatian polemicist, R. Jacob Emden.(13) R. Hayyim subjects this deviation to thorough criticism and, by means of *reductio ad absurdum,* exposes its essential antinomian nature. Nevertheless, R. Hayyim does not disapprove in principle of Hasidic *devekut* as such, during prayer — which he emphatically does during the study of Torah.(19) Rather, he permits it as long as it is kept in rein and the Halakhah is not violated. He seeks to contain, not outlaw, Hasidic *devekut.* His response is, ''Yes, but.''

One of the key issues between the two contending groups was the study of Torah, classically considered the most important precept of Judaism.(16) This characteristically rabbinic version of the *bios theoretikos* is considered normative rather than the prerogative of an educated elite; all Israelites must study Torah. The significance of study of Torah relative to prayer underwent a transvaluation in Hasidism.(17) The differences between the Hasidic and Mitnaggedic visions were most succintly crystallized in their various definitions and evaluations of the concept of *talmud torah li'shmah,* the study of Torah ''for its (own) sake.'' The Talmud prefers Torah studied with proper motivation *(li'shmah)* over Torah studied without the proper motivation *(she'lo li'shmah),* and yet maintains that even if one studies for the wrong reasons, he ultimately will study for the right reasons.(18)

What does *li'shmah* mean? Several definitions are admissible: in order to practice what is being studied in the sacred text; for the love rather than only the fear of God; for ''the sake of Heaven''; to fulfill the commandment to study Torah; in order to understand the material studied.

Very early, however, the Hasidic teachers gave a new definition to this concept, connecting it to the key Hasidic precept of *devekut. Torah li'shmah* was interpreted as Torah study accompanied by, and for the purpose of stimulating, *devekut.*

Here, however, a new problematica arose, one not encountered in the realm of prayer. For study of Torah is the service of the Lord through the medium of the intellect, and analytic reasoning is an absorbing preoccupation which does not easily abide, and cannot flourish in the midst of, an active affective experience. Study and *devekut* are, therefore, in apparent conflict with each other. Can they be reconciled? If not, which deserves preference?

Two schools of thought appeared. One perceived a clear conflict between both values — the classic principle of study of Torah on one side, and the Hasidic demand for *devekut* on the other — and made a choice in favor of *devekut.*(19) Thus R. Menahem Mendel of Peremyslyany writes: ''Another great principle is not to study too much ... If we remove our thoughts from *devekut* in the Lord and study much, the fear of the Lord will, Heaven forbid, be forgotten by us ... Therefore one must study less, and (instead) meditate always on the greatness of the blessed Creator . . . ''(20) What might to the casual reader seem a minor shift in emphasis is indeed, in the context of Rabbinic Judaism, a radical innovation.

The second school, however, did not — or felt it could not — consider the two values as mutually exclusive. The Besht, R. Dov Ber of Mezeritsch, and R. Yaakov Yosef of Pollonoye therefore suggested a novel theory, namely, that the two can somehow be undertaken simultaneously. Human awareness can, with sufficient practice, be split into two parts, the affective and the cognitive, each operating in its own sphere at the same time. This ''double consciousness''(21) is no easy matter but, they maintained, it can — and must — be done.

A more determined polemicist seeking to make a telling debator's point, would have seized on the first theory and held it up as proof of the heretical character of Hasidism. It is, of course, possible that R. Hayyim was not aware of this radical position. It is more likely, however, that in the highly charged atmosphere of religious hostility, all such deviant opinions would have been ferreted out and held up to opprobrium.

R. Hayyim addresses himself to the second school, the one identified with the Besht and the Great Maggid.(22) Logically and analytically he refutes the Hasidic definition of *Torah li'shmah* as *devekut,* disallowing it on the basis of the authoritative sources of the rabbinic tradition and revealing the absurdities implicit in the Hasidic orientation. The practice of double-consciousness is, he maintains, untenable, considering the all-absorbing nature of the cognitive act required in the study of Torah.(23)

For himself, R. Hayyim follows a dual approach. First, in keeping with classical rabbinic view, he considers the study of Torah as such as an act of *devekut* — the communion with the word and will of God, for Torah is the revealed *logos* — even without any conscious religious experience or even awareness.(24) Second is what might be called the ''Dissociation Principle.'' While *devekut* is subordinate to study of Torah — the affective always remains secondary to the cognitive medium as the most desireable way to communion with God — it retains its validity. But the experiential and the intellectual realms must be dissociated from each other, and one must take special care not to allow religious rapture to spill over and inundate the rational activity of the Jew. The two may coexist in the same personality, but cannot be practiced simultaneously.

The assertion of the Dissociation Principle is important if we are to discern R. Hayyim's technique in the dialogue. He has not denied the validity of *devekut* as a conscious religious experience, not even as the characteristically Hasidic ecstasy. He has, rather, set clear limits which, while they may allow for the practice of Hasidic *devekut,* will in effect retain the primacy of the study of Torah, which he considers absolute, even as in other areas he strives for the protection of the integrity of Halakhic norms.

In yet one more related area do we find evidence of this "yes, but" method. R. Hayyim considered the principle of study of Torah to be jeapordized not only by *devekut* as an experience but also as a literature and a discipline. By this I mean that R. Hayyim was unhappy with Hasidim who, in the time they did make available for study, paid too little attention to the classic Scriptural and Talmudic (especially Halakhic) texts which are considered the true subject matter of *talmud torah,* and diverted it instead to ספרי יראה ומוסר 'works of piety and *Musar.*'' Hasidic pietism and its emphasis on intention, inwardness, and interiority had elevated the prestige of the devotional works of spiritual edification, character perfection, and the arousal of religious emotion — collectively known as *Musar* — at the expense of the study of Halakhah.

R. Hayyim, in his *Nefesh ha-Hayyim,* criticizes this imbalance. Yet he by no means denigrates the value of this literature. On the contrary, he is sufficiently respectful of *Musar* to have caused a major historian of the *Musar* movement to consider R. Hayyim a spiritual father of *Musar* — which first emerged as a movement two generations later.(26) But here again R. Hayyim seeks to limit the time alotted to *Musar* rather than to deny its worth altogether.

Now, I have suggested elsewhere(27) that R. Hayyim's criticism of the excessive attention paid to this literature is directed primarily at two sub-groups of this genre. One of these is the pre-Hasidic devotional works, such as the famous *Shenei Luhot ha-Berit* of R. Isaiah Halevi Horowitz, and other such books, especially during the century preceding the emergence of Hasidism. The second sub-group consists of the early classics of Hasidic writings, which were printed and reprinted and distributed in great quantity in Galicia and the Ukraine beginning in 1780.

If this assertion is correct, then R. Hayyim turns out to be moderate to a surprising degree, for what he is saying is that whereas such Hasidic tracts should not displace the classical halakhich texts to any appreciable degree, they are legitimate representatives of a sacred literature universally accepted from the time of the appearance of the *Hovot ha-*

Levavot by the revered R. Bahya Ibn Pakudah in the early Middle Ages. In effect, the very works interdicted by his colleagues and his teacher, some of which were publicly burned, are now obliquely accepted by R. Hayyim who implicitly offers them his imprimatur as valid exemplars of *Musar*. Again we find the "yes, but" approach.

III

Both Hasidism and the leading theoreticians of Mitnaggedism firmly anchored their theologies in Lurianic Kabbalah. The exact relationship of the various key personalities in the early period of the Hasidic movement to the arcane mystical system of R. Isaac Luria (1534-1572) is problematical. But certainly both sides affirmed their allegiance to Lurianism; indeed, the charge of lack of fealty to Lurianism was often made by one side against the other.(28)

The particular mystical doctrine which shall concern us here is that of *Zimzum* or self-contraction. Only the briefest summary of the concept can be offered here, with all the disadvantages of oversimplification. For further and more detailed information, the reader may consult the various works of Prof. Gershom Scholem, particularly his *Major Trends in Jewish Mysticism.*

The Kabbalah posits an Essence of God that is totally without distinction or differentiation in Its absolute perfection. In this aspect, called *Ein-Sof* ("that which is without end"), God is unknowable and indescribable, devoid of all attributes, even of volition. The turning outwards of the *Ein-Sof* takes place by means of the emanation of the Ten *Sephirot*, the divine spheres which are the self-expression of the *Ein-Sof.*

The problem arises, however, that the *Ein-Sof*, by virtue of His very absoluteness, leaves no space for creation; the existence of any area or object that is not *Ein-Sof* constitutes an infringement of His infinity. Hence, Luria asserts that preceding the emanation of the *Sephirot* there took place an act of *Zimzum*, of constriction or self-limitation, whereby the *Ein-Sof* entered into Himself, leaving room, as it were, for the creative process to take place by the emanation of the *Sephirot* into the primordial "space" which thus emerged.

Later Kabbalists were divided on whether the *Zimzum* was to be taken as an actual event or whether it was meant figuratively. The leading advocate of the literalist interpretation was R. Immanuel Hai Ricchi, with R. Joseph Ergas (both in the first half of the 18th century) expounding the position of the symbolists.

Now, R. Shneur Zalman was deeply committed to the figurative interpretation of *Zimzum*. There are, he wrote, some who are "scholars in their own eyes, may God forgive them, who erred and misinterpreted in their study of the writing" of Luria and thus accepted *Zimzum* literally.(29) It is usually accepted that this and similar references are to the Gaon.(30) Indeed, the Gaon's position on *Zimzum* is not completely clear. There are those who assert that the Gaon was a symbolist,(31) but he nowhere explicitly states such a view. However, Teitelbaum(32) has correctly demonstrated that the Gaon's interpretations of the doctrine cannot be taken as simply literalist. The Gaon applies *Zimzum* not to the *Ein-Sof* itself but to the divine Will and Providence which, while they are removed and emanated from the *Ein-Sof,* may still be called "*Ein-Sof.*"(33)

R. Shneur Zalman formulates his symbolist position by invoking a dichotomy first proposed by that other luminary of the Safed mystic brotherhood, R. Moses Cordovero. This is the distinction between מצדו–מצדנו "from His side" and "from our side." From the vantage of the *Ein-Sof,* as it were, the *Zimzum* never occurred. It is only "from our side" that we must project this act of self-limitation upon the *Ein-Sof.* From God's point of view, *Zimzum* was merely an act of concealment — an epistemic, not an ontic constriction. From man's view, *Zimzum* was thus an act of revelation.

Hence, R. Shneur Zalman is clearly a symbolist, using this dichotomy as the basis of his figurative interpretation. The Gaon does not mention this distinction in regard to *Zimzum* and, at the very least, cannot be categorized unequivocally as asserting an allegorical interpretation of Luria.

Now, R. Hayyim is unambiguous in his espousal of the metaphorical view, and makes liberal use of the bifurcation first applied to *Zimzum* by R. Shneur Zalman. "The word *Zimzum,*" he writes, "means not a removal and movement from one place to another, an entry and joining of Himself to Himself, as it were,"(34) but must be understood symbolically, and viewed bifocally: "from His side" and "from our side."

On this key mystical doctrine, we thus find R. Hayyim agreeing with the leading Hasidic theoretician rather than with his own teacher, the Gaon of Vilna. Moreover, there is a rather startling similarity of language in the writings of R. Hayyim and R. Shneur Zalman.(35) Even further, R. Hayyim follows R. Shneur Zalman in his acosmism or illusionism ("from His side" there exists no real world, for all is *Ein-Sof*); in the identical exegesis of אין עוד (Dt. 4:39) as "there is nothing else" (implying acosmism) rather than, "there is none other" (i.e., no other gods); and in the identical interpretation of the Zohar's explanations of the *Shema* and the verse that follows it in the daily prayers.(36)

Yet it would be erroneous to conclude from the above that R. Hayyim was a crypto-Hasid. R. Hayyim's agreement only goes so far, and no further. At a crucial point, his "but" follows his "yes" in time to salvage his fundamental Mitnaggedic position on the utter integrity of Halakhah and its protection against any incipient antinominaism.

On this key mystical doctrine, we thus find R. Hayyim agreeing with the leading Hasidic theoretician rather than with his own teacher, the Gaon of Vilna. Moreover, there is a rather startling similarity of language in the writings of R. Hayyim and R. Shneur Zalman.(35) Even further, R. Hayyim follows R. Shneur Zalman in his acosmism or illusionism ("from His side" there exists no real world, for all is *Ein-Sof*); in the identical exegesis of   (Dr. 4:39) as "there is nothing else" (implying acosmism) rather than, "there is none other" (i.e., no other gods); and in the identical interpretation of the Zohar's explanations of the *Shema* and the verse that follows it in the daily prayers.(36)

Yet it would be erroneous to conclude from the above that R. Hayyim was a crypto-Hasid. R. Hayyim's agreement only goes so far, and no further. At a crucial point, his "but" follows his "yes" in time to salvage his fundamental Mitnaggedic position on the utter integrity of Halakhah and its protection against any incipient antinomianism.

It is well-known that one of the major contributions of Hasidic theology is its emphasis on divine immanence. "The whole world is full of His glory" (Isa. 6:3) became the *locus classicus* of Hasidic religious philosophy. God, the Hasidim hold, is present everywhere and in everything, even in dust and stones — even in sin iteself. This immanentism is fraught with antinomian possibilities. Thus, to take an example which R. Hayyim seized upon in his critique, the belief in the immanent omnipresence of God led certain Hasidim to violate the halakhic proscription of meditating in words of Torah or other sacred thoughts in unclean places. But if God dwells everywhere, even in the lowliest of places, why not think holy thoughts every place? The issues *per se* may hardly seem earth-shaking, but R. Hayyim correctly perceived in it an antinomian dynamic which, were it allowed to develop unchecked, would undermine the whole structure of Halakhah which is based on clear distinctions between the sacred and the profane and the various gradations in between.

R. Shneur Zalman integrated his Hasidic immanentism in his larger system. He defined the Zohar's terms for immanence *(Memalei Kol Almin)* as differentiated, and transcendence *(Sovev Kol Almin)* as uniform. Thus, God is present in the world in different degrees, depending on the value or spiritually absorptive capacity of every item in creation; whereas in His transcendence, He is uniform and beyond cognition.

R. Hayyim too uses these Zoharian terms for immanence and transcendence, but with one change — which Teitelbaum noticed but the important consequences of which he did not appreciate.(37) R. Hayyim switches definitions: he considers immanence uniform and transcendence differentiated.(38) It is here that we come to the crux of the disagreement between Hasidism, as represented by R. Shneur Zalman, and Mitnaggedism in its exposition by R. Hayyim.(39)

For R. Shneur Zalman, transcendence is uniform and hence is uncognizeable. He assigns transcendence to "from His side" in the mystery of *Zimzum*, thus affirming its superior ontic quality as the source of the divine creative energy. Immanence is considered differentiated and the source of the multiplicity of values in the world, for it is finite and "from our side." As such, it is spiritually inferior to transcendence but — and this is crucial — it represents man's vision of the real world, the phenomenal world of "revelation," and hence existentially is most significant to man as *Homo religiosus.* It is immanence rather than transcendence, therefore, that becomes the metaphysical basis of Hasidic thought and the source of the rationale for tis characteristic fervor and enthusiasm — its *devekut.*

When, however, R. Hayyim — who follows R. Shneur Zalman so closely on *Zimzum* — defines immanence and transcendence in the exactly opposite ways, he is really challenging the immanentist basis of Hasidim and reasseerting the transcendentalist quality of Jewish religious thought and experience. Thus, R. Hayyim considers immanence as uniform, "from His side," and hence an expression of acosmism. Immanence denies the reality of our mundane existence and experience and, in this sense, is a spiritually superior form. However, it is thereby effectively removed from the arena of man's religious life, which must be based on a real, concrete, differentiated world of multiple values — which is R. Hayyim's definition of transcendence. It is this latter, which is "from our side," which is the realm of man's religious quest and his encounter with the divine will. R. Hayyim thus emerges with a transcendentalist rather than an immanentist world-view, one that is more congenial to his major concern for the integrity of the revealed Halakhah, and one more suited to his "sober" religious temperament.

Hence, while the Gaon dismisses immanence peremptorily and considers the verse "the whole world is full of His glory" as denoting Providence, R. Hayyim accepts the Hasidic view of *Zimzum*, the acosmism and immanence elaborated by R. Shneur Zalman — but, by equating immanence with acosmism, he effectively removes it as a factor in Jewish religious consciousness and salvages the Halakhah which he perceived as threatened by a run-away immanentism. The immanence-acosmism moment is in dialectical tension with the transcendentalist affirmation of multi-valued reality and its ontological validity, but while the former can lay claim to being "from His side," it is "His" will that we live our lives "from our side" — and it is this halakhic affirmation of our phenomenal world which is our response to God in His transcendence, which in turn is His medium for communicating His will in discrete form for man to follow and implement in his world.

R. Hayyim's characteristic method is thus present in this difficult and obscure realm of theology and mysticism as well. He will grant as much as he can, undeterred by polemical zeal, and hold back forcefully when he reaches what he considers the true core of his differences with Hasidism: the inviolability of Halakhah and the supremacy of Torah.

NOTES

1. His work on the subject, *Shalom al Yisrael,* was first published in Zhitomir in 1868, and has been reissued in Jerusalem, 1970.

2. *Shalom al Yisrael,* III, p. 14.

3. See, in greater deatils, in my "**מוולוז'ין ובמחשבת הדור**" **תורה לשמה במשנת רבי חיים**" (Jerusalem: Mosad Harav Kook, 1972), pp. 9-25. (This work will hereinafter be referred to as *TL.*)

4. *TL,* pp. 2-8.

5. See Mordecai Wilensky, *Hasidim U-Mitnaggedim* (Jerusalem: Mosad Bialik, 1970), pp. 106-110, and especially n. 27.

6. *TL,* pp. 10-13.

7. M. Buber, *Tales of the Hasidim* (N.Y.: Schocken, 1947) I, p. 28.

8. G. Scholem, *Major Trends in Jewish Mysticism,* (New York: Schocken, 1941), p. 340.

9. Two incidental but revealing clues to R. Hayyim's conciliatory approach to Hasidism deserve special mention. First, the *Nefesh ha-Hayyim* bears certain remarkable similarities to the *Likkutei Amarim* of R. Shneur Zalman in its literary structure: each begins Part I with a mystical anthropology and concludes with a description of the successive restrictions imposed by the Halakhah upon the freedom to achieve *tikkun* by extra-halakhic means, and Part II begins with the theme of the love of God (*TL,* p. 42). Second, R. Hayyim never mentions the Hasidim by name, either collectively or individually. Instead, he uses a code-word: **אלה אשר קרבת אלקים יחפצון** "those who desire the nearness of God." This remarkably felicitous choice combines a reference to

Hasidic immanentism, an expression of R. Hayyim's paternal understanding and forgiveness of unwitting deviations, and a rather ironic and satirical judgment on Hasidic excesses, if we are to judge by the Scriptural context of the phrase in Isaiah 58:2 (*TL*, pp. 34f).

10. *TL*, p. 36. A measure of his concern for communal peace is his advice to travellers to Palestine to pray in the Lurianic version rather than the Ashkenazic, following the Hasidim, at a time when Mitnaggedic pamphleteers were excoriating the Hasidim for abandoning the Ashkenazic rite in favor of the Lurianic or Sephardic (*TL* 13, n. 48).

11. Hence, R. Hayyim's oblique reference to the Hasidim as הָעוֹלָם רוֹב, "most of the world" *(Nefesh ha-Hayyim* 4:2).

12. See Scholem's "*Devekut*, or Communion with God," originally published in the *Review of Religion*, XIV (1949-50), 115-39), and more recently reprinted in his *The Messianic Idea in Judaism* (N.Y.: Schocken, 1971), pp. 203-226. Joseph Weiss has written on *Devekut* in his Hebrew study, "*Reshit Zemihat Derekh ha-Hasidut*, "in *Zion*, XVII (1951), pp. 46-105.

13. In his *Mitpahat Sefarim* (Altona, 1758). See *TL*, p. 16. This custom apparently spread, especially in the third generation of the movement, and later became the source of conflict among various Hasidic groups. See Aaron Wertheim, *Halakhot ve'Halikhot be'Hasidut* (Jerusalem: Mosad Harav Kook, 1960). pp. 88-93; *TL*, pp. 15-20.

14. *TL*, p. 187, n.3; p. 192.

15. While apparently withholding any broad disqualifications of the ecstatic prayer-experience demanded by Hasidism, R. Hayyim himself opts for the normative pattern of worship, legislated by the Halakhah, as the heart of prayer, even while subscribing to the Lurianic concept of the highest form of prayer as being theocentric: a supplication for the healing of the Shechinah which, in sympathy with man, suffers for man's deprivations. This latter view is shared by the Besht, R. Yaakov Yosef of Polonnoye, and other Hasidic masters. R. Hayyim symbolizes this most exalted form of prayer by the *Korbon Olah*, the burnt offering which was completely consumed on the altar: in both cases, all is done for the sake of Heaven, with man obtaining no personal benefit. The Talmud (*Ber.* 26b) records two differing opinions as to the source of the institution of prayer: the three daily services were ordained by the three patriarchs of Israel, or they were established as equivalents of the two daily sacrifices in the Temple (making only two of the services obligatory, and the third optional). Whereas the later Halakhists decide in favor of the latter, they clearly do not dispute the former but prefer to remain with both opinions. Most authorities on the philosophy of prayer make use of both Talmudic opinions. Yet R. Hayyim exclusively relies on the view that relates prayer to sacrifice. I suggest that the reason for this is his assertion of the supremacy of the normative over the pneumatic — the sacrificial rite had to conform punctilliously to halakhic regulations — even when the intention of the worshipper optimally had to reach the heights of self-abnegation. See in detail in *TL*, p. 68, n.254.

16. Mishnah, *Peah* 1:1.

17. See my "Study and Prayer: Their Relative Value in Hasidism and Mitnaggedism," in *Samual K. Mirsky Memorial Volume* (N.Y.: Yeshiva University, 1970), pp. 37-52.

18. Full documentation and elaboration may be found in my *TL*, devoted primarily to this theme.

19. This point of view is associated with R. Menahem Mendel of Peremyslyany, R. Pinhas of Korecz, R. Meshulam Feivush of Zbarazh, R. Yehiel Mikhel of Zlotchov, and others. See Joseph G. Weiss, ישראל בעש"ט" in "תלמוד תורה לשיטת ר׳ ברודי י . לכבוד היובל תפארת ישראל – ספר pp. 151-168.

20. *Hanhagot Yesharot* (Lwow: 1792). The last line of this passage is revealing: "And one should not think many thoughts, but one thought." The author is obliquely disqualifying the idea of simultaneous study and *devekut* — the "double consciousness," about which see later.

21. This felicitous term is used by both Weiss, *loc. cit.*, and R.J.Z. Werblowsky, *Joseph Karo: Lawyer and Mystic* (London: Oxford University; 1962), p. 158.

22. R. Shneur Zalman is much more restrained in combining *devekut* and study of Torah. See *TL*, p. 157.

23. R. Hayyim does not deny the possibility of double-consciousness as such. He himself recommends this practice and reads it into the Mishnah דרך ארץ יפה תלמוד תורה עם (*Avot* 2:2): one can cogitate in Torah even while he is engaged in the ordinary pursuits of making a living (R. Hayyim, *Ruah Hayyim* to *Avot* 2:2). However, this does not imply approval of the Hasidic notion of double consciousness which applies to two mental activities, *devekut* and study of Torah, each of which uncompromisingly demands full concentration and attention.

24. Such too is the explicit view of R. Joseph Karo. See Werblowsky, *op. cit.*, p. 159; *TL*, p. 192.

25. See, in greater detail, in *TL*, pp. 190 ff.

26. *TL*, pp. 204 ff.

27. *TL*, Appendix B.

28. *TL*, pp. 20-24.

29. R. Shneur Zalman, *Likkutei Amarim*, II:7. There are similar formulations throughout his writings.

30. M. Teitelbaum, *Ha-Rav mi-Ladi u-Mifleget HaBaD* (Warsaw: 1913), II, p. 87. So Prof. Mordecai Wilensky in his splendid work, *Hasidim U-Mitnaggedim*, I, p. 196f., referring to the famous letter by R. Shneur Zalman to his followers in Vilna in 1797.

31. R. Abraham Simhah of Amstislaw, in his letter appended to Luzzatto's *Derekh Tevunot* (Jerusalem: 1880), who ascribes R. Hayyim's clear advocacy of the figurative view to the teaching of the Gaon.

32. *Op. cit.*, II, pp. 87 ff.

33. Appendix to the Gaon's Commentary on the *Sifra di-Tzeniuta* (Vilna: 1882).

34. *Nefesh ha-Hayyim* 3:7.

35. Thus, R. Hayyim, *loc. cit*: סילוק והעתק ממקום למקום R. Shneur Zalman (*Likkutei Amarim*, II, 7): את עצמו אינו לשון So (in *Likkutei Torah* to Nitzavim, p. 49b): ממקום זה"ה שהקב"ה סילק למקום עליון דאין הפי׳ כפשוטו כהסתלקות הדבר

What is puzzling about his similarity in language is that the latter work by R. Shneur Zalman was first published after R. Hayyim's demise in 1821, and the first, while printed in 1797-8, did *not* include this particular passage, which for some reason was omitted and remained in manuscript form at least as late as the early part of this century. May we conclude that R. Hayyim somehow had access to the as yet unpublished manuscripts of R. Shneur Zalman?

36. R. Shneur Zalman, *Likkutei Amarim* II, 7; R. Hayyim, *Nefesh ha-Hayyim* 3:6, and gloss to end of 3:11.

37. Teitelbaum, *op. cit.*, II, p. 92, n.5.

38. *Nefesh ha-Hayyim* 3:4.

39. On this point see my *Faith and Doubt* (New York: Ktav, 1971), pp. 153-155, and *TL*, p. 71f.

PART III

TOLERANCE IN EAST CENTRAL EUROPE

Abraham G. Duker

FRANKISM AS A MOVEMENT OF POLISH-JEWISH SYNTHESIS

The Founder and His Sect

Jacob Frank (1726-1791) proclaimed himself the God of the true faith and the Messiah of the Jews.(1) He recruited his own Frankist sect from among the Shabbateans, the Cabbalistic followers of Sabbatai Zevi, the notorious false Messiah, who was forced to join Islam under the threat of death in 1666. Frank similarly, became a Roman Catholic in 1759 to escape a church trial for heresy. Like some Shabbateans who followed their master into Islam, hundreds of Polish Frankists were marched to baptismal fonts with great pomp and ceremony. Moslem or Christian, the conversion of both groups was formal, as they retained their beliefs in their own cabbalist versions of messianic Judaism ("The Higher Torah"). The new Moslems soon attained high positions in the Ottoman Empire and some of their descendants were active in the Young Turk movement. The new Catholics also advanced economically, culturally, socially and politically in Poland and have produced outstanding persons in Polish life.(2) However, the Polish Frankists had less staying power as a sect than their Moslem antecedents, some of whom continued to be identified as members of the Doenmeh Konyosos sect as late as 1970. A few even emigrated to Israel after the attainment of Jewish statehood. In Poland, the Frankists, with very few exceptions, if any at all, were absorbed into the Polish-Catholic community by the end of the 19th century.(3) None could be identified as followers of the sect during the interbellum years, 1918-1939.

The main question raised here is: why in the face of the full and irretrievable absorption of the Frankists in Polish society the solution of assimilation by baptism for large numbers of Jews has been resisted, if not utterly rejected, by Polish society, at the very time when the descendants of the former sectaries have been attaining their final integration into Catholic Polishness through intermarriage? The answer can be found only through the consideration of Polish society's general readiness to accept non-Poles, non-Catholics and non-Christians as legitimate elements in the Polish state and nation: in other words, the root of the answer lies in Polish nationalism. The latter's connection with the Roman Catholic faith has been so intimate that religious deviations in Polish nationhood have, at best, been accepted grudgingly and conditionally, with some exceptions, of course. Yhe Jews have and conditionally, with some exceptions, of course. The Jews have accept the Frankists as true Poles depended first on their behavior as inidividuals and as a group. Through most of the group's existence, social and marital separatism was too obvious and offered the ready excuse that their isolation went much further, thus accentuating their alleged Jewishness. Polish public opinion became conditioned in the next stage to judgment on the basis of impressions concerning the Frankists' separatism, despite its steadfast weakening.

A new factor entered in the middle of the nineteenth century, namely, the transformation of antisemitism in Poland from mainly religiously motivated views into racial, racial-religious, and finally, racial-religious-folkish ideological solutions of the Jewish problem. These changes brought theoretical and speculative antisemitic interpretations of Frankism, possibly more far-reaching than that of the Nazis, as will be mentioned later. It is my intention to bring out, within the limited space allotted, the main lines as well as examples of the developments. A more conclusive examination requires much more space and time. The allotment of the latter is not in my hands.

Ambivalent Acceptance

The Frankists' baptism met with the enthusiastic response of the Catholic clergy and of many aristocrats. The unprecedented conversion, seemingly voluntary, of a fairly large number of Jews was viewed as a beginning of a miraculous abandonment of Judaism in favor of the true Christian faith and as the forerunner of an expected larger mass conversion. This, despite the continuous barrage of justified criticism of their separatism and of their alleged reluctance to mix with true Catholics(4) and what appeared to have been worse, their addiction to Jewish practices, including a taste for Jewish cooking.(5) The welcoming attitude continued to be expressed throughout the nineteenth century despite recurrent attacks against the Frankists.(6)

As I have pointed out, references to the Jews in Mickiewicz's Lec-

tures on Slavic Literature (1842-44) at the College de France and other
allusions during his Towianist period point to Frankist influence in the
poet's view of their role as the catalyst in a messianist solution of
Poland's future or to a mystical Frankist-Towianist synthesis or
symbiosis between the Jews and the Poles.(7)

Not only mystics viewed Frankism as the way of solving the Jewish
problem. In 1844 Adrian Krzyżanowski stated that "the teaching
confessed by the Frankist sect had been and continues to be the only
effective instrument of reforming and changing the Polish, Ruthenian
and Lithuanian Jews into a great mass worthy of the name of man."(8)
In his 1866 book on the Frankists, E. Hipolyt Skimborowicz expressed
doubts in the continued existence of the sect.(9) In 1878, Wacław
Aleksander Maciejowski repeated Krzyżanowski's statement. He denied
that Frank was an impostor and emphasized his role in bringing the Jews
to the Catholic Church.(10)

Renewed interest in the Frankists in the 1880's was sufficient to
stimulate the publication of a compilative pseudonymous work by the
conservative Walery Skimborowicz, denying the charges of their
continued separatism.(11) A review in the Polish language Jewish
Warsaw weekly opined that there was nothing new in the book.
However, it also cited an opinion from one of the "largest dailies"
(Polish and unnamed) to the effect that "among the Frankists, particularly in the later generations, there were many outstanding and
deserving men. This movement brought benefit to society, because it
made possible the inflow of new forces into many fields that are very
useful, and in a few cases, of the first rank."(12)

Kraushar, an assimilated Jew, and the author of the basic and
irreplaceable biography of Frank and history of his movement, held
that "the descendants of the first followers of the 'Master,' having
become real and faithful Christians and citizens of their country, already
in the second generation severed all threads of the tradition of the
precepts of the agitator, and today, after the extinction of more than five
generations, their great grandchildren have nothing in common and
wish to have nothing in common with their historical past."(13)

In his review of Kraushar's work, the great historian Tadeusz Korzon
stressed the gratitude that Poland owes to Frank "for the refashioning of
several thousand Jews into true Poles, even in the first, in the second or
third generations."(14) Even the rabid antisemite Antoni (Anton von)
Marylski told in his history of the Jews in Poland that "out of the
disintegrating sect a certain small part has been permeated with the
principles of the Christian faith and since 150 years ago drowned in the
sea of Polish life. the other, larger part, clung of Judaism and was drawn
into the ranks of the Hassidim."(15)

Even during the antisemitic Interbellum era, 1918-1939, a popular encyc' ped'a, published in 1930, informed the reader that "after the death of Ewa in 1816 the mystification ended. The Polish Frankists, very rich people, later made connections with many houses of the Polish *szlachta* (gentry), contributing to these houses drops of Jewish blood."(16) A weightier encyclopedia, published in the same year, also stated that "the Frankist sect in Poland enjoyed many considerations of Polish society. Almost all the neophytes received Polish names, many were granted nobility. In time they became completely assimilated."(17)

No attention has been paid in Polish writings, and for that matter in Jewish literature, to the Frankists' inner struggle, the psychological and generational conflicts during the process of abandoning their faith and group life and of substituting the self-image of a chosen elite, proud of its Jewish past and convinced of its destiny of blessings and rewards, for that of a coterie of spiritual and social beggars, avidly and competitively social climbing who had to prove themselves worthy of gracious acceptance and therefore having to dissociate themselves from their two pasts, the Jewish and the Frankist.

As they prospered and attained prominent positions following their post-baptismal emancipation, the Frankists faced increasingly bitter opposition. The Catholic clergy suspected their piety; middle classes and artisans resented their competition and the successes that backed their social climbing; the aristocrats and gentry did not want them as owners of neighboring rural estates. Suspicions of their separate group existence continued long after their religious and group ethnicity had disappeared. Social isolation kept them together and helped to bolster the suspicions. Together with other converts, states Shatzky, they were accused in 1794 of espionage on behalf of Russia.(18) Their unpopularity is reflected in folk sayings.(19) Anti-Frankist propaganda in pamphlets and literature contained various types of accusations.(20) The emergence of mystic cults and movements in Europe, which very possibly helped to hold the sect together, also served to raise suspicions against the Frankists. The involvement of a few individuals in the French Revolution and the image of Napoleon as an anti-Christ called attention to the suspect converts.(21) Mistrust called forth "Hep, Hep" street cries. There were personal insults. Juljan Ursyn Niemcewicz called Dominik Krysiński, an important attorney, a "Jew" in public in 1831.(22) The situation was not better in the Great Emigration that followed the Insurrection, where activities of a few radicals of Frankist descent created a furore of insults.(22a)

The tsarist regime was also suspicious of the sectaries. Alexander I, always interested in the conversion of the Jews, had his eye on the Frankists. His Warsaw spy, Macrott reported to him regularly about them.(23) The Tsar also was supposed to have ordered them to be called "Frankists."(24) I have not been able to use Soviet archives. The few studied printed sources, however, reveal a continued tsarist interest. An 1847 publication of the Ministry for Internal Affairs by I.I. Grigoviev takes the sect's continuity for granted, with communities in Moldavia and Turkey and a reputation for honesty, acknowledged even by their enemies.(25) Other repercussions will be discussed later.

World Rule

Frank hinted to his followers that he would soon occupy the thrones of the Holy Roman and Ottoman empires and prophesied his world rule, as befits the Messiah. While it is quite likely that he believed in these predictions, it is also possible that he had made them in order to strengthen his followers' confidence in him at a time of adversity.(26) As early as 1820, an anti-Jewish brochure expressed the dread that "the several million Jews, together with the neophytes might rise in a revolution, with the appearance of a Jew or a convert with great genius,"(27) a fear of a Jewish and convert plot recurrent not only among Poles. During his anti-Jewish stage the poet Adam Mickiewicz prophesied in his classic *Ksiegi Narodu* that the idolaters (the ruling governments) would be eliminated by the real revolutionaries, "Jews or persons of the Old Testament," who will judge the "idolaters by the law of Moses and Joshua, and Robespierre and Saint-Just, exterminating them from old man to suckling child . . ."(28)

Jan Czyński was the only Frankist to have been truly interested in the welfare of the Jews and to have fought consistently for their emancipation.(29) However, he too contributed to the spread of the notion of Jewish world rule through his popular novel which appeared in 1833-34 in Polish, French and English.(30) More widely read, direct and effective was the great poet Zygmunt Krasiński's *Nieboska Komedja* (Undivine Comedy), a drama published in 1835 and an important early modern antecedent of the Protocols of the Elders of Zion. The theme, as I have stated elsewhere, is a "revolutionary plot against Christendom and the social order to be executed by a secret cabal of Jewish converts to Christianity. Their aim was world rule by Jews and their method — a proletarian revolution against the remnants of Aristocracy."(31) While the converts in the drama have generally been identified as St. Simonists by students of literature, there are good reasons for presuming that the author also had the Frankists on his mind. These early Polish variations on the theme of an alleged Jewish world rule plot are given not only as illustrations of anti-Frankist suspicion, but will also serve as background for a brief treatment later on the revaluation of the place on the Frankists in Polish history by that particular school of addicts of racism and antisemitism that had much to say in Polish scholarship and public opinion in the 1930's, very much under the influence of the then rising star of Nazism, not that its followers lacked original initiative. Some of them have not given up their agitation in exile.

It may be assumed that small fragments of the Frankist sect continued to exist at least during the first half of the 19th century. This is testified by Polish and Jewish writings, tsarist policy and contemporary reportage on Eastern Europe. In my opinion, the mysterious messianic Napoleonic "numerous Israelite sect, half Christian, half Jewish" which according to Adam Mickiewicz's 1842 statement existed in the 1830's or early 40's can be identified as Frankist.(32) At best, however, the sect consisted then of a relatively few remnants. Most Frankists, it may be assumed, were no longer "believers" in Frankism; instead they were skeptics and doubters, with some sincere Catholic believers.

Continued Separatism

The separationist past, family structure, child rearing, acceptance by Polish society ranging from suspicion to outright rejection, and deliberate dissociation from Jews served as the chief unifying ties among the Frankists, regardless of their religious aspects of sect continuity. (We shall not enter into an examination of the retention of Judaism among the non-baptised faithful in their own way, while ostensibly continuing orthodox Jewish practices and even Talmudic learning.) (33) The prohibition against outside marriages goes back to Frank's dictates. Self-cognition as an elite group continued to discourage outside marriage, just as later the desire to avoid marital complications stemming from radically differing religio-cultural and familial backgrounds, with contempt for Jews as an inbuilt culture pattern among most Catholics and Poles. Preferences for marrying converted Jews continued, therefore, after the abandonment of the Frankist faith. As I have pointed out elsewhere, "it is proper to view the Catholic Frankists from a sociological angle as a well-established, self-sustaining and closely knit group."(34)

We shall now briefly consider the possible stages in the fascinating dual process, the gradual abandonment of the faith in Frankism, combined with the retention of group solidarily, generation after generation. There were cases of doubt in Frank's divinity or messiahship during his lifetime among the faithful. An unusual case was the expose of Frank's doubtful adherence to Catholicism by an erstwhile believer who thereby laid claim to his own sincere conversion.(35) Scepticism in his divinity and messiahship must have grown after Frank's death. It became more widespread after his daughter Ewa's demise. Enlightenment, time-distance from the forefathers and increasing Polish acculturation-assimilation helped to spread doubts in the truth of the faith.

With their integration in the culture of the Polish upper and middle classes, the Frankists increasingly shed their limited Jewish Cabbalistic (Higher Torah) identity, practices and culture patterns. Again, it can be assumed that soon after Frank's death, some of the faithful began to view him as their mentor and emancipator rather than the Almighty. As among some non-baptised Frankists, the shadier aspects of the Sect's early history were eventually forgotten, while gratitude to Frank for their liberation continued to be retained well into the nineteenth century.(36)

The more "Jewishly" inclined Frankists, in the Cabbalistic sense, of course, of the third or fourth generations, possibly even of the second, who had lost their faith in Frank would have found it difficult if not impossible to return to the Jewish community and to join the closest trend, (Cabbalistic) Hassidism, by that time strange and bizarre, particularly to those brought up on the Enlightenment ideas, which included a good dose of deprecation of Judaism, the Talmud, and, therefore, also the Jews. Thus intellectuals, the learned and the thinking among the Frankists could not accept an orthodoxy of any faith, including Judaism. Conversion to Judaism was prohibited and when permitted, return to the ancestral faith would have brought with it a reassumption of the status of a second-class human being that came with joining the Jewish people. It also would involve a return to the strict Orthodox way of life, held in contempt by the Frankists, aggressively antinomian since their beginnings. The memory of the persecution of their ancestors by the "Talmudic" Jews lingered on. Only the most idealistic would have been willing to face such a drastic change. Cases of return of non-baptised Frankists to Orthodox Judaism seem to have been rather rare.(37)

A bitter struggle between the more "orthodox" Frankists and the enlightened ones or those inclined to accept Catholicism and to marry outside the fold must have taken place in every family on different levels. Again, data are few. We can only surmise their extent from a case or two in the Wołowski family. Celina Szymanowska-Mickiewicz admired her aunt Julia's "true and quiet but sincere religion." Celina confessed that she was the cause for her aunt's "so many sufferings and persecutions "(38) I have no doubt that Celina's illness and miraculous cure by Andrzej Towianski, the mystic, in whom her husband Mickiewicz believed, had a background of religious-ethnic Frankist complications.(39)

Abandonment of belief in Frankism as a religion could rarely have resulted in an immediate sincere conversion to Catholicism. A transitional rational and deistic stage can be visualized. It is difficult to assume that enlightened individuals who went through the trying struggle involved in the abandonment of the mystical Cabbalistic messianism would turn as a reaction to Catholicism, a hated alien religion, into which their ancestors had been forced in order to save their lives. Only the less educated and non-intellectual might have been culturally prepared by the Frankist non-Christian Cabbalistic trinitarianism for the acceptance of Catholicism.

Obvious are the difficulties in child-rearing under varying conditions of multiple Marranoism in a seemingly increasingly liberal yet unfriendly world. Frankism required the transmission of a tradition of a conspiratorial elite and could not exist without family solidarity. Ties of kinship continually had to be strengthened by marriage within the sect and within extended family clans. Later, in the assimilationist stage, unions were also preferred with persons in fairly similar situations, namely non-Frankist converts from Judaism and their descendants.

It must have taken generations of acculturation and cultural assimilation as well as a good dose of applied pragmatism to arrive at the decision that it was time to bring up the children as true Catholics, without any doubts or secrets — the final break with Frankism as a religion. In many cases, such a decision did not bring with it automatic acquiescence to allow or encourage outside marriages. Parents were reluctant to risk a loss of protection for their children, upon sending them for life into the enemy camp.

Complications in Accepting Christian Beliefs

Eventually the nominally "Catholic" Frankists ceased to be Jews, even of the "Higher Torah". The doubters and sceptics continued to carry out the required and later the customary practices of Catholicism's more visible rites, typical of the early Frankist pattern. Let the future novelist playwrights and filmmakers attempt to portray the sectaries' inner conflicts, the ambivalence of the early generations, hovering between the Judaism of yesterday and the Frankist around-the-corner realization of the living Messianic promises to themselves, the truly chosen people, salvation in their own lifetime that had brought them immediate liberation from the ghettoes, discrimination and restrictions. The cost of separation from their near and dear Jewish relatives and the reluctant abandonment of their own way of life, facing the prospects of contempt, hatred and persecutions by the Jews were repaid with venom and vindictiveness. Thus Frank forced his followers to accuse their fellow Jews of practicing ritual murder of Christians.(40)

It is impossible to find direct information about the gradual replacement of Cabbalistic Judaism by Roman Catholicism, perfunctory or sincere, but always convenient and profitable, and of the parallel abandonment of Jewish Cabbalist Shabbatean ethno-cultural belongingness in favor of Polishness, or, sociologically speaking, the final and irrevocable assimilation of the Frankists into Polish Catholic society. One can only imagine the struggles about religious beliefs and practices that went on between parents and children, grandparents and grandchildren, brothers and sisters, different branches of the same families.(41)

It may be surmised that some insight into such family conflicts can be gained from an examination of similar situations and crises in Jewish families that have been going on since the Shabbatean outburst. Reflections on more recent disagreements between generations and individuals not only concerning religious beliefs and practices but also about ideological differences. Clashes have been common in Orthodox Jewish families on the subject of the varying punctilliousness of observances, intellectual interests outside the traditional religious areas as well as about personal associations. Such conflicts in the areas of Frankist beliefs and group belongingness must have taken place also in Frankist families during the processes of polonization, Catholicization and liberalization. Conflicts similar to those between Hassidim and Mitnagdim or clashes among family members concerning changes to different Hasidic *rebbis* must have taken place in Frankist families when the group began to split into smaller splinters, as had happened among the Moslem convert Doenmeh sect, although we know nothing specific about such splits in the Polish sect.

Emancipation's major cultural dilemma, the search for a balanced integration in the Jewish and surrounding cultures, the fundamentalist and more so the secularized or liberalized Christian ones that have led culturally emancipated Jews to assimilation, career baptism and westernization of Jewish culture, may well have been faced by the Frankists along similar lines, though on different levels. We can also surmise that among the subjects of conflict among the Frankists were interpretations of Jewish messianism and Cabbalistic teachings, their place in the new nineteenth century and questions of the degrees of belongingness to the Jewish people and sharing in the Jewish faith, in the Cabbalistic sense, of course, the extent of Catholic practices required for a safe and comfortable daily life, and the Frankist and Jewish practices that should be transmitted to children.

During the assimilationist stage debates could have ranged on the adjustment to the hostile world around them and on the continuation of the practices of mutual protection and their limits. By that time class divisions and success in social adjustment among the Polish nobility and upper classes had made their contribution to the weakening of group solidarity. No doubt, some Frankists were concerned with the situation of the Jews, particularly in Poland. Actual involvement in remedial action required a good deal of bravery and very likely had been suspect of interfering with the acceptance of the group and its full assimilation in Polish life.

The processes of abandoning the more visible aspects of the Jewish culture in favor of those of the Polish understandably appear to have been less painful than those involved in shifting from the Frankist brand of Judaism to Catholicism. Linguistic transformation came first. It may be possible that the youths who served their Master in his court in Offenbach retained some command of a Germanized Yiddish, at the very least in order to be able to communicate with their non-baptised fellow initiates from Bohemia-Moravia, and that some Frankists maintained a modicum of Yiddish for business reasons.(41a)

Clearly, Polish became the chief language among the faithful, certainly in the second, if not the first generation. It is possible that the teaching of Hebrew was maintained for prayer, the study of the Bible and cabbalistic writings as well as for scholarly interpretation of the sect's Cabbalistic studies and principles and communication with the Doenmehs. How long such instruction continued is not known. Nor have Frankist prayers been retained in Polish translation, unlike the situation in the Doenmeh sect. Polonization was rapid not only because of economic, residential and Marrano-like life realities. Poland was Frank's favorite country. He viewed it as the basis of his messianic mission and operations.(42) This created religious receptivity to the land and language. Moreover, use of the Polish language presented fewer possibilities of clashes of values between the old and new cultures. Its knowledge was an economic necessity, and not at the very least, a chief protection in the difficult technique of living in a double Marranoism.

Next to the language came Polish patriotism, easily acquired at an early stage from Frank's teachings about Poland, to the sect a visible symbol and proof of belongingness. Consequently, youths of second generation and the younger first generation participated in the Kościuszko Insurrection for Poland's independence.(43) Frankists rose in rank in Napoleon's armies.(44) Participation in military service at these stages could also have been motivated to a considerable extent by Frank's teachings on military preparation as a means of the sect's attainment of power. The social rise of the Frankist families and their connections are attested by nobilitizations as early as 1793.(45) (The ancient Lithuanian practice of the almost automatic nobilitizing of converts was abolished in 1764.) These are indications of not only the possession of wealth, but also of a high degree of acculturation. Therefore, Teodor Jeske-Choiński's assertion that ''not many of them — the Frankists — spoke Polish . . . and knew how to write it until 1810'' could have pertained only to grandparents and aged relatives.(46)

The number of Frankist participants in the Insurrection of 1830-31 was expectedly larger than that than in the Napoleonic Wars. They appear to have been mainly of the third generation. Some occupied high positions, including a General, Jan Krysiński, a Colonel, Jan Czyński, several adjutants to generals, army physicians, and other commissioned officers.(47) One may surmise that the motivation for these acts of volunteering was derived more from Polish patriotism and less from Frankist messianic urges. By this time, the Frankist Franciszek Wołowski, uncle of Mickiewicz's wife Celina, was an outstanding conservative Sejm leader.(48) The number of the participants in the 1863 Insurrection was too large to be listed by me in ''PFD.'' Among the many Frankist insurrectionists was General Antoni Jezioranski. His namesake, Jan Jezioranski, the Revolution's Commissioner of Communication, was hanged by the Russians together with the Revolution's dictator Romuald Traugutt.(49)

There can be little doubt that by this time the Frankists have been reaching their last stage of religious and ethnic group separatism and were ready spiritually and intellectually for the final stage of physical merger through intermarriage. Emotional acceptance of this irretrievable step was to come more hesitatingly as I have tried to explain.(50)

The Frankists as a Social Group

In face of the weakening of the Frankist faith, most sectaries remained a close group bound by a mutual past: the awareness of the antinomial revolt against traditional Judaism that had led them out of ghetto misery to freedom and prosperity, a civilized social life, economic rise, blood relations by marriage, the hostility and distrust of Polish-Catholic society and in consequence, mutual defense interests, regardless of religious changes.(51) There were always exceptions. But those involved in the sect remained sufficiently large in numbers to constitute a socially self-sufficient group. A high birth rate, and the few conversions of Jews in the upper classes to Christianity, mainly Protestantism, made it possible to continue and enabled the Sect to maintain its cohesion without having to marry outside the group.

Some families evidently broke away early, but not many as early as in the second generation. According to Swierczewska, the Krysiński family was at the head of "the enlightened Israelites, who did not endorse these Frankist tendencies" of "transofrmation into an ordinary religious sect with elementary Hebrew-Christian beliefs."(52) However, no proof was presented by her.

Jeske-Choiński dated the Frankists' decision to cease their existence as a group to 1810, after their loss of faith in Frank and Ewa and with the emergence of a second and third generation, educated in Piarist schools. To quote, "now all the Frankists had become Catholics and Poles, which has not prevented them from holding themselves as one family . . . Only the youngest, contemporary Frankist generation is no longer faithful to the commandments of their master, and even mixes its blood with its Aryan coreligionists."(53)

In 1919, Choiński again mentioned the Frankists' admiration for Frank. While some "until today cannot forget the leader of their ancestors and . . . carry his portraits in their wallets or purses," there are also some "who had forgotten about their 'Messiah,' have been clinging to their new fatherland, have served her and continue to serve her as proper citizens, patriots, learned men . . . They have generally been active in the bar."(54) Choiński presents no proof for the magic year 1810.

Expansion of Class of Wealthy Jews

What disturbed this gradual and ideal absorption process? Tsarist economic policy after the 1830 Insurrection exacted heavy fines and troop maintenance costs from the Kingdom. These led to the rise in the value of money and to the growth of banking, particularly Jewish banks. The abolition of the customs fees between Russia and the Kingdom (1850), of the *Geleitzoll*(Daily entry tax for out-of-town Jews, 1851), and the development of railroads stimulated further the capital's growth and served to increase its Jewish population. The Crimean War (1853-55) added to the economic upsurge. These developments caused the rise of numerous Jewish plutocrats, industrialists, businessmen and bankers. Government monopolies, including that of the kosher meat tax that plagued the poor Jews, also enriched the new Jewish class of wealth.(54a)

With economic rise came rapid acculturation and assimilation. Polish replaced German as the language of enlightenment and westernization. The new "progressive class of Jews" avidly sought participation in Polish culture and the Polonization of their co-religionists.(55)

As in other continental countries of emancipation and the struggle for it, acculturation was a temporary stop on the road to complete assimilation, that often ended with baptism.(56)

Some converts retained their interest in the "improvement" of the Jewish masses and contributed to Jewish charities. However, most of them cut their ties with the Jewish community. Assimilationist Jewish self-deprecation and self-hate was often turned into antisemitism, often right after the visit to the baptismal font. While converts and their offspring usually married their own kind, intermarriages began to appear also with members of the Polish upper classes, causing both satisfaction and chagrin on the part of Poles, depending on their liberalism, nationalism, racism, and their own relationships to the persons concerned or involved.

As in other societies, support of the arts, theater, and concerts was a method of attaining respect and contacts in social cimbing that would lead to political rights and social equality. As usual, such Jews and converts became avid theatre and concert goers and supporters. Arguments in favor of equality were at first based on their self-assertion as ethical and useful citizens. Later, such rights were increasingly claimed on the basis of democratic principles. Their political demands and high visibility, too often viewed as evidence of upstart brazenness and vulgarity, were resented by the Polish upper and middle classes, particularly by the declining *szlachta* (gentry) and by the compeing Catholic urban elements.

In the words of the antisemitic historican Kazimierz Bartoszewicz:

> The share of the Jews in the economic movement was large . . . Their fortunes grew from day to day, and they therefore played an increasingly large role in communal and social life, particularly so, because the ranks of their intelligensia slowly increased. . . . The Jew banker, industrialist, factory owner, entered in direct relations with the landowners and the official circles. The Jew bookseller and publisher began to influence the fate of literature and science, which even found their maecenases among the Jews; for instance, Mathias

Rosen and Leopold Kronenberg supported financially the *Biblioteka warszawska,* foremost scholarly and literary periodical. Increasingly, the ranks of Christian employers became dependent on the Jewish plutocracy. Jewish physicians enjoyed an extensive practice, and some enriched Polish medical literature; for instance, Ludwik Natanson edited the *Tygodnik lekarski* (Medical Weekly) . . .

Here Bartoszewicz listed some names of Jewish bibliographers, the artist Alexander Lesser, the musicians, Wieniawski. To cite further:

Jews were increasingly encounted in social life, particularly the ones insulting termed *meches* (converts); there were also cases of such people entering in family relations with the nobility, including the crimsoned . . .(57)

Nostalgia for Poland's agrarian economy with its traditional aristocracy-centered way of life was expressed in hostility to "materialism" and stimulated by idealized Slavophilism. There was sympathy for young aristocrats, who were forced to seek employment in the new industrial and commercial enterprises owned by Jews or converts. Hostility was fed by the cultural assimilation and influence of marriages of converts with the nobility, viewed in these quarters as the final proof of the decline of the Polish traditional way of life.

The Jewish War of 1859

Hostility came to a head in a dispute, tendentiously termed by Bartoszewicz: "the Jewish War of 1859." It was precipitated by poor attendance at the December 26, 1858 concert of the Naruda (Nerude) sisters, Czech instrumentalists, in contrast to a later crowded concert by a Jewish artist. A citation from a feuilleton by Józef Kenig in *Gazeta warszawska,* of January 4, 1859, illustrates the resentment of the anti-assimilationist Poles:

She lacks an eagle nose, a dark complexion, black hair, and other characteristics of non-Aryan ancestry . . . Her name does not end with berg, blatt, kranc, stern or similarly, she therefore lacks the title for support from the side of that mysterious alliance, which has saddled itself upon entire Europe, especially amidst us, and clinging closely together, pushes ahead everyone of its own, whether a banker, a tenor, a speculator, or a violinist.(58)

The younger assimilated Jewish set resented the attack on its Polishness and human dignity. Anonymous letters, some threatening, attacked the writer and editor, Antoni Lesznowski. In a collective letter 23 prominent Jews requested a retraction. The next well-attended Naruda concert was turned into an anti-Jewish demonstration, The debate persisted. Lesznowski sued in court the signers of another letter

who were found guilty and were given mostly three month sentences.
Both sides appealed against what they viewed as a mild or strict verdict,
respectively. The sentences were not carried out. Democratic public
opinion was shocked by the court's expression that stressed that ''(the
Jews) do not tend to merge with the nation, which accepted them
hospitably and had fed them for 800 years.'' It pointed to ''their love of
the golden calf,'' dislike of civilization. It called them ''newcomers.'' It
sharply condemned the ''Israelite idea'' shown in the anonymous
letter, in which fun was made of the Poles, presenting the Jews before
them as the example of ''the only representatives of good sense and love
of God in this unhappy land.''(59)

The dispute became widespread at home and abroad in the ''Great
Emigration''. The democratic *Przeglad rzeczy polskich* (Review of
Polish Affairs) and *Demokrata polski* defended the Jews. The latter
emphasized the polonization of the younger Frankists. The rightist
Wiadomości polskie (Polish News) supported Lesznowski for a brief
period. The debate in which some Jewish emigrés participated was
ended with a pro-Jewish brochure by the elder statesman, the great
scholar, Joachim Lelewel, in 1860. The next year witnessed joint
patriotic demonstrations of Jews and Poles in Warsaw. These ushered in
a period of fraternization, the prelude to the 1863 Insurrection, with a
wide participation of Jews.(60)

The ''Jewish War'' seemed to have spared the Frankists, to judge by
Bartoszewicz's study.(61) There was an anonymous threat against Józef
Ignacy Kraszewski that as the new editor of *Gazeta warszawska,* the
newspaper purchased by a rich Jew, he would remain alone ''with
Klaczko, Wołowski and Leo, just converts.''(61a) This labeled the
established Frankist leader Wołowski as no better than any recent
convert. In the Emigration, the *Demokrata polski* commented that ''the
younger generation of the Frankists is constantly manifesting nobler
hearts and loftier sentiments. And one could say bravely that the
children among them are born with a true Christian nature.''(62)

Defense Tactics

The Polish-Jewish brotherhood that preceded the Insurrection and
lasted through it continued to be expressed and even practiced to an
appreciable degree during the period of positivism. However, anti-
positivist feelings revived the hostility against the Jewish and convert
''plutocracy'' in the later 1870's and early 80's. The new antisemitism
was fully directed against the converts, in line with its latest racist
version. The Frankists became concerned with the threat of the in-

terruption of their peaceful final stage of absorption in Polish society. New tactics had to be devised.

As long as they had been true believers, their defense tactics, or, shall we say, their public relations, followed the chief line of Marrano behavior, avoidance of public attention. Press and pamphlet attacks forced them to issue a defense brochure as early as 1790.(63) During the period of transition from Frankism to Polishness and Catholicism they continued the policy of avoiding the limelight. Thus when a translation of Julius Brinken's German novel on Frank began to be serialized in the periodical *Biblioteka warszawska* (Warsaw Library) in 1845, the Frankists stopped its publication, with negative results.(64) The tsarist government satisfied the curious by publishing it in Russian in 1892.(65)

Racisim and Anti-Frankist Fears

The 1880's and 90's saw a revival of interest in the Frankists.(66) The new propaganda against the wealthy converts forced them to back Skimborowicz's psudonymous apologetic book in 1893,(67) written with the purpose of stressing the Frankists' normalcy as Poles and thus dissociating them from the new upstarts. The perusal of Kraushar's classic *FFP* proves its purpose of putting an end to any doubts concerning the continuity of the sect.

Rejection of Other Converts' Intermarriage

The new racial-religious antisemitism developed into a mass movement, stimulated by profit-prone agitators even in respectable intellectual and social quarters. Popular propaganda and serious anthropological and sociological studies alike emphasized, following the new antisemitic European style, the seemingly eternal and irrevocable racial differences between the Jews and the "Aryans", with Slavs and Poles receiving their attention. In consequence, offspring of the mixed marriages between Frankists and presumably racially pure Poles were forced to protect the integrity of their own Polishness and to retain open opportunities for mixed marriages for their own children. This could be done either by waging an uncompromising struggle against the new nationalism and racism or by joining the war against the presumably insincere non-Frankist converts. The following brief treatment of Frankist writers of the second school, who were fully integrated into Polish culture to the extent of accepting its folk and racist aspects, is an attempt to examine another area of Frankist adjustment, so many of which remain to be explored.

Wacław Szymanowski (1821-1866) represents a Frankist pre-racist approach to the Jewish problem. He was a third or fourth generation Frankist married within the group. His daughter, however, was married to a convert from Judaism. Szymanowski was an editor *(Kurjer war-szawski,* 1848-1866), a writer of fiction and poetry, and a successful playright. Of his many works, only two seem to deal with Jewish themes. His 1855 drama, *Lichwiarze* (Usurers), portrays a sordid Jewish money lender, who managed through adroit and heartless deals to rise from poverty to great wealth. The man forgets his past and leads the vulgar ostentatious life of the *nouveau riche.* The author admits that there were only twenty such usurers in entire Warsaw. He also praises Jewish industriousness. Nevertheless, the picture emerges of a sordid Jewish stereotype.

Szymanowski's other work of present interest is the drama, *Salamon,* portraying the vicissitudes of a 16th century Jewish cabballist in Krakow. His daughter who decides to abandon Judaism and marry her Christian lover is killed by her Jewish intended. Here Christianity is presented as the higher religion. However, the work contains some moving passages about Jewish life, determination of the Jews to survive, longings for the Holy Land, and, not unexpectedly for a person of Frankist background, praise for Caballah.(68)

Symanowski's novel came before the real crisis. It presents an attempt of a full-blooded Frankist to appear as a good Polish nationalist. Perhaps he could not be called a real anti-Semite, but he is a representative of a generation that could still avoid it.

By the 1880's, Frankist assimilation has gone so far that it was reported the the younger Frankists felt insulted when reminded of their Jewish, very likely Frankist, descent. This was quite in contrast with the attitudes of the older generation that displayed pride in its ancestry.(69)

Kazimierz Zalewski (1849-1919) editor, popular playwright, theatrical critic and stage director, joined in the 1870's the fashionalbe condemnation of rich converted Jews. In his comedy *Z postepem* (With Progress, 1874), Baron Silber, a rich convert banker, dared to offer his daughter's hand to an impoverished count of ancient lineage. The would-be son-in-law replies that his blood is not for sale to "a poison snake, a low Iscariot."

Even more critical of the new converts was Zalewski's comedy *Góra nasi* (Up with Our Own, 1885). The villain Pomper, a baptised millionaire, industrialist, merchant and great philanthropist is running for mayor. His opponent is the ethnically pure hero Dolski, a journalist "indifferent" to an individual's religion, but a firm upholder of tradition, family merits and above all, Polish nationality. To him Pomper is neither a Jew nor a Christian, but belongs "to a caste of humans who are interested only in self-enrichment . . . . You are a member of one nation only, true, a strong and powerful one, the nation of financiers, a nation that will be agreeable to any form of government, to any rule." Pomper argues that Christian Polish society objects to the Jews' rise in the professions, to their participation in Polish culture and even in services to the country, except for one area: commerce. The Jews' only weapon is money that buys their way into Polish society; hence, their concentration on money-making. He points to his own great philanthropic contributions, his ability, efficient administration and experience. These are acknowledged by his adversary who claims that his own ancestors' patriotic martyr careers, his good nature, honesty and insutriousness will counter-balance Pomper's assets.

Mieses, in his presentation of these two works, offers his thesis of the Frankists' need for the rejction of the recent converts for the sake of acceptance by Polish society.(70)

The evidence is clear. Antisemitic literature became popular and profitable merchandise with the rise of literacy and the spread of anti-Jewish agitation throughout Poland. Zalewski had to do his share in attempting to avoid the identification of the old converts with the new ones, that could prevent the Frankists' final absorption in the Polish upper classes.

Kazimierz Przerwa Tetmajer (1865-1939 or 1940), poet, writer and acknowledged representative of the "young decadent generation" at the turn of the century presents another stage and type in the adjustment of descendants of Frankists, the "half-Poles" in the racist sense. (I dislike the use of the horrible word *Mischling*, but such treatment was applied in some situations.) His mother was fully of Frankist descent. His father was of impeccable aristocratic Christian ancestry who also had a fully "Aryan" son, Kazimierz's half-brother, by his first wife. It stands to reason that Tetmajer's condemnation of marriages of daughters of rich converted Jews to aristocratic Christians stems from his personal experiences of the tragedies involved in such unions.

His published novel *Panna Mery* (Miss Mery, 1901) portrays the marriage of an attractive and gifted daughter of a rich convert to the aged Count Czortsztynski. The couple is confronted with the calamity of the birth of a baby of "Semitic" appearance. The poor boy was expectedly rejected not only by relatives and servants, but also by his own parents. The father even refused to look at him. The mother, conflicted and not too fond of the child, seeks escape from her misery and disinterest in her husband in a love affair. The mesalliance is discovered. The Count calls his wife *Żydówka* (Jewess), a drastic insult in these days and circles. Divorce follows. Mery finds some solace in the God of the Old Testament.

Clearly, Tetmajer sized up the tragedy of racism. However, he failed to condemn it. Nor were the plutocratic converts the only object of his repulsion. In 1919 Tetmajer attacked brutally the noted Galician literary critic and historian Wilhelm Feldman, alluding to him as *"faktor i pachciarz literacki"* (a broker and Jewish literary tenant.) Feldman was not even a convert. He was an assimilated Jew and a great Polish patriot. On the other hand, Tetmajer also wrote on Old Testament themes, displaying a good deal of sympathy for biblical characters.

It is hard to tell what could have been Tetmajer's reaction to the announcement that Feldman was baptised on his death bed, I suspect, at his son's decision. This practice has not been infrequent among children who had been raised as Christians by non-baptised parents or who had converted to Christianity on their own. Tetmajer also portrayed Feldman as the sleazy "Pfefeldman" in his 1909 novel, *Krol Andrzej* (King Andrew).(71)

We have dealt with one aspect of this complicated problem of the later their self-legitimization as Poles. However, there were the others who defended the Jews. The most famous of them was Tadeusz Boy Żeleński.(71a) He and others surely deserve the attention of the researcher, just as do many other problems and personalities mentioned or treated in the present article.

"Intellectuals" Go Racist

The final blow to any possibilities of mass absorption of Jewish converts to Catholicism in Polish life were the Protocols of the Elders of Zion. This fabrication became the chief weapon of all antisemites after World War I and continues to be a leading one today, both in its original version — a Jewish plot to defeat Christianity and capitalism by the introduction of a communist order and the new opposite version, as maintained in the Soviet and other "socialist" areas, a Zionist colonial plot to defeat socialism and restore imperialistic capitalism under Jewish control, I have little to add to what I have written in my "PFD."

Interbellum Poland's antisemites saw an organic continuity between Frank's meanderings about world rule and the Protocols. Among the chief propagators of this preparation for genocide were the progromist agitator, Father Stanislaw Trzeciak and Jedrzej Giertych. Trzeciak characterized Frankism as a Jewish "national political maneuver in the invasion of Poland." He described Frank who had been fought bitterly by the Jewish community as its *chacham* (rabbi) and emissary. Frank's ritual murder accusations were viewed by Trzeciak as merely "a strategem to obtain the confidence of the Poles." He saw a continuous plan for Jewish domination "beginning with Frank through the Wise Men of Zion until today's communists." To him the Bolshevik revolution was proof positive to the truth of Frank's predictions of the world's upheaval and reconstruction.(72)

Giertych is still an active antisemitic propagandist in Great Britain. His latest contribution is the diting of the rabidly propagandistic work, Koneczny's "Jewish Civilization," a tawdry and academically irresponsible Polish follow-up of Houston Stewart Chamberlain's *Foundations of the Nineteenth Century* and an important weapon for the continuity of genocide propaganda against the Jews.(73) Giertych has many other antisemitic works to his credit or rather discredit. I shall deal with just one of the many, his analysis of Polish revolutionary efforts through Poland's history.(74)

Giertych presented all Polish revolutions as Masonic Jewish plots. He portrayed Kościuszko as an instrument of Masonry and asserted that "Talmudist Jews" had financed Frank as part of the plot. Another writer, Stanisław Didier, disregarded the distinction between the Frankists and earlier and later converts.(75) Henryk Rolicki, a more careful historian, operated by innuedos and pointed questions, rather than by direct accusations.(76) Ponisz went even futher in his arguments that the children of assimilated or baptized Jews remain "atavistically" Asian Jews, with but a few exceptions. His solution called for complete isolation of the Jews in preparation for their exile from Poland.(77) He sought support from Thomas Aquinas' teachings on the segregation of the Jews, an excuse given by the Vatican in 1941 for its indifference to the introduction of racism in Vichy France.(78) Father Józef Kruszyński, another harbinger of genocide, was restrained by his Catholic view on racism and by his conviction of the effective assimilation of the Frankists in Polish society from mentioning them in some of his books. He, nevertheless, followed the customary Nazi propaganda line of the Jewish plot for world domination.(79)

These are but a few examples of the treatment of converts and of the Frankists as an actual problem in Interbellum Poland's antisemitic propaganda.

That period has also witnessed racist attacks on Poles of Frankist descent who have made great contributions to Polish life. A good example is the treatment of the composer Karol Szymanowski who had been forced to defend his music against the accusation of Jewish influence.(80) One may, therefore, venture to predict that Frankism will continue o serve as an important weapon in the armory of antisemitism.

As early as 1835, Józefat Bolesław Ostrowski in his attack on Czyński's defense of the Jews stated that their "separate nationality" had ordered them to "strive for world domination." Taking into consideration Czyński's origin, the Frankist implication may not be too far-fetched. In view of the interest of officials of the Russian Ministry of the Interior in the Frankist movement and of their role in the promotion of the plot of the Elders of Zion,(81) the Frankist experience as a basis for the concoction of that canard deserves serious consideration. The German Nazis did not venture that far in racism. Their encyclopedia had nothing to say about the Frankists.(82)

The Frankist experience was also produced for theory about the creation of a new improved Polish people, through Polish-Jewish intermarriages.

In 1911, the poet Antoni Lange (1861-1929) could, in his "On the Contradictions of the Jewish Question" come out with an appeal for a complete biological and psychological merger between Jews and Poles, the "Semitization" of the Poles through joining the two stocks. He held that the merger of the two great races would create a new God (not of the Old Testament) and a new race, with Mickiewicz and Chopin as the examples of this synthesis.(83)

This was one of a number of attempts at a solution of the Jewish problem in Poland following the example of the Frankists. This ethnic-racial element in Lange's proposal was in the style of prevailing theories of his times, except that he included the Jewish group, not religion among the gifted races. Research in this area with due consideration of the role of the Frankist experience will bring out some interesting data.

Early in the twentieth century, Neo-Towianists tried to work out a basis for a sincere assimilation into Polishness and Catholicism for some mystically inclined escapist Jews. However, Towianism too became tainted because of its belief in the Jews as one of the three leading groups, France, the Slavs (Poles) and Israel, the Jews.(84)

It is difficult to establish a definite policy of identification of the descendants of Frankists as such in present day Poland without more extensive research. A few examples may suffice. Just as Józef Frejlich identified Czyński as of "Jewish descent, but born and raised in the Roman Catholic religion" in his 1938 biographical article in a most prestigious reference work.(85) Krempowiecki was identified by Witold Lukaszewicz, 38 years later as one "born in a nobilitized neophyte family."(86) There is no mention of the Frankist descent of either one.

On the other hand Syga's and Szenic's valuable revelatory work on Szymanowska is candid about her origin and family transformation.

The popular. *Wielka Encyklopedia powszechna* (Great General Encyclopedia) tells frankly, though not always accurately, about the Frankists, acknowledges their rapid assimilation, a few decades after Ewa's death, and identifies certain political leaders as Frankist, including Czyński and Krempowiecki.(88) Julian Krzyżanowski, author of a standard history of Polish literature, refers to Tetmajer's origin only on his father's side.(89) Winklowa's 1967 biography of Boy-Zeleński(90) gives geneological data, but the latest work about him does not mention his Frankist descent.

We shall now return to our original main question concerning the rejection by important elements in Polish society of a seemingly acceptable assimilationist solution through mass baptism or perhaps more so through group baptism.

On the Frankist side, a limited and increasingly broadening synthesis of Polishness and Cabbalistic Jewishness existed as long as it involved predominantly cultural rather than religious integration. Frankists participated in Polish culture and politics while retaining their Cabbalistic Judaism. The realization of their messianic dream very like was conveniently postponed just as it has been among some of the acculturated and comfortably situated Orthodox or Conservative Jews in many places, with special theories developed to justify such a convenient *modus vivendi.* After the Frankists had given up their belief in the "Higher Torah" and in their own special place as a group in mankind's history, any synthesis of multi-cultural living came to an end, as they were culturally and even religiously Poles — at worst non-practicing Catholics — like some others of non-Jewish descent, but without doubt, Poles and Catholics.

More is to be said about the Polish side that distrusted the Frankists, even after their complete assimilation. With the rise of reaction and racism, important elements and sectors among the nationalists, possibly, in particular, among the National Democrats (Endeks) resisted such acceptance. (Another problem worthy of investigation, particularly in view of their strong Catholic stance.) Such resistance was of course hypothetical.

The parallel with the German experience is striking. The Germans had to face a moderate mass (not group) baptism at the end of the 18th and early in the 19th centuries. (I am leaving out the Lutheran rejection of an 18th century proposal of a mass conversion to a modified Protestantism by a leading Jew in search of rights.) As in other countries and societies of Emancipation and or acculturation there was also a steadfast stream of individual converts to Christianity, even during the early years of Hitler's rule. The Nazis, confronted with the problem of the racially part Jews, had a pragmatic solution: The Nuremberg Laws that defined as a Jew any person with one Jewish grandparent. By the prohibition of "race-mixing" of any sort between Jews and "Aryans", the Nazis froze the absorptive capacity in German society for Jews of any kind, baptised or unbaptised, but legitimitized as proper "Aryans" those who had chosen their grandparents wisely.

In Polish society, the problem of geneological limits of acceptability or absorption was settled for the Frankists and converts in general through a process of accomplished facts, though not to the wishes of the extremist antisemites.(Again I must leave out the problem of Catholics of Jewish descent who were segregated in the Warsaw Ghetto under Hitler and went to Auschwitz with other Jews.) The settlement could therefore be termed hypothetical so far as the antisemites were concerned. Nevertheless, that point of view is significant as the extreme antisemites' popularity in Interbellum Poland and even in the present Emigration should not be underestimated in the West. True, they never had the chance to introduce racist legislation. It would be interesting to study their thinking about it.

It is noteworthy that the present Polish regime's almost final mass expulsion of Jews from Poland as alleged Zionists, following the Six Day War of 1967, included many active communists with records of bitter hostility to Zionism. With the exiling came propaganda that is still continuing and is hardly a step away from a leftist version of the Protocols. The action is fairly close to the realization of the mono-national-religious-ethnic-cultural order advocated by the radical nationalists in the Interbellum years.

Another melancholy reflection: Jews acculturated in modern cultures present a larger target for hostile envy than the old-fashioned Orthodox Jews, as they participate in many areas closed to the Orthodox of their own volition. The acculturated or westernized or Russianized-Sovietized-Jew participates in economic, political and cultural life and competes with non-Jews in many areas. Not the least is the additional factor of sex competition which does not exist for the traditional Jews. To judge by the popularity of Streicher's pornographic propaganda in Germany, harping on the seduction or marriage or downfall of the innocent "Aryan" blond by or to the dark evil Jew was an important factor in Nazism's ability to capture the public mind, perhaps next to the tale of the Protocols' alleged plot of "Judaizing" the genuine German Nordic civilization.

More questions have perhaps been raised than answered, but this should be understandable and legitimate in view of the scandalous disregard by serious historians and textbook writers of the history of the Jews and of antisemitism, particularly in Eastern Europe; in their wider implications these are of universal significance to all mankind, not only in times of extraordinary adversities. There is room for a study of the valiant struggle of the decent elements in Polish society against thie interbellum epidemic of racist and religous nationalism.

NOTES

1. The best introduction to Frank and Frankism is Gershom Scholem's *Kabblah*, New York, Quadrangle, 1974, pp. 287-308; consisting of the author's articles in the new *Encyclopedia Judaica*, Jerusalem, 1972; article on Frank, etc., is in vol. vii, cols 55-72. Other important publications are: Alexander Kraushar, *Frank i Frankiści polscy 1726-1816* (Frank and the Polish Frankists, 1726-1816), Krakow, 1895 *(-FFP)*, 2 vols; Scholem, *Major Trends in Jewish Mysticism*, New York, 1946 and subsequent editions; his classical essay, "Mitzva ha-baah be-avera . . .," *Kneseth*, Tel Aviv, vol. ii, 1937, pp. 347-92 (with footnotes); in English, "Redemption Through Sin," in his *The Messianic Idea in Judaism and Other Essays on Jewish Spirituality*, New York, 1971, pp. 71-141 (footnotes omitted); the very important, Mateusz Mieses, *Polacy chrześcijanie pochodzenia żydowskiego* (Polish Christians of Jewish Descent) *(-PCPZ)*, Lwow, 1939, 2 vols.

2. On Sabbatai Zevi, see Scholem's publications, to which I am glad to add the English translation of his classical biography, *Sabbatai Sevi: The Mystical Messiah*, Princeton, 1973. For latest bibliography, see his *Kabbalah, op. cit.*, pp. 285-86.

3. The only extensive study devoted solely to this subject is my "Polish Frankism's Duration: from Cabbalistic Judaism to Roman Catholicism and from Jewishness to Polishness," *Jewish Social Studies*, vol. XXV, 1963, pp. 287-333 ("PFD"). It will appear hopefully without the many earlier typographical errors, in a collection of my studies in Polish-Jewish history and relations. Ktav Publishing House in New York will be the publisher.

4. "PFD," pp. 290-293.

5. *Ibid.*, p. 300.

6. *Ibid.*, and below, pp.

7. *Cf.* my "The Mystery of the Jews in Mickiewicz's Towianist Lectures on Slav Literature," *The Polish Review*, vol. vii, 1962, pp. 40-66, (-"MJ"-); my "Jewish Volunteers in the Ottoman-Polish Cossack Units during the Crimean War," *Jewish Social Studies*, vol. xvi, 1954, pp. 203-18, 351-76.

Cf. also the basic, Roman Brandstaetter's "Adam Mickiewicz's Jewish Legion," *Miesiecznik żydowski* (Jewish Monthly), Lodz, year ii, no. 1, Jan. 1932, pp. 20-43; no. 2, Feb., pp. 112-32; and no. 3, March, pp. 225-248.

8. *Cf.* his *Dawna Polska* (Ancient Poland), Krakow, ed. 1, 1844, pp. 51-66.

9. *Żywot, skon i nauka Jakuba Józefa Franka* (Life, Death, and Teachings of Jacob Joseph Frank), Warsaw, 1866, p. 3.

10. *Cf.* his *Żydzi w Polsce, na Rusi i Litwie . . .* (Jews in Poland, Ruthenia and Lithuania . . .) Warsaw, 1878, pp. 79-80.

11. Zygmunt Lucyan Sulima, *Historya Franka i frankistów* (History of Frank and the Frankists), Krakow, 1893. *Cf.* also Jacob Shatzky, *Geshikhte fun jidn in Varshe* (History of Jews in Warsaw) *(-Warsaw)*, vol. i, New York, 1947, p. 299.

12. *Izraelita*, vol. xxviii, no. 46, November 12 (24), 1893.

13. *Cf.* his *FFP*, vol. i, pp. 31-32. On his tendentiousness, *Cf.* Jacob, Shatzky, "Alexander Kraushar and His Road to Total Assimilation," *Yivo Annual of Jewish Social Science*, vol. vii, 1952, pp. 146-47 (originally published in *Yivo bletter*, vol. xxii, 1943); Mieses, *PCPZ*, vol. ii, pp. 12-18.

14. *Kwartalnik historyczny* (Historical Quarterly), vol. xvi, 1898, p. 430.

15. *Cf.* his *Dzieje sprawy żydowskiej w Polsce* (History of the Jewish Question in Poland), Warsaw, 1912.

16. *Encyklopedia powszechna ultima thule* (General Encyclopedia Ultima Thule), vol. iii, Warsaw, 1930, p. 682.

17. *Cf.* Gutenberg, publisher, *Wielka illustrowana encyklopedia powszechna* (Great Illustrated General Encyclopedia), vol. v, Krakow, 1930, p. 537.

18. *Cf.* Shatzky, *Warsaw*, vol. i, p. 299.

19. *Cf.* Emanuel Ringelblum, *Di poilishe jidn in oifshtand fun Koshchushko* (The Polish Jews in the Kosciuszko Insurrection), Warsaw, 1937, pp. 183-84, 189, n. 13, 18.

20. *Cf.* Władysław Smolenski, *Stan i sprawa żydów polskich w XVIII wieku* (The Situation and the Question of the Polish Jews in the 18th Century), Warsaw, 1876, p. 36; Kraushar, *"FFD,"* p. 300, n. 78, 79, 38; p. 290, n. 20.

21. Teofil Syga and Stanislaw Szenic, *Maria Szymanowska i jej czasy* (Maria Szymanowska and Her Times) *(-MS)*, Warsaw, 1960, p. 158. This valuable publication is very important for insight into changes in the sect as seen in the Wołowski family.

22. *Cf.* my "PFD," pp. 308-09.

22a. *Cf. ibid.*, p. 314ff and notes 28, 69 below.

23. *Cf.* Syga, *MS*, pp. 15, 465-67, 479-80. His reports are available in the Warsaw Archiwum Akt Dawnych. Regrettably, I had no time for sifting for this purpose the many volumes of his reports during my last visit there in 1967.

24. *Cf.* Peter Beer, *Geschichte, Lehren und Meinungen aller bestehenden religioesen Sekten der Juden und die Geheimlehre der Kabbalah*, Bruenn, 1823, vol. ii, p. 319.

25. *Evreiskiia religioznyia sekty v Rossiyi* (Jewish Religious Sects in Russia), St. Petersburg, 1847, Press of the Ministry for Internal Affairs, p. 203.

26. *Cf.* my "PFD," p. 306, for references from Kraushar's *FFP*.

27. *O Żydach i judaizmie (czyli wykrycie zasad moralnych tudziez rozumowanie żydow)* (About the Jews and Judaism (or the Exposition of the Moral Basis and Understanding of the Jews)), Siedlce, 1820, cited by Mieses, *PCPZ*, vol. i, pp. xxx-xxxi.

28. *Cf.* my "Adam Mickiewicz's Anti-Jewish Period. Studies in the Books of the Polish Nation and of the Polish Pilgrimage," in *Salo Wittmayer Baron Jubilee Volume*, Jerusalem and New York, 1975, vol. i, pp. 318-319.

This may have been Mickiewicz's attempt to dissociate himself from Jews, a subject on which we shall touch later. It might have also served to identify the few radical émigré Frankists as followers of the Old Testament, presumably in contrast to the bulk of the sectaries who were obviously persons of the New Testament.

29. On Czyński whose activities I have described elsewhere, see my Columbia University doctoral dissertation, "The Polish 'Great Emigration' and the Jews. Studies in Political and Intellectual History" (-"GE"), Publication 1627, Dissertation Series, 1956, University Microfilms, Ann Arbor, Mich. References to other publications on Czyński, including mine, will be found in my "PFD", p. 298, n. 72b; p. 304, n. 102.

30. Jan Czyński's novel *"Crown prince Konstanty and Marija Grudzińska or The Polish Jacobins"* exaggerates the influence of the Jews in Poland at the time of the 1830 Insurrection. It may have been a deliberate reversion to the old Frankist tradition and the false messiah's dreams of glory at the time of an outburst of faith in the people's revolutions. The novel's Polish title is *Cesarzewicz Konstanty i Marja Grudzińska czyli jakubini polscy.* I read the Leipzig, 1876, edition. *Cf.* my "GE," pp. 91ff. A new edition appeared a few years ago in Poland.

31. Quoted from my "MJ," p. 53 (as in note 7), where Mickiewicz's criticism is described. The comedy has been fairly popular on the Polish stage and has been translated into many languages, one of the latest being the Arabic, by Mohammed Saleh El Bondack (Beirut, 1959), with a preface in French by Hector Klat, describing it as a true prediction of the authentic Protocols of the Elders of Zion (pp. 9-10).

There is no mention of these aspects of the possible origin or at least antecedents of the libel in the standard work, Norman Cohn, *Warrant for Genocide; The Myth of the Jewish World Conspiracy and the Protocols of the Elders of Zion,* New York, 1967, and subsequent editions.

32. *Cf.* my "MJ," p. 57, For other evidence, see my "PFD," pp. 289-296.

33. On the continuity of Frankist beliefs among some non-baptised Frankists well in the second half of the 19th century, a subject into which I cannot enter now, see my "PFD," pp. 296-297; and Scholem, *Kabbala, op. cit.,* pp. 306-307.

34. *Cf.* my *"PFD,"* p. 301. For statistics of Frankists, ranging from conservative figures of several thousand in Warsaw at the end of the 18th century to Smoleński's and Mieses' much higher figures (24,000), see my *"PFD,"* pp. 301-02, particularly, n. 90.

34a. For changing attitudes to intermarriage in one family group, the Wołowskis, that may present a good example, see, *ibid.,* pp. 320-23.

35. One Jacob Goliński, formerly called Rabbi Glinianski, and baptised in 1759, deposited in 1776 a lengthy complaint addressed to Empress Maria Theresa to the effect that Frank was not a true Catholic. *Cf.* Kraushar, *FFP,* vol. ii, pp. 24-43. Some financial dealings with Frank were also involved.

36. This view helps to explain reliable reports about Christian Poles who carried in their watchcases miniatures of Jacob or Ewa Frank in the 1920's or the 1930's. I was told of this by the martyr historians Emanuel Ringelblum and Isaac (Ignacy) Schiper in 1933 or 1934.

37. Naphtali Dembitz, an American, author of *Jewish Services in Synagogue and Home* (Philadelphia, 1898) and uncle of Justice Louis D. Brandeis,

returned to Orthodox Judaism. *Cf.* Alpheus Thomas Mason, *Brandeis, A Free Man's Life*, New York, 1946, p. 441. I met one of Dembitz's descendants in Israel. He was a member of a religious kibbutz. American Jews of Frankist descent also belong to other Jewish religious groupings, and, conversely, some of their relatives are Christians.

38. Letter of Celina to Julia, June 17, 1847, in Wladyslaw Mickiewicz, "Moja Matka," (My Mother), in *Przeglad Współczesny* (Contemporary Review), vol. xix, no. 54, Oct. 1926, p. 125.

39. On Celina's background, illness and cure, *cf.* my "PFD," pp. 320-30. I have stressed the absence of Catholic allusions in prayer in the family correspondence. However, I have since found a letter of hers with a distinct Catholic prayer. I hope to refer to it in my forthcoming volume. For the fullest treatment of Towianski's attitudes to Jews and his work among them, see my "GE,", p. 229ff. and my "MJ."

40. On the Frankists' vindictive ritual murder accusations, a *cf.* Kraushar, *FFP*, vol. i, p. 221 ff.; Meir Balaban's Hebrew, *Toldot ha-tenua ha-frankit* (History of the Frankist Movement), Tel Aviv, 1934-35. 2 vols. On the good memory of antisemites in 1859, the centennial of the ritual murder accusation, *cf.* my "PFD," p. 331. On its utilization in 1913 in connection with the Beilis trial, see, *ibid.*, I regret my inability to pursue the matterfor 1959, although it may have been too early then for antisemitism's sufficient recovery since its presumably decisive defeat in 1945.

Polish nationalists have made ample use of thie canard before, during and after World War I, particularly during the inter-war years, and after 1945. See, for example, its treatment in Feliks Koneczny's posthumous *Cymilizacja żydowska* (Jewish Civilization), Wydawnictwo Towarzystwa Imienia Romana Dmowskiego, no. 9, London, 1974, 440 p. (double column, small type), in which this protège of Arnold Toynbee reiterates his belief in the canard that should be viewed in our own times as propaganda for genocide on the basis of his own "researches", in antisemitic literature, of course. He also reasserts his conviction of the existence of a Jewish world rule plot. This work, written in Krakow, under the Nazi occupation, was published by the Roman Dmowski Association and bears the endorsement of a number of Polish dignitaries, including prominent men of the cloth, among them Americans. I am grateful to my friend Samuel Shneiderman for having brought the book to my attention.

In contrast to the modern would-be-genociders and their dupes, the Vatican at the time of the Frankist blood libel accusation continued its position of exonerating the Jews from this charge. *Cf.* Cecil Roth, Ed., *The Ritual Murder Libel against the Jews: The Report by Cardinal Lorenzo Ganganelli* (Pope Clement XIV), London, 1935.

41. *Cf.* parts dealing with the Wołowski family in my "PFD," pp. 317-30, and Syga and Szenic, *op. cit.*, as in my note 21.

41a. On an interesting possibility of the retention of Yiddish in the 1840's, see my "PFD," p. 326.

42. *Cf.* "PFD", pp. 306-07, where references are given to Kraushar, *FFP*.

43. Mieses cites at least four or five names in *PCPZ*, vol. i, p. 59; vol. ii, pp. 45, 55, 97, 98. *Cf.* my "PFD", p. 310, n. 127. It is possible that the "Jacobin" Jakub Jasiński was a Frankist, according to anti-Semitic historians. *Cf.* Didier as in "PFD," n. 146, and Mieses, *PCPZ*, vol. ii, pp. 190-91.

44. It is possible that Capt. Jan Dembowski was a general and his namesake

Joachim was adjustant to Prince Joseph Poniatowski. *Cf.* Mieses, *PCPZ*, vol. ii, pp. 97-98. However, their Frankist origin is open to question.

Scholem brings out that George Alexander Matuszewicz, Dutch artillery commander under Napoleon, was the son of a leading Frankist. *Cf.* his *Beth israel b'polin* (The House of Israel in Poland), Jerusalem, 1954, vol. ii, p. 71. His name is not mentioned in Mieses, *PCPZ*. For suspicions concerning the Poniatowski family's partial Jewish origin, *cf. ibid.*, pp. 172-74.

45. Sulima (as in n. 11) lists the new nobles at the end of the book.

46. Teodor Jeske-Choinski, *Neofici polscy,* (Polish Neophytes), Warsaw, 1903, pp. 68, 70-71.

47. *Cf.* my "PFD," p. 311, n. 132, based mainly on Mieses, *PCPZ*. Mieses also lists in another work the Frankist brothers, Major Ludwik Maciej Dembowski, Captain Jan Dembowski, later generals in Napoleon's legions, their brother Joachim, and Captains Jan Krysiński and Jan Czyński. *Cf.* his *Udział żydów w wojnach Polski przedrozbiorowej* (The Participation of Jews in Pre-Partition Poland's Wars), Warsaw, 1939, pp. 214-22. There were also quite a few Jewish participants, including commissioned officers. *Cf. ibid.*, p. 271.

48. On Wołowski, see "PFD," pp. 304, 316ff; and, of course, Mieses, *PCPZ*, vol. ii.

49. *Cf.* my "PFD," p. 311, on the basis of Mieses' *PCPZ.*

50. We may also infer that the Sect's decline could have been temporarily checked by what may have appeared to some as significant messianic signs, for instance, the Napoleonic wars, the calling of the Sanhedrin, Jewish messianic movements and expectations, such as the Tarniks in 1840 and calculations for 1848 and 1860. An example of an encounter of this sort is described in my "The Tarniks (Believers in the Coming of the Messiah on 1840)," in the *Joshua Starr Memorial Volume. Studies in History and Philosophy*, New York, 1953, pp. 191-201. I have accumulated more material on this subject since then.

51. We must go back again to the Wolowski clan, as in n. 41, 48.

52. "Jan Czyński, a Political and Literary Figure and Publicist of the Times of the Great Emigration (1801-1867)," in Towarzystwo Literackie Im. Adama Mickiewicza, Oddział w Łodzi (Literary Association Named after Adam Mickiewicz, Lodz Section), *Prace polonistyczne* (Polonistic Works), series viii, 1950, Wroclaw-Lodz, 1951, p. 112. However, *cf.* my "PFD," p. 303, n. 94, where I cited Mieses on the marriage of Leon Krysiński, an outstanding lawyer (b. 1847), who "first broke Frankist tradition by marrying a Catholic of Slavic Descent, Maria Przyluska" (*PCPZ*, vol. ii, p. 55). Perhaps, Mieses implied the first marriage of a male, because the earliest case of exogamous marriage was that of Tekla Labecka and Count Jerzy Marcin Lubomirski, with Frank's permission (*FFP*, vol. ii, pp. 120-22). This marriage was an exception. It would appear, however, that Frank's rule had been broken in the second generation. Thus, General Jan Dembowski (b. 1775) married a Visconti woman *(PCPZ,* vol. i, p. 98). Similarly, General Józef Szymanowski (1770-1867), supposedly a very pious Catholic, married Matylda Poniatowska. *Cf.* n. 44. For other possible causes, see the same reference in my "PFD."

53. *Neofici polscy, op. cit.*, pp. 68, 70-71. He cited names of seven such prominent families.

54. *Historya żydów w Polsce* (History of the Jews in Poland), Warsaw, 1919, p. 158.

54a. *Cf.* Ignacy Schiper, *Dzieje handlu żydowskiego na ziemiach polskich* (History of Jewish Commerce in the Polish Lands), Warsaw, 1937, pp. 457-91. *Cf.* also Bina Garntsarska-Kadary, "The Jews and the Factors in the Development and Location of Industry in Warsaw," *Gal Ed*(Witness Stone. A Collection on the History of Polish Jewry), Tel Aviv, vol. ii, 1975, pp. 25-58 (English Summary, pp. VIII-X). *Cf.* also contributions by I. Schiper, Adolf Peretz, and Alexander Haftka in Ignacy Schiper, Ed., *Żydzi w Polsce odrodzonej*(Jews in Restored Poland), Warsaw, 1933, vol. ii, pp. 432-63, 479-541; Ryszard Kołodziejczyk, *Kształtowanie sie burżuazji w królestwie polskim (1818-1850)*(Formation of the Bourgeoisie in the Kingdom of Poland (1815-1850), Warsaw, 1957. Some of the other side of the picture is shown in Adam Wein, "Limitations of the Influx of Jews to Warsaw (1815-1862)," in *Biuletyn* (as in n. 29), No. 49, 1964, pp. 3-34.

55. Among 45 works published in Polish by Jews between 1832 and 1859, nineteen were of Jewish content. The weekly *Izraelita*(The Israelite) appeared in 1865 and lasted until 1913. *Cf.* Hilary Nussbaum, *Szkice historyczne z życia żydów w Warszawie* (Historical Sketches from the Life of the Jews in Warsaw), Warsaw, 1881. The bibliography of works of 68 authors is on pp. 182-96. The breakdown is by Shatzky, *Warsaw*, vol. ii, pp. 161-74. *Cf.* also Sara Zilbersztejn, "The Progressive Synagogue on Danilowicz Street in Warsaw," *Biuletyn*(as in note 29), No. 73, 1970, pp. 31-57.

56. The percentage of white collar and upper class people among the baptised rose to 70 between 1832 and 1870. *Cf.* Shatzky, *ibid.*, p. 43 ff.

Ample references on adjustment to Emancipation will be found in Abraham G. Duker and Meir Ben Horin, Eds., *Emancipation and Counter-Emancipation: Selecteed Essays from Jewish Social Studies*, with an introduction by Salo W. Baron, New York, Ktav Publishing House and Conference on Jewish Social Studies, 1975. Especially useful will be my "Selected Bibliography on Jewish Emancipation and Counter-Emancipation," pp. 359-413. Neither space nor time permit the citation of particular references. However, Theodore Lessing's *Der juedische Selbsthass*, Berlin, 1930, is still basic and penetrating.

57. Kazimierz Bartoszewicz, *Wojna żydowska w roku 1859. Poczatki asymilacyi i antisemityzmu*(The Jewish War in the Year 1859. The Beginnings of Assimilation and Antisemitism), Warsaw, 1913, pp. 1-2. *Cf.* also Shatzky, *Warsaw*, vol. ii, pp. 199-208; Hilary Nussbaum, *Historya żydów od Mojżesza do epoki obecnej*(History of the Jews from Moses to the Present Epoch), vol. v, *Żydzi w Polsce* (Jews in Poland), Warsaw, 1890, pp. 411-16; and the characteristically named chapter, "The Polish-Jewish War," in Samuel Hirszhorn's *Historja żydów w Polsce, 1788-1914*, (History of the Jews in Poland . . . 1788-1914), 1921, pp. 151-61; Hilary Nussbaum, *Z Teki weterana warszawskiej gminy starozakonnych*(From the Portfolio of a Veteran of the Warsaw Community of the Old Testament Believers), Warsaw, 1880.

58. Bartoszewicz, *op. cit.*, p. 37.

59. *Ibid.*, p. 81, and other mentioned publications. The letter in question was obviously a falsification.

60. The debate in the Emigration is described in Bartoszewicz, *op. cit.*, My treatment of it is yet to be published. The most up-to-date coverage of the entire affair will be found in Eisenbach, *Kwestia rownouprawienia*, *op. cit.*, p. 259 ff.

61. *Cf.* Bartoszewicz, *op. cit.*, p. 91. I have had no opportunity to peruse

Kraszewski's voluminous correspondence for these years, which may reveal some more data on the subject.

62. On the Jewish participation in the Insurrection, see A. Eisenbach, D. Fajnhauz and A. Wein. *Żydzi a powstanie styczniowe. Dokumenty i materiały* (Jews and the January Insurrection. Facts and Materials), Warsaw, 1963.

63. Kraushar, *FFP*, vol. i, p. 22. *Cf.* also Artur Eisenbach, Jerzy Michalski, Emanuel Rostworowski and Janusz Woliński, *Materiały do dziejów sejmu czteroletniego* (Materials on the History of the Quadrennial Diet), Wrocław, 1969 (published by the Institute on History of the Polish Academy of Sciences). It contains major publications of that period.

64. Kraushar, *FFP*, vol. i, p. 1.

65. *Sekta yudeev-sogaristov v Polshie i zapadnoi Evropie. Iosif Frank, Evo uchenie i posledovateli. Istoricheski razskaz* (The Jewish Zoharists' Sect in Poland and Western Europe. Joseph Frank, His Teachings and His Followers. A Historical Tale), St. Petersburg, 1892. A brief biography of Brinken in included on pp. iii-iv.

66. MY "PFD", p. 293-95, based on Shatzky's "Kraushar," *op. cit.* and other sources.

67. *Cf.* Sulima, *op. cit.*, as in n. 11.

68. *Cf.* Mieses, *PCPZ*, vol. ii, pp. 218-25.

H. Wilczynski in his *Jidishe typn in der poilisher literatur* (Jewish types in Polish Literature) Warsaw, 1928, lists with very brief descriptions other comedies by Zalewski on the same theme of intermarraiges with rich converts.

69. *Cf.* my "PFD," p. 294, n. 49.

Of course, there were earlier antisemitic Frankists. One of them was Tadeusz Krempowiecki, the radical emigre and target of Mickiewicz's satire, who together with Czyński was the cause of an anti-Frankist campaign in the Emigration, in which Mickiewicz had joined. The acceptance of Mickiewicz as a true Pole was not too difficult. However, his wife Celina fared much worse. In the long run, however, their acceptance helped the Frankists.

A word must be said about the deliberate destruction of documents, in which the poet's son Władysław seems to have specialized. *Cf.* my "PFD," esp. p. 324, "GE," and my other works on Mickiewicz, and, of course, Taduesz Boy-Żeleński's works. I have used his classical *Bronzownicy* (Bonze-platers), Warsaw, 1930. The essays in it are republished in his *O Mickiewiczu* (About Mickiewicz), Warsaw, 1949, and more generously in *Brazownicy i inne szkice o Mickiewiczu* (The Bronze Platers and Other Sketches about Mickiewicz), Warsaw, vol. iv, of his *Pisma* (Writings), with an introduction by Maria Habion. On Żeleński, see also my "PFD,", p. 324, n. 209; and Barbara Winklowa, *Tadeusz Żeleński (Boy): twórczość i życie* (Tadeusz Żeleński (Boy): Creativity and Life), Warsaw, 1967.

70. *Ibid.,* p. 289.

71. *Ibid.,* pp. 232-41. On Feldman, see Ezra Mendelsohn, "Wilhelm Feldman and Alfred Nossig; Assimilation and Zionism in Lwow," *Gal Ed*, vol. ii, 1975, pp. 89-111 (English summary, pp. xi-xii).

71a. *Cf.* notes 69, 90.

72. *Mesjanizm i sprawa żydowska* (Messianism and the Jewish Question), Warsaw 1934, pp. 97-98, 332, 86. He was the author of many other works.

73. *Cf.* above n. 40.

74. *Tragizm lósow Polski* (The Tragedy of Poland's Fate), ed. 2, Pelplin, 1937, pp. 196, 69.

75. *Rola neofitów w dziejach Polski* (The Role of the Neophytes in Polish History), Warsaw, 1934, pp. 31-45.

76. *Zmierzch Izraela* (The Decline of Israel), Warsaw, ed. 3, 1933. A trenchant answer to this work is S.J. Imber, *Asy czystej rasy* (Aces of a Pure Race), Krakow, 1934, pp. 101-220.

77. *Sprawa żydów w Polsce ze stanowiska narodowego i katolickiego* (The Jewish Question in Poland from the National and Catholic Point of View), Czestochowa, 1938, pp. 24-25, 37, 53-69, 72, 76. In the same anti-Frankist genre is Marjan Morawski, *Zrodlo rozbiorów Polski* (The Source of Poland's Partitions), Poznan, 1935. Among other works dealing with the problem of converts in Poland that may pertain to our interest and which I had no opportunity to examine are Białkowski, Leon, *Żyd o neofitach polskich* (A Jew About the Polish Neophytes), Warsaw, 1939,; Tadeusz Korwin (Piotrowski), *Szlachta neoficka* (Neophyte Nobility), Krakow, 1939, and *idem, Szlachta mojżeszowa* (Mosaic Nobility), Krakow, 1933.

78. *Cf.* Report of Leon Berard, French Ambassador to the Holy See, to Marshall Petain, September 2, 1941, *Le Monde juif,* Paris, October, 1946, pp. 2-4; excerpts in Leon Poliakov, *Harvest of Hate,* Syracuse, 1954, pp. 299-301; and in my letter in *Jewish Chronicle,* London, July 19, 1963; my *Jewish Community Relations . . .* New York, 1952, pp. 54, 113; and earlier letters to editors and items to which I have no access at present.

79. *Rola światowa żydowstwa* (Jewry's World Role), Wloclawek, 1923. Published by the General Bookstore and Printing House of the Diocese, the book "exposes" the "Jewish plot" for world conquest, involving the Alliance Universelle Israelite. It cites fabricated appeals to Red Army units. His book, *Antysemityzm, antyjudaizm, antygoizm* (Antisemitism, anti-Judaism, Anti-Goyism), Włocławek, 1924, similarly published by the Diocesan Press, also omits the mention of the Frankists. It emphasizes, however, the charge of the international "Judaization" of western Christian culture and the need for an international solution of the Jewish problem. I have not read all of Kruszyński's works.

80. *Z pism* (From Writings), ed. by Teresa Bronowicz-Chylińska, Krakow, 1958, pp. 52-53, 57. The article in question relates to an attack in 1922-23.

81. *Cf.* note 65.

82. *Sigilla Veri. (Ph. Stauff's Semi-Kirchner); Lexikon der Juden, Genossen und Gegner . . .,* Erfurt, vol. ii, 1929, pp. 388-400.

83. *O Sprzecznościach sprawy żydowskiej* (About the Contradictions of the Jewish Question), Warsaw, 1911. *Cf.* also Mieses, *PCPZ,* vol. ii, pp. 62-70.

84. Jacob Shatzky, *In shotn fun doires* (In the Shadow of Generations), New York, 1947, pp. 30-45; my "GE," p. 226.
Some pro-Towianist writings by converted Jews are: Andrzej Baumfeld, *Andrzej Towiański: Dwa odczyty* (Andrew Towiański: Two Lectures), Lwow, 1904; *idem, Towiański i Towiańism* (Towiański and Towiańism), Krakow, 1908; Wacław Bojomir Mutermilch, *Na przełomie dwóch epoch* (At the Crisis of Two Epochs), Krakow, 1916; *idem, Mesyanizm polski a kosciół katolicki* (Polish Messianism and the Catholic Church), Krakow, 1916; *idem, Parakletyzm (Epoka ducha swietego) a kwestja żydowska* (Parakletism (The Epoch of the Holy Spirit) and the Jewish Question), Warsaw, 1920; Jednacz (pseud.), "The Jewish Question in the Light of Polish Messianism . . ." *Pochodnia* (The Torch), vol. i, 1919, pp. 165-77.

85. *Polski słownik biograficzny* (Polish Biographical Dictionary), Krakow, vol. iv, 1938, pp. 378-78.

86. *Ibid.*, vol. xv, 1970, pp. 300-302.

87. *Op. cit.*, as in n. 21.

88. Vol. iv, 1964, pp. 7-8.

89. *Dzieje literatury polskiej od poczatków do czasów najnowszych* (History of Polish Literature from the Beginnings to the Lastest Times), Warsaw, 1970, pp. 461-65.

90. Andrzej Z. Makowiecki, *Tadeusz Zeleński (Boy)*, Warsaw, 1974.

Ezel Kural Shaw

THE OTTOMAN ASPECTS OF *PAX OTTOMANICA*

THE POLITICAL, PRACTICAL AND PSYCHOLOGICAL ASPECTS OF *PAX OTTOMANICA*

Faced with the possibility of climatic changes that may contribute to future famines in hitherto agriculturally prosperous areas, it is easier to understand the plight of Central Asian Turks of a millenium ago. Wave after wave, the migrating peoples swept over the praries to the North of the Caspian Sea, and they penetrated the South through the mountain passes of the Hindi Kush. Dynastic considerations and succession based on heredity were not a way of life for the nomads: they forged ahead, under whatever leader could promise and provide greener pastures.

Whether they went North or South, the migrating Turkic peoples had their first extensive experience with densely settled areas only after they reached territories formerly occupied by the Roman Empire or peoples who themselves had been neighbours to the Romans. Those who took the northerly route eventually blended with the peoples of Europe. The processes of Romanization, Slavization, and Christianization absorbed the Huns, the Guzzes, the Patzinaks, and the Avars; the Bulgars, Magyars, and Finns shed their Asiatic vestiges. The relatively peaceful assimilation of these groups can perhaps be attributed to the lack of a cohesive and exclusive European entity at the time of their appearance. Except for the harrassment experienced by the settled peoples, their merging into the medieval scene was relatively uneventful.

The story of those who followed the southern route varied somewhat. They, too, experienced a change, but this change was more sudden than the gradual absorption that was taking place in Europe. The Shamanistic religious practices were superceded by Islam. The *cuius regio, eius religio* principle was at work long before the Peace of Augsburg of 1555; once the leaders of the nomadic peoples accepted the new faith, the rest adapted the change. Conversion meant absorption into Islam, but not into the two complex and distinct cultures, Arabic and Persian, that Islam had come to be identified with. Under their leaders, and charged by a new ideology, the Turks moved on to the conquest of new lands.

The new religious identity had upstaged the nomadic peoples' ethnic consciousness, but the practical need of carving new territories beyond areas already under the sway of Islam made the leader a focal point of loyalty and identity. Islam preached the brotherhood of all believers: so they were Moslems and *gazis* rather than Turks. As the nomadic idea of yemporary leadership made way for a settled and stable administrative outlook based on dynasticism, the new identity was expressed not in ethnic terms, but with reference to the immediate ancestors of those who had provided guidance. First it was Seljuk, than Osman who provided an appelation that designated a settled, organized territorial formation. Significantly, until almost the end of the nineteenth century, the term "Turk" was used in Europe to denote the barbarian, and since the Ottoman ruling class did not think of itself in ethnic terms, it took no offense. Thus the Ottoman sense of identity was based on religion, and the issue of toleration was of no relevance in ethnic or racial terms. Distinctions, to the extent they were discernible, arose from religious affiliation, occupational status, and location of one's home town.

Other factors that influenced Ottoman attitudes to the "outsider", namely the none-Moslems who lived within the Empire, can be viewed in three categories:

a. The Roman-Byzantine heritage. Once beyond the territory already settled by the Arabs and the Persians, the Seljuks, and later the Ottomans, found themselves in the lands of Rum, or former Roman territory, lands that had participated in Pax Romana. As the nomadic elements, examplified by the *akincis,* raided the adjacent lands, the runners of the Ottoman State developed roots that fed on the institutions and practices generated by the preceding civilization. For instance, the Venetians had established close trade relations with the Byzantines and had been allocated a quarter along the Golden Horn.(1) As followers of the Latin, Roman Catholic, Christianity, the Venetian community had been set apart from the Greek Orthodox Byzantine community. Furthermore, they enjoyed exemption from imperial Byzantine law. Thus, the principle of extraterritoriality, associated with the capitulatory rights extended to France during the reign of Suleyman the Magnificent and to other western states eventually, had its historic roots in the Byzantine period, in recognition of religious differences between the Venetians and the Byzantines, as well as other merchant communities that kept colonies in Constantinople. This idea of historic continuity is further strengthened by the existence of early trade agreements between the Ottomans and the Venetians, drawn soon after the Ottoman conquest of Constantinople.(2) These agreements follow the Byzantine pattern of making special concessions to the religious needs of the commercial settlements in Ottoman territory. In short, respect for the customs of different peoples and the provision of accommodation and autonomy for people of a different creed were part of the tradition of the area.

b. The Islamic tradition. Pre-Ottoman Islamic empires had extended over vast territory, where followers of monotheistic religions had been recognized a special legal status. The term *dimmi*(3) was used to designate non-Moslems living in an Islamic state. As the Sheriat or Islamic religious law, was inapplicable to the *dimmis*, they were permitted to live according to their own religious law and pay a special poll tax, *cizye*, in lieu of military service. The rapid expansion of the Islamic empires had been facilitated by this moderate approach that did not build up resentment or strong resistance. Secure in what mattered to them most, religion, regions changed hands from one ruler to another, and occasionally from a semi-anarchic condition to one of relative stability.

c. Exigencies imposed by current reality. As the Ottomans expanded, they needed a supply of manpower, both for the cultivation of the land and the manning of the army. They appreciated a solvent treasury and the importance of a regular tax system. At least in the first centuries of Ottoman rule, this resulted in an enlightened and realistic policy of making use of all available resources without drastic alteration of existing institutions.

The Ottoman state developed into an Empire in the fifteenth century, reached its most extensive boundaries in the sixteenth, and managed to hold on to most of the vast territory throughout the nineteenth century. The consolidation, or annexation, of smaller and often rival political units meant the suspension of military hostilities within the new imperial structure. At the cost of being deprived of their political leaders, who were often assigned positions of responsibility within the Ottoman military or even administrative structure, the local populations experienced a transfer of responsibility. The defense of the area no longer rested with them, and to the extent that masses could be free in a pre-industrial society, they were left to their own devices. They were given autonomy in their socio-religious activities. The chief concern of the central administration was to ensure that economic activity — agriculture, crafts, trade — would continue uninterrupted, so that taxes could be collected and supplies replenished.

So, the peace that was experienced by the subject peoples of the Ottoman Empire was one that came through the equal application of pressure on all, a pressure that discouraged defiance yet left room for life and even growth. Pax Ottomanica, a term coined by L.S. Stavrianos,(4) prevailed from the Ottoman conquest of Southeastern Europe to the period when nationalism established its own claim over the varied peoples of the area. Almost half a millenium under Ottoman rule was hardly something any of the subject nations were grateful for, and in the nineteenth century the anti-imperialist tendencies of the age of nationalism would allow no such thoughts or feelings. Yet the very fact that ethnic and religious identity had been preserved through centuries of alien rule was something both the rulers and the ruled could be proud of in the final count. The political, practical, and psychological issues related to this Pax Ottomanica illustrate the concept of toleration in action.

Ottoman advances and conquests in Europe in the fourteenth and fifteenth centuries display a pragmatic character. Aside from making a careful inventory of the territory acquired and the taxes that might be expected from the area in the future, the main change that was introduced was the establishment of the Ottoman Sultan as the suzerain in the area. The relative rapidity of the expansion and the need for soldiers made a total change in the administration of the area impractical and undesirable. In return to cooperating with the new ruler, the notables were given the opportunity to participate in the Sultan's future expeditions. Conversion to Islam was not a prerequisite for fighting under the command of the leader of the *gazis*. It was only after the defeat of Ankara in 1402, when Bayezid lost to Tamerlane and the "conquests" in Europe seemed to slip out of Ottoman grasp overnight, that the temporary nature of alliances with the Christian princes from the European holdings became evident.

The early Ottoman Sultans needed to develop an institution that would balance the Turkish aristocracy and strengthen the position of the ruler. The organization of the Janissaries, the collection, conversion to Islam, and the training of young Christian boys as a loyal core to the Sultan's army arose from this need. A fifth of the booty in the newly conquered areas was considered the ruler's share. Extending the principle to the population in the conquered areas, the "gathering" *(devshirme)* of young boys from families that had more than one son, was utilized to establish a well-trained central infantry in the service of the Sultan. The boys were taken to the capital, educated in the principles of the Islamic religion, and trained for service in administrative or military capacity.

Except for the practice of the *devshirme* system, the local population in the newly conquered areas experienced no religious pressure or coercion. In a way, conversion to Islam would deprive the Ottomans of the lucrative poll tax collected from non-Moslem subjects. Of the two institutions that structure society most effectively, relgion and state, the loyalty of the masses in this period was primarily to the church. The Ottoman conquest presented no real challenge to the established way of life.

By the middle of the sixteenth century, Ottoman conquests had stabilized, and the basic features of the socio-political set up that was to dominate the structuring of Ottoman society to the nineteenth century established. The functioning of the Ottoman system depended on the successful coordination of institutions for the optimal political and economic advantage to the state. Once a pattern developed, the state tried to preserve it and discouraged change.

Ottoman administration has been characterized variously as theocratic, autocratic, and despotic. Though these terms are of some value in describing the role of religion in the conducting of the affairs of the state, or the attempt of the sultan to concentrate power in his hands, the amount of control the state exerted over the subjects was diffuse. In fact, it can be argued that the Ottoman power structure was a federal organization based not on geographic, but on religious grouping, Ottoman society was divided into two major classes, the rulers and the ruled. All the subjects of the empire who were not of the ruling class, Moslem as well as non-Moslem, were called *rayas*, meaning the Sultan's protected flock. The Moslem religious law provided the main guidelines for the state and regulated the behavior of the Moslem subjects. Non-Moslems were left outside the scope of the Sheriat, therefore they had to resort to their own religious precepts. So in civil matters such as marriage, divorce, birth, death, inheritance, property, and the like, the subjects were granted communal autonomy based on their religious affiliation.

The subject class was divided into sub-groups according to religion. Each sub-group, called *millet,* was placed under the leadership of its own head of religion. The dealings of the central administration with the *millets* were carried out through these communal leaders. In the sixteenth century, four major *millets* were recognized by the central administration:

1. The Moslem *millet,* under the guidance of the *ulema,* or men of learning in matters of religion.

2. The Orthodox Greek *millet,* under the Patriarch. One practical consequence of the conquest of Constantinople had been that the

scattered autonomous Orthodox churches in Southeastern Europe, and through the churches the people, were bundled together for administrat've purposes. The extension of the ecclesiastical and secular jurisdiction of the Patriarch of Constantinople to areas already acquired by the Ottomans strengthened the Orthodox Church. Ironically, the Patriarchate became stronger than it had been under the Byzantine Emperors.

3. The Armenian *millet*, under the Catholicos. The Armenian *millet*, aside from the Monophysite Armenians, included others who had been declared heretical by the Greek Orthodox Church. From the early centuries of Christianity, the ethnic identity of the Armenians had been sheltered by their adherence to Monophysitism, their deviant theological stand preventing their absorption by the Greek-Hellenic civilization that surrounded them.

4. The Jewish *millet*, under their Rabbi. Within the Jewish *millet*, there were four main doctrinal and social divisions. The first two consisted of groups who had lived in the middle East before the influx of European Jews in the fifteenth and sixteenth centuries. They were "divided doctrinally into Rabbanites, those that revered the Talmud, and Karaites, those that did not."(5) Most of those who came from Europe accepted the leadership of the Rabbanites, but those coming from Spain and Portugal formed the third distinct community, the Sephardim, who talked a fifteenth century Spanish dialect known as Ladino. The Sephardim kept the traditions of Moslem Spain. The ones who came from Germany and Central Europe were the fourth group, the Ashkenazim. The Sephardim came in such large numbers that they gradually dominated the institutions and traditions of the Jewish community. Their most distinguished and wealthy members such as Dona Gracia and Don Joseph gained considerable influence at the end of the sixteenth century, in the courts of Selim II and Murad III.

The comparison of the *millet* system to a federalism based on autonomous religious communities under their own leadership is further strengthened by the different social, cultural, and economic functions fulfilled within the *millet* system. Each *millet* established and maintained its own institutions. Education and social security were taken care of by the community, through the church and the guild systems, and the *millets* had their own schools, hospitals, hotels, and hospices for the poor and the aged. It should be remembered that the arrangement was true for the Moslem as much as the non-Moslem *millets*. In many instances, these institutions lasted into the twentieth century, though the advent of secularism and the new concept of the responsibilities of a centralized and secular state made the *millet* system itself obsolete.

The Christians and Jews in the Ottoman empire were required to pay the poll tax. The tax was collected from each province as a whole. The individual *cizye* was levied according to the wealth of the *dimmi*, in three categories: high, middle, low. The tax was on each adult *dimmi* who had property or income. In addition to the *cizye*, there were occasional taxes imposed on non-Moslem communities. The arrival of a new governor or a Moslem religious festival might be used as an occasion for collecting gifts in cash or in kind. The Porte, or the central administration in Constantinople, continuously issued orders to the provinces to forbid governors from requesting or collecting extraordinary dues, fees, fines, or taxes, but the frequency of such orders is one indication that admonitions from a distance were not effective. The impact of Ottoman administration — Pax Ottomanica — on the different parts of the empire was as good as the series of governors or administrators assigned to the area, often the Moslem and non-Moslem equally suffering from the maladministration of a Pasha, or flourishing under the firm or progressive approach of an occasional dedicated administrator.

In matters of justice, ecclesiastical courts were in charge of cases arising among members of the same *millet*. When members of different *millets* were involved, they had to appeal to the Sheriat court. Problems that arose between two *millets* were often referred to the central administration that would act as an arbiter after examining the claims made by each community, and taking into consideration charters and special privileges that may have been granted to the communities in the past. It was not just the sultan's pleasure that decided how the matter should be settled, but it was traditions established for generations, and promises made by past rulers that determined the outcome of a dispute. It was those in the service of the sultan, the members of the ruling class, that had to fear the absolute power of the sultan over their person and property: the "protected" status of the subject class prevented the ruler from taking action against the raya without cause.

When a Moslem and a non-Moslem were involved in a court case, the matter was taken to a Sheriat court where the judge, or *kadi* would listen to the parties and pass judgment according to the Moslem religious law. It was understood in such cases that the testimony of the non-Moslem witness would be given less credence. One of the main aims and accomplishments of the Tanzimat reform movement of the nineteenth century was the limination of such discrimination. Judiciary reform in the Ottoman empire was a least conspicuous but most noteworthy sign of the growing secular orientation of Ottoman administration. Secularism, and its twin ideology, nationalism, were two challenges that the traditional *millet* system could not survive.

How did the non-Moslem subjects feel about the *millet* system? Did they have a chance to be heard at the central level? The man of religion acting in his capacity as administrator within his community, was the liason between the subjects and the central government. On the one hand, he collected the poll tax for the state, on the other hand he transmitted the requests of his community to the central administration. Permissions, concessions, renewals of special privileges, or the obtaining of particular favors for the community was handled by the head of the *millet*. The ruler might have had a reputation for being despotic and autocratic, but at the local level it was the man in charge of the religious affairs that had control over the activities of his flock. The *devshirme* system, never applied to the *dimmis* in Istanbul nor to the Armenian and Jewish subjects, was discontinued after the seventeenth century, the Janissary organization being supplied by Moslem children whose parents paid large sums to guarantee a position of power and prestige for their sons.

The non-Moslems were subjected to sumptuary legislation that was enforced with varying vigour, often being allowed to lapse or leaving room for circumvention. Heights of buildings, the colors that could be worn by different *millets*, the carrying of weapons were each at times subject to restrictions. The interference of the state did not confine itself to the consumption habits of only the non-Moslems. To strengthen the image of the state as protector of the Moslem religion, the state often took strict measures to enforce fasting among the Moslem subjects during the month of Ramazan, and to prevent the drinking of wine and the smoking of tobacco. As these activities were not forbidden to the non-Moslems, the existence of visual distinctions, such as the colors used in their wearing apparel, helped the officers in charge of law enforcement. The high point in the use of sumptuary legislation in the Ottoman Empire came under Murad IV (1623-1640).

In an effort to rid the capital and the empire from gangs of bullies who disturbed the public peace by their obnoxious and immoral behavior, Murad IV shut down coffee houses, forbad the use of tobacco, and ordered that nobody should be on the streets after dark without a lantern. The death penalty was used speedily and indiscriminately against anyone who was caught disobeying the regulations. Fasting during the month of Ramazan was enforced by the state, and any Moslem caught eating during the fasting hours was beheaded or hanged on the spot. Under these conditions, the enforcement of sumptuary legislation pertaining to wearing apparel was a necessary precaution to distinguish the non-Moslem who did not have to fast from the Moslem who could lose his life for not observing the fast. The extreme measures of Murad

IV created a reign of terror, especially among those in his service, but failed to bring about the reign of virtue.(6)

When demands for reform in the *millet* system came in the nineteenth century, what the different *millets* requested was not the abolishment of the poll tax, or equal opportunity in holding military and administrative offices, but an extension of their own political rights within their own *millet,* a broadening of the decision making group within the community, and secularization of their *millet* administration. The call was not for the destruction of the traditional arrangement between the *millets* and the central government, but for the democratization of the *millet* from within.(7)

The subject class was also classified according to occupation. Aside from the men of religion and educators, there were the cultivators, craftsmen, and merchants. Cultivators and craftsmen, as producers of wealth, were especially subject to state regulation of their activities. They were not allowed to change their residence or occupation, vary the crops, the method of tilling the soil, or the execution of a craft. The opposition to innovation was probably at its strongest when the government feared a hazard to the socio-economic fabric of society.

Ultimate ownership of land rested with the Sultan, as part of his sovereign rule, but in practice the holdings were distributed to Moslem and non-Moslem *rayas* for cultivation and this was certified by deeds recorded in cadastral registers. If the land was held directly from the state, the tax went to the central government; if the revenue had been assigned to a *timar* holder in return to his services, he collected the tax. Fiscal fluctuations that started in the sixteenth century and the economic decline that followed introduced numerous flows in the tax collection practices of the Ottoman Empire. The state resorted to the use of tax farmers. Often these were local people who purchased the right to collect the tax from the area and managed to turn the transaction into profit for themselves. The tax farmer was often of the same religion as those from whom he was collecting the tax, but his superior economic status set him above the cultivators. The suffering came not from religious discrimination, but from the corruption that was made possible by the lack of effective state control at the lower levels and the lack of an alternative efficient system.

In towns and urban centers, the craftsmen were organized in guilds, or *lonca.* Some of these guilds were confined to members of one religion, some included persons from different religions. The guilds determined a person's place in relation to his occupation. They performed social functions, often in alliance with popular religious orders. They maintained professional ethics and applied the moral standards that supplemented the principles imposed on the individual by his religion. A main purpose of the guild was to maintain the standards of the craft and pass the job and skills from one generation to the next. The guilds controlled quality, price, and profit, and they handled the members' relations with other guilds or with the government. Alongside the *millet* organization, the guilds provided another nuclear association to which an individual could belong.

Necessities of everyday life and work invariably created situations and relations beyond those indicated by government or guild regulations. Professor O.L. Barkan's study of the registers kept during the construction of the Suleymaniye Mosque in Istanbul spotlights the artisans and the craftsmen at work.(8) The ledgers reveal lists of names, places of origin, areas of specialization, wages, and work periods which fall into a pattern. The practical workings of Pax Ottomanica come alive in the process of building the monument designed by Sinan the Architect. A sampling of observations and conclusions presented in the Barkan study shows the Moslem and non-Moslem subjects involved in the process:

1. Attendance was at its peak on Thursday, payday. The Moslems did not work on Fridays, and Christians stayed home on Sundays. Construction work ceased altogether during the Moslem holidays, and Christian workers observed Easter and Christmas. Fluctuations in the attendance of individual workers further indicate that they could stay away from work for personnel reasons such as illness, other business, or to observe a lesser holiday. They were not obliged to come to work every day. Their schedule was flexible.(9)

2. Slightly over half the workers employed in the construction of the mosque (over a period of six years) were Christians(51), the rest were Moslems(49). This balance between Moslem and Christian disappeared when the workers were grouped in terms of their special skills. 83 of the masons were Christians, while the Christians made up only 11 of the stone cutters and stone workers.(10) Though one can see a concentration of specialization, neither group was exclusively of one *millet.*

3. Workers were identified with reference to their birthplace when there were two men of the same name. Over half of those whose birthplaces were indicated came from various quarters in Istanbul, but these areas were the ones recently populated by colonization and settlement from older urban centers within the empire. The Christian masons were primarily from the Aegean coast, the Prince Islands, and the Ionian Islands.(11) Thus one practical result of the Pax Ottomanica was to make talent anywhere in the empire available for the glorification of the capital.

"Konstantaniyye" as the Ottomans called it, or Istanbul, was a special city where Pax Ottomanica found its full expression. The metamorphosis from the Byzantine to the Ottoman capital was symbolized by a change in the skyline: minarets punctuated the rolling hills, and the Moslem call to prayer replaced the sound of church bells. Yet the basic zoning of the city in relation to administrative, commercial, and residential use exhibited an impressive continuity.(12)

Historically, one of the factors that had drawn foreigners to Constantinople had been the harbor facilities offered by the Golden Horn, the delta of a river that separated the old city from the extended city, Pera and Galata. The conquest had introduced a large Turkish element into the old city, where the administrative zone was, but Galata remained a hub of commercial activity. French, English, Dutch, Venetian, and Genoese merchants, collectively termed the "Franks", enjoyed trade privileges that had been recognized by special agreements since earlier times and institutionalized by the capitulations introduced in the sixteenth century and renewed and perpetuated to the twentieth. The capitulations, aside from dealing with commercial matters, made possible the recognition of foreign colonies as autonomous in the conducting of their own internal affairs. This provided the Franks with an arrangement similar to the *millet* system valid for the Ottoman subject class. In Galata, professions that catered to the needs of a harbor city, ranging from inn keeping, banking, storage, construction, and repair to the running of taverns and places of entertainment provided income for the local population. Few Turks lived in Galata, and the existence of numerous churches and synagogues testified to the large number of Greeks, Armenians, Jews who had settled there.

Above Galata, beyond the walls that surrounded the city, lay Pera, with an abundance of gardens and vineyards. In the sixteenth century the area was sparsely populated. At first there were a few Genoese residences and some dervish convents. By the seventeenth century, foreigners discovered the outstanding location of Pera with its view over the old part of the city and the Marmara Sea. A new residential area developed along a straight and narrow street. Settled by the Franks and the Greeks, Pera had little contact with Ottoman Turks until the nineteenth century. Pera was and remained a little Europe, isolated from the surrounding culture. It was a residential quarter, with beautiful gardens and numerous Catholic churches. It was only natural that in time ambassadors to the Porte should choose Pera as the seat of their embassies.

The development of residential settlements in Istanbul demonstrate a few tendencies that contributed to the elimination of friction among peoples from different backgrounds. First, without any designation by the government of a specific locality as exclusively set aside for one group, people from a similar background tended to congragate in the same quarter. Those who moved to the capital formed little colonies and maintained their customs, mannerisms, and regional dialects. Moslem colonies frequently identified themselves with their place of origin, such as Trabzon, Kayseri, Konya, or Rumelia. Second, the institution of schools attached to the specific church or synagogue, the designation of areas as cemeteries, the specialization of different communities in different crafts made the autonomy recognized to religious communities a practical and desirable way of life. Thirdly, the presence of foreigners, the capitulations, and the active commercial life in Constantinople affected the cultural and political evolution of the non-Moslems as well as having an impact on their economic life. Aside from trade contacts, the Greeks, Armenians, and the Jews of the capital acted as interpreters to the diplomatic envoys and to the Palace. As bankers, Armenians and Jews kept contact with banking establishments in Europe. As physicians, many Jews came to know people in the Palace, including the Sultan, and this could be used to establish contact between the Palace and the world outside. For all the sense of superiority the Moslems had for belonging to the same religion as the Sultan, the non-Moslems in the capital nurtured a feeling of sophistication derived from their insight into what was going on in the outside world.

Each religious community guarded jealously its own rights and privileges. Problems were at a minimum when there were no conflicts of interest. The issue of conversion of churches to mosques was a sensitive one. Churches and synagogues that had been built prior to the Ottoman conquest and that had not been converted to a mosque at the time of the conquest were recognized as the property of the religious community, and could not be converted into mosques at a later date. The building of new places of worship and repair or addition to existing structures were subject to permission. Restrictive though the ground rules were, in practice these rules were not strictly observed. So long as change did not involve friction among the different *millets,* the central government was not likely to interfere.

Areas where problems arose most frequently were places that had been settled by a variety of religious communities for a long time and where there were conflicting interpretations of jurisdiction, encroachments, and claims of who was there first. Disputes arose among the various Christian communities for their rights at the Holy Places in Jerusalem. These were brought to the attention of the Sultan as early as the sixteenth and the seventeenth centuries. long before the issue was built into international stature prior to the outbreak of the Crimean War, 1854-1856. An order sent to the *kadi* of Jerusalem in July 1613 settled the question on the repair of a shrine on the Mount of Olives in favor of the Armenians:

> the (re)building of the walls (of this shrine) and their restoration to their original condition and ancient state, the mending of its floor-covering (doseme), and the repair and restoration of the dome itself are the privilege of Armenian Christians living and domiciled in Jerusalem. And the other infidels (Christians) may only (?) come and visit the said place in accordance with their false rites. And neither the Muslims nor anyone from the outside is allowed to interfere and meddle with what they (the Armenians) have in their possession at present. Concerning all this they hold numerous noble firmans, imperial charter(s) (ahd-name), and legal certificates (hucec). Therefore when(ever) it became necessary to (re)build (the shrine) and restore (it) to its original condition, the above named Armenians used to do it by legal permission. Now, however, some Muslims, solely in order to gain money and to annoy and tyrannize over the said infidels, have come with the intention of living there . . . My order has therefore been issued that no interference contrary to the sacred law is to take place . . . .(13)

The document is interesting in conveying the full implication of the term toleration. The Christian form of worship is not approved of, but recognized and sheltered in accordance to Islamic tradition. The Sultan's decision is not based on his pleasure, but on the traditions and practices inherited from the days of his ancestors.

Another document of the period granted permission for the repair, "without, however, adding anything to it", of

> the ancient monastery known as Mar Saba, (which is) situated in the desert region east of the city of Jerusalem . . . a monastery of Serbian (Sirb) monks. In the course of time . . . some of its parts have become dilapidated and are on the verge of falling into ruin . . . Since the monks are not able to repair and restore it, its walls have fallen down and it has become ruined. As a result Bedouin brigands find it possible to shoot arrows at the troubled monks and pell them with stones. And they (the monks) do no harm and give no offense whatever to anyone . . . (on the contrary,) they serve the wayfarers who pass through the desert by offering them water and bread . . .(14)

It was Pax Ottomanica that made it possible for the Serbian monks to live in a monastery in the Holy Land, and the Ottomans saw themselves as the custodians of the religious legacy of the land. Perhaps it is not surprising Jerusalem was one of the hardest places where the Ottomans tried to preserve order. The existence of shrines sacred to Jews, Christians, and Moslems alike should have inspired the groups to live in peace, but trouble was the more frequent outcome. In response to a petition from two Shaikes, a firman to the Kadi of Jerusalem said that the Frankish monks at the sanctuary in Bethlehem had prevented some Moslems and non-Moslems from hanging lamps at Christ's birthplace, and ordered that the Frankish monks should not "without reason hinder anyone who wants to hang up lamps and perform a pious act at the said place and not let them vex and molest a single person".(15)

The distribution of churches in Constantinople itself reflected the continuing cosmopolitan composition of the population. In the seventeenth century, according to Evliya Chelebi, there were thirty Orthodox churches in the city, including the Bosphorus area. The Armenians had nine, five in the city, and four in the suburbs. Catholics had two churches in the city at the beginning of the seventeenth century, but by the second half of the century their churches were to be found only in the Galata area, numbering somewhere between five and nine. The synagogues were over thirty in number.(16)

Pax Ottomanica provided limited social and cultural contact among the different groups that lived in the empire. The different *millets* came into contact under circumstances that made close understanding of one another unlikely to develop. One practical outcome was stereotyping. Both reflecting the image that existed in the popular mind and reinforcing the continuation of the concept, was the stereotyping that came across the screen: in the Ottoman case, the screen that reflected the characters in the shadow puppet theater, the Karagoz.(17) Stereotyping was not confined to the *dimmi*. Aside from the Frank, the Jew, the Greek, the Armenian, there were the Albanian and the Arab, the Kurd, the man from the Black Sea region, and from Central Anatolia. Dialectical differences were used to bring to life the two-dimensional world of shadows and reflections. The *dimmis* were characterized by their costume, occupation, accent, and attitude. Exaggeration and caricature were part of the show, and humor a way of relieving the stresses that existed between different groups.

The reliance on costume and linguistic perculiarities to introduce particular characters in the Karagoz plays was an extension of real life observation into the world of play. First, sumptuary legislation, regulations as to what Moslems and non-Moslems were allowed to wear, attempted to provide visual distinction among the different groups. Second, the socio-cultural isolation of the *millets* had fostered distinct differences in pronunciation, differences that persisted at least until the nationalization of education in the twentieth century.

The church played an important role in preserving the culture and language of each *millet*. Whatever the degree of control the Patriarchate in Phanar, along the Golden Horn, had over the provincial Orthodox churches, the practice of the Orthodox church to allow services to be conducted in the language of the locality was to assure the preservation of the identity of the different peoples in the Balkans. In time, the issue of toleration in Bulgaria and Rumania was to manifest itself not so much as a matter between the orthodox subjects and the Moslem Ottoman administration, but as resentment on the part of the Slavic peoples of the dominance of Greek culture and influence in the administration of the Orthodox Church.

In the nineteenth century, the Bulgarians were in the midst of a controversy as to whether Church Slavonic or the living language should be accepted as the national language, while the Patriarchate chose to ignore the linguistic and cultural aspirations of the area and insisted on appointing Greek-speaking bishops to important church positions in Bulgaria. Lulled by the peace and quiet the *millet* system had provided over the centuries, Ottoman mentality, administrator and intellectual alike, was very slow in assessing the strength of national feeling. As the secular expression of nationalism in the Balkans was in terms of Pan-Slavic ideology sponsored by Russia, the early stages of the demand for an independent Bulgarian Church was misunderstood by the Porte to mean growth of Russian influence. It was against the historical, fiscal, and spiritual interests of the Patriarchete in Istanbul to give up its jurisdiction in the area, so the agitation within the Bulgarian church was allowed to take its course.

A memorandum presented to Ali Pasha in April 1870 tried to present arguments that would convince the Porte to the advantages to be derived from the establishment of an independent Bulgarian Church. It was pointed out that the latest proposal of the Greek Patriarchate, that ecclesiastical autonomy to Bulgarians should be contingent upon the establishment of geographical boundaries within which this autonomy should be exercised, would in fact create a political Bulgaria. Yet this was

> not the view of the Bulgarians. These ask in their names for privileges from the central government. They speak for Bulgarians everywhere, wherever they may be, not in a Bulgaria that does not exist. It is repugnant to them to set a territorial limit to which the privileges would be attached. They are loyal subjects of His Majesty, and the whole empire belongs to them equally with the other subjects. They don't have a territory and they cannot have it. But they are and wish to stay a religious community.(18)

The argument, presented only eight years before the Congress of Berlin which made Bulgaria into an independent state, is reflective of the awareness of the subject peoples of their separate identity as *millets*, while they could benefit from being part of a vast empire, from whatever remained of Pax Ottomanica. The sincerity as well as the validity of this argument at this late date may be questioned, nevertheless it must have contained some elements of persuasiveness and credibility to those who would rather not face the reality of nationalist aspirations, and see the separatist movement only in a religious context.

Pax Ottomanica left its imprint on different aspects of life in the empire. Popular mystic orders of various kinds cut across religious barriers. There was a mutual veneration of saints, visiting of shrines, offering of candles and incense. There was a sharing of customs, and even superstitions. The practices of one community affected the other. For instance, though not veiled, Christian and Jewish girls and women led a secluded life. The value systems of the different communities, their concept of morality, their attitudes were alike. The individual identified himself with his religious community, the *mahalle* or quarter of the twon where the community was settled, and the gupd to which he belonged. The community had its own mosque or church, its school, firefighters, market, and even workshops. The self sufficiency of the *mahalle* eliminated the need for an over-all municipal organization until the nineteenth century.

Though continuity and stability were emphasized, there were opportunities for horizantal and vertical mobility. Restrictions on change of occupation or of location were difficult to enforce, and the ambitious and the adventuresome could take the road to the nearest urban center, and from there often to the capital. Anyone with ability, after acquiring the necessary training and qualifications, could make it to the ranks of the ruling class.

By the end of the nineteenth century, Pax Ottomanica was an anachronism for several reasons. First, the age of nationalism that had swept over Europe in the aftermath of the French Revolution was unmerciful to the weakened and faltering empires that had lost contact with their intitial invigourating and inspiring drive for power. Second, the secular outlook that had moved in with the Enlightenment movement of the eighteenth century had depreciated the value of religious toleration that one found in the Ottoman Empire at the height of religious persecutions in Europe, in the sixteenth and seventeenth centuries. With religion no longer a central issue between the Catholic peoples of Europe and the Orthodox peoples of the Balkans, trade relations that flourished during Napoleon's Continental System could develop further, into cultural and personnal ties with the West. Third, the cosmopolitanism that technology and industrial growth introduced ushered an age of internationalism. Imperial boundaries that were used for protection in the past were now found restrictive, or at best useless in an age when free trade seemed to provide everyone with an equal chance. Fourth, the psychology of toleration which had existed within the Ottoman territories was built on a foundation of self-assuredness on the part of the Ottomans: they felt ''tolerant'', acted ''tolerant,'' were ''tolerant'' because they believed they were superior and could lose nothing by acting in a magnanimous way. Once their confidence in themselves was shaken as a result of repeated defeats and of remonstrations of the Big Powers in behalf of various religious communities within the empire, their attitude was bound to change. The Ottomans were being told how they should administer the subject peoples, what type of institutions they should introduce, and what type of rights they should recognize to the non-Moslems living within Ottoman territory.

Toleration at gun point reverses the delicate balance on which the concept depends. In the course of the nineteenth century, one by one the subject peoples demonstrated that they would not be content with toleration, pacification, not even extended representation: they wanted to be on their own. ''Pax Ottomanica'' had nothing left to offer. Even the Moslem subjects of the empire began to break away and assert their separate identities. The Constitution of 1876 was bound to fail: it did not recognize that stating ''All subjects of the Empire are, without distinction, called Ottomans, whatever religion they profess'' (Article VIII) would not reverse the separatist trend set by nationalism. Those who had been ''tolerated'', now that they were feeling strong, did not feel elated or grateful for being called ''Ottoman''.

Pax Ottmanica had served a purpose. Through the centuries of religious persecution in Europe, it had provided an asylum, a refuge. Europe had matured into accepting religious diversity, or so it seemed. Many groups that were able to maintain their identity within the Ottoman complex for centuries were eager to develop their own national states. Toleration left its own after-taste: a bitterness on the part of those who had been ''tolerated'', and a shock on the part of those who found their historical role in the survival of different cultures unappreciated. Without getting trapped in historical determinism, within the context of historical development, Pax Ottomanica can be seen as a practical outcome of converging traditions that had outlived their purpose and effectiveness by the end of the nineteenth century.

NOTES

1. Deno John Geanakoplos, *Byzantine East and Latin West,* (New York, 1966), 16.

2. Resat Ekrem, *Osmanli Muahedeleri ve Kapitülasyonlar,* (Istanbul 1934), 30.

3. On the dimmi and the millet system in the Ottoman Empire in the sixteenth century see H.A.R. Gibb and Harold Bowen, *Islamic Society and the West.* (London 1957) vol. I, pt. II, 207-261.

4. L.S. S.avrianos, *The Balkans Since 1453,* (New York 1958), 112ff.

5. Gib and Bowen, *Islamic Society . . .*, vol. I, pt. II, 218.

6. Gibb and Bowen, *Mufassal Osmanli Tarihi,* (Istanbul 1960), vol. IV, 1886ff.

7. On reforms of the *millet* system, see Roderick Davison, *Reform in the Ottoman Empire, 1856-1876,* (New Jewsey, 1963), 114-135.

8. Omer Lütfi Barkan, *Süleymaniye Cami ve Imareti Insaati* (1550-1557), (Ankara, 1972), vol. I.

9. *Ibid.,* 166.

10. *Ibid.,* 142.

11. *Ibid.,* 145f.

12. On Istanbul in Ottoman times, see Robert Mantran, *Istanbul dans la Seconde Moitie du XVIIe Siecle,* Faris, 1962.

13. Uriel Heyd, *Ottoman Documents on Palestine, 1552-1615.* (London, 1960), 181.

14. *Ibid.,* 179.

15. *Ibid.,* 184.

16. Robert Mantran, *La vie quotidienne a Constantinople au temps de Soliman Le Magnifique es de ses successeurs,* (Paris, Hachette, 1965), 302.

17. On Karagöz, see Metin And, *A History of Theatre and Popular Entertainment in Turkey,* (Ankara, 1963-1964).

18. Public Record Office, London, Foreign Office archives, 195 998, memorandum from Ivantzo Efendi to Ali Pasha.

Stanford J. Shaw

THE OTTOMAN MILLET SYSTEM: AN EVALUATION

The *Millet* system, as it developed in Ottoman times, was a product of the traditional Middle Eastern social system, developed since ancient times to meet the peculiar political, geographic, religious and economic structure of the area. It was characterized by an extremely limited scope of government, involving primarily the functions of keeping order, defending boundaries, collecting taxes, and assuring the religious and cultural autonomy of all the different groups in the Middle East. Everything else was left to the people to deal with as they wished through their own autonomous institutions, formed according to economic occupation and religion, and organized according to their own laws and traditions. The government's function in relation to these groups was no more than to make sure that the system worked and to collect what is needed to support itself. Government therefore was only a very small part of the way things operated in the Middle East. It had little impact on the average subject even when it did perform its functions. And in the intervals between empires, when the formal political structures created by governments were inactive or completely absent, it was this underlying social substructure of Middle Eastern society which replaced it and softened the effects of the resulting political and military anarchy. This traditional Middle Eastern system was taken over and institutionalized by the Ottomans and then extended outside the area into the conquered areas of Southeastern Europe where it was superimposed over, and sometimes combined with, the established social and political structures of the area.

The primary purposes of the *Millet* system, as it was extended throughout the Ottoman Empire, were to provide for the basic needs of the people — education, health care, social security, justice, communication and the like — without burdening the government, and to keep the different religious, social and economic groups apart in order to prevent the conflict which otherwise would have arisen in such a highly heterogeneous society. These purposes were almost entirely fulfilled. Everyone was given a place in society and accepted it. Society worked and worked quite well, even in the long centuries of Ottoman political decline. There was, indeed, very little conflict among the peoples caused the non-Muslim subjects of the Sultan to begin to slaughter their Muslim brothers and to invite retaliation in kind.

What was particularly striking in the *Millet* system was the decentralized form of government which it imposed on the Empire. Europeans for centuries tended to think of the Ottoman Sultan as an Oriental Despot, despotic head of a highly centralized despotism. In fact, the reverse was true. Most powers of government went to the religiously-oriented *Millets* and to the economic and social guilds formed by the subjects. Even with the functions left to the Sultan and executed by the Ruling Class, its members were autonomous in their functions and could not be interfered with by their ruler so long as they did their duty in accordance with the secular and religious laws of the Empire. The Sultan's "despotism" was limited to his ability to appoint and dismiss the officials of government and to confiscate their properties, making their situations in life, therefore far less secure than those of the rayas of the Sultan, his "protected flock", who were protected by both the secular and religious law. It was only in the 19th century as a result of the impact of the West that the Ottomans established a centralized system of government which extended its scope into the areas formerly ruled by the *Millets* and guilds, and thus stimulated the nationalist reactions which inevitably destroyed the Empire.

Considering how decentralized the Ottoman system was, what held it together so long? First was the person of the Sultan, who was revered as a leader, albeit on different grounds, by rulers and subjects, Muslims and non-Muslims, alike. Second was the loyalty of the *Millet* leaders, who were given far greater secular as well as religious authority over their followers under Ottoman rule than was possible for them in Christian states. There was no Ottoman misrule of their subjects in the true sense of the term. There was, rather, a benign neglect, since the subjects were ruled by their *Millet* leaders, who thus were left to misrule as they did during the later centuries of Ottoman decline. Finally, in many ways the most important element which held Ottoman society together was the guild system, which brought together different people of different religious groups into organizations which reflected common economic interests. The guilds transcended the official differences, enabled people to know and understand each other and to share each others ways of acting and thinking across the bounds imposed by religion so that they could and did become elements of a common Middle Eastern Civilization.

Stephen Fischer-Galati

JUDEO-CHRISTIAN ASPECTS OF *PAX OTTOMANICA*

Like all historical slogans *Pax Ottomanica* defies precise definition and general acceptance. In its broadest sense it implies an age of satisfaction· of the basic desiderata and needs of the inhabitants of the Ottoman Empire and a corollary acceptance of Turkish rule. Chronologically, the period of the *Pax Ottomanica* is generally equated with the "Golden Age" of the Empire encompassing the century-and-one-half which followed the conquest of Constantinople in 1453.

Both the concept of *Pax Ottomanica* and its specific duration, however, have failed to gain broad recognition among historians of the Ottoman Empire, for a variety of reasons. For one thing, the *Pax* itself was a function of war. For another, the concept is incompatible with the traditionally negative views pertaining to the Turks and their empire which have been held by chroniclers, polemicists, and historians since at least the fifteenth century. Thus, to ascribe positive qualities to the Infidel or Terrible Turk and his governance represents revisionism of the most unacceptable kind to most traditional and contemporary interpreters of the character of Ottoman rule and purpose. Such positive assessment also rejects the alleged historical rationale of the subject peoples of the Empire, i.e. the struggle for religious and or national liberation from the arch-enemy of Christendom and national self-determination — the Ottoman Turk. And these almost all-pervasive interpretations of Ottoman history are particularly evident in analyses of the status of the non-Moslem communities of the Empire, the Christian and to a lesser degree also the Jewish.(1)

In trying to ascertain the validity of the concept itself, as a reflection of the nature and significance of Ottoman rule over Christian and Jewish communities, it is necessary to test the validity of a variety of dogmatic assessments of the nature of the Ottoman Empire and purposes of its rulers in the light of historic evidence.

The anti-Turkish polemic which has so obscured the history of Christian, Jewish, and even Moslem communities under Ottoman rule has two basic roots and exponents. The oldest is the Christian, steeped in theological considerations albeit with political implications if not necessarily politically motivated at all levels of expression. In an extended form it comprises variations by humanists, Christian and "Pagan," and by political thinkers, Christian or secular, whose theories and appraisals of the Ottoman purpose and order were often inspired by an unrealistic understanding of the realities of life and society under Ottoman rule and, at least in the fifteenth century, of the realities of life and society in Constantinople and in the Byzantine Empire.

Not less virulent is the polemic generated and carried on with a modern crusading spirit by historians and others who are expounding the ideological and political tenets of modern nationalism and or communism whose very *raison d'être* is condemnation of Ottoman rule for arresting the national and social evolution of the conquered Christian peoples.

The anti-Turkish polemics have stimulated pro-Turkish reactions erring in the opposite direction. And the search for the truth is compounded by the lack of reliable information for the period of *Pax Ottomanica* because of the insufficiency of the records whether Turkish, Jewish, or Christian. Thus, in attempting to ascertain the truth certain fundamental assumptions, perhaps arbitrary and polemical themselves, will be made. First, it will be assumed that the contemporary external observers of the Ottoman scene in the fifteenth and sixteenth centuries lacked close access to the Christian and Jewish communities of the Ottoman Empire and had only limited knowledge of the workings of the Ottoman state. Second, it will also be assumed that these observers ascribed unrealistic qualities to life and society in the pre-Ottoman period. The idyllic attributes bestowed upon the Eastern empires, whether Byzantine, Bulgarian, Serbian, or Bosnian, fail to recognize the differences between the relative evolution of East and West which had occurred long before the conquest of Constantinople by the Turks. And these assumptions will be extended chronologically to modern historians who have chosen to regard the peoples of Southeastern Europe, before but particularly after the Conquest, as fighters for social and national liberation, as nationalists and or socialists by instinct and as revolutionaries by nature. Finally, we will assume that the Turkish sultans from Mohammed the Conqueror to Selim II were not necessarily men of unusual brilliance or deliberate champions of reconciliation of social and political conflicts, whose personal qualities and heroic feats represented a conscious and permanent commitment to the *Pax Ot-*

tomanica or, for that matter, that the *Pax Ottomanica* could have been effective in more advanced societies at almost any time during its duration.

The denigration of the Turkish conquerors, based on minimum evidence and maximum prejudice, antedates the fall of Constantinople. It is a product of the traditional image of all Moslems as ''blood-thirsty salacious heretics who, thanks to the deception of the lusty heresiarch Mohammed, had devoted themselves to the service of the Devil.''(2) Most of the diatribes directed against Mohammed the Conqueror and the sacking of Constantinople in 1453 reflect this basic prejudice. Even such relatively enlightened humanists as Aeneas Sylvius Piccolomini, who identify the destructpn of Greek civilization by the Infidel as perhaps the most tragic aspect of the conquest, were prone to stress ,he masacring of upward of 40,000 inhabitants of the city, the cruelties inflicted upon the survivors by the conquerors, and the need of a Holy War.(3) And similar sentiments were echoed by Bessarion and a spate of Greek scholars, ecclesiastics, and diplomats who had made their way to the West in the fifteenth century.(4) Toward the end of the fifteenth century the virulence of the polemic had lost none of its intensity as more and more humanists, clergymen, and military adventurers were using the Turkish threat as a tool for self-promotion, for urging crusades and other forms of military action against the Infidel, for keeping alive the fears generated in the West by the very presence of the Turkish conqueror on European soil. The voices of those who recognized the inaccuracy of these views were generally muted by the chorus of anti-Turkish propagandists.

Such objective accounts as are available, mostly travelers' tales by apolitical yet Christian pilgrims imbued with the standard western views of the Infidel, depict a more positive image of the Turks and of their activities. Typical of the best was that by Bernard von Breydenbach, the cannon of the Cathedral of Mainz, which was first published in 1486. Breydenbach's *Peregrinationes in Terram Sanctam*(5) stresses *inter alia* the religious toleration exercised by the Turks toward Christian and other inhabitants of the vast empire. Even more realistic is the account of another German pilgrim Arnold von Harff, who conducted his pilgrimage in 1496, whose positive appraisals of Turkish mores, religion, and life are in direct contradiction with those generally held by his West European contemporaries.(6)

The prevailing negative appraisals of Ottoman rule and policies, albeit outside and beyond the narrowly religious context stressed by the men of the fifteenth century, are also to be found in the work of later historians of the Ottoman Empire. The uniform presumption of the existence of a

"Turkish yoke," propounded by authors using both western and "national" sources, assumes massive discontent among Christians and Jews with most aspects of Turkish rule and of the Ottoman governmental structure, particularly with the so-called "Christian Institution." Even writers of the caliber of Steven Runciman and Nicolae Iorga tend to give more credence to negative accounts such as Crystobulus' than to positive such as Konstantinovich's, to subscribe to notions of Turkish primitiveness and stupidity, and to accept axiomatically the proposition that a superior civilization, i.e. the Byzantine, was forcibly displaced by or amalgamated into a non-civilization, i.e. the Ottoman, to the detriment of the former.(7)

The common bond linking fifteenth century observers and later students of the Ottoman Empire is the presumption that the Christian inhabitants lost more as a result of the Ottoman conquest than they gained from it. The millet system is regarded as regressive and discriminatory; the *devşirme* system is almost universally condemned on moral and or on religious grounds. To best illustrate the validity of these assumptions, historians of the Empire have equated presumed discontent with revolutionary manifestations by oppressed Christians. Despite the valiant efforts of such modern historians as I.C. Dostian, Bistra Cvetkova, Fan Noli, A. Grecu, and others to depict hajduks, tribesmen, peasants, voevods, magnates, or patriarchs as men driven to violence by fanaticism, desperation, or hope, as men ready to make the supreme sacrifice for the defense of usurped rights and liberties, it is difficult to accept the validity of such interpretations of Christian purpose and Ottoman rule.(8) The few sources at our disposal are at best inconclusive for the fifteenth century and, at worst for these historians, subject to interpretations basically favorable to the Turkish rulers. The Constantinople Patriarch, for one, even according to contemporary Greek accounts, fared well under Mohammed and his immediate successors and the sources also reveal that the Serbian and other Christian communities derived direct benefits from both the *devşirme* system and the religious policies of the sultans of the second half of the fifteenth century.(9) Nevertheless, the elevation of the social, political, and in many ways also economic status of the peasant masses through the actions of Mohammed the Conqueror and his successors is as a rule ignored by contemporaries and downgraded by later historians. Even for the sixteenth century when contacts between Western Europe and the Ottoman Empire increased, when a "normalization" of relations if not necessarily a *détente* occurred, when accounts by diplomats and travelers as well as by Christian chroniclers within the imperial domains became more plentiful and somewhat more reliable, only a marginal dent in the *a priori* negativism which characterizes descriptions and analyses of the Ottoman order can be noted.(10) And there are good reasons for this.

The principal ones are related to the crisis in the Universal Church focussing on the German Reformation. Luther, and many of his ideological followers and political supporters, assigned a special role to the Turks in theology, polemic, and political practice. The basic theological position was that the Turks were the "scourge of God" sent by the Almighty to punish an erring Christendom.(11) That view was hardly original as it provided even pre-Reformation theologians, polemicists, and political leaders with a ready explanation of the reasons for the fall of Constantinople and the "enslavement" of Balkan Christendom by the Infidel. Subsequent modifications, most notably the equating of the Papacy with the Infidel as dual threats to Christianity and common targets for destruction by the true faithful, were merely embellishments of standard distortions of the realities of Christian life under Turkish rule during the early years of the Reformation. The Turks, at least until the fourth decade of the sixteenth century, continued to be regarded as cruel oppressors of Christians and sworn enemies of Christendom by devout and committed Catholics and Protestants alike. Therefore, the numerous *Flugschrifte*, plays, poems, and sermons concerning the Turks of this period are essentially useless for correct appraisal of the Turkish order.(12)

Other sources of non-Ottoman provenance do, however, afford a more "scientific" if not completely reliable account of the status of Christian and Jewish communities in the Empire. The sources are "secular" to the extent to which they are drafted by political emissaries of western rulers, by travellers, and by political writers concerned with other pursuits than the exposition of dogma. The most reliable are the diplomats' and tradesmen's accounts. The reports of various emissaries sent to the Porte by western monarchs, of men like Antonio Rincon, Ogier Ghiselin de Busbecq, or Jean de la Forest, are a major source of information about the *Pax Ottomanica.* So are the reports of Venetian ambassadors and of tradesmen of all nations dealing with the Turks.(13) These accounts generally provide descriptions of life in the Ottoman Empire as well as of policies and practices toward Christians and Jews. We are told, *inter alia,* that during the sixteenth century, and particularly during the reign of Suleiman the Magnificent, the Turks exercised religious toleration, used moderation in political and fiscal matters, encouraged advancement of moslemized Christians within the Christian Institution, and lent support to the commercial and cultural activities of Jews, Sephardic or Ashkenazic, who had migrated from the

Spain of Ferdinand and Isabella and from other parts of Europe to find haven in the Ottoman Empire. These contentions are confirmed also by indigenous sources from the Christian and Jewish millets, by account of Romanian chroniclers and voevods, and by the writings of Moslem authors and official recorders.(14) Their validity was recognized by contemporary political essayists such as Bodin and Montaigne, albeit for reasons unrelated to express concern with the affairs of the Ottoman Empire and of its subjects as such.(15)

Later students of the Empire, particularly Halil Inalcik and A.H. Lybyer, have displayed an equally positive attitude toward Turkish rule in the sixteenth century.(16) In fact, even among the historians of the twentieth century who are most critical of Ottoman rule there is a reluctant tendency to recognize improvement in the condition of the subject peoples of the Turks during the first half of the sixteenth century.(17) Neverhteless, the majority of modern and sixteenth century writers on Turkish imperial problems have based their work on the classic anti-Ottoman account of the Croatian polemicist Batholomew Georgevic whose *Miseries and Tribulations of the Christians Held in Tribute and Slavery by the Turks*(18) became a best seller in numerous editions and languages after its original appearance in 1544.

Commentators on Ottoman affairs, regardless of biases, however recognized that conditions in the Empire changed for the worse after the death of Suleiman. The battle of Lepanto of 1571 whether depicted as a military disaster for the Turks, as God's punishment of the Infidel, as a symbol of Christian superiority over Islam, as a manifestation of the bankruptcy of the Ottoman system or, by more objective standards, as an alteration of the balance of military power in the Mediterranean, has been recognized as the dawn of the new era of "decline" of the Ottoman Empire.

The concept of decline, with its implications for the *Pax Ottomanica,* had in fact been formulated by informed observers of Turkish affairs even before Lepanto.(19) To French and Ventian diplomats, to Habsburg emissaries, to travellers of various nationalities, to leaders of several component units of the millet itself and of the Romanian provinces, and to Turkish officials and military men the decline in Ottoman power and the corollary alteration of internal conditions within the Empire was apparent since the middle of the sixteenth century. The stabilization of the Turkish frontiers in Eastern Europe as recorded in the Habsburg-Ottoman agreement of 1547 served as evidence to the astute of the weakening of the Ottoman military state and, as such, of impending change in the nature and fundamental relationships which characterized the *Pax Ottomanica.*

Such foreboding phenomena as unrest among Janissaries, Suleiman's relations with Roxelana, the questionable succession of Selim II, Selim's own relations with Don Jose Nassi, the rivalry of Nassi and Mohammed Sokolli were all known and appreciated in the West and were even regarded by a few analysts as determinant factors for the symptomatic defeat at Lepanto. The events following Lepanto were broadly publicized by gleeful prognosticators of the inevitable collapse of the Ottoman order and liberation of the enslaved Christians as well as by those judicious observers who realized all the more clearly that the Turkish sultans and the Ottoman system itself could no longer cope with the military and economic problems which were facing the Empire in the last quarter of the sixteenth century.(20) The prolonged war against the Habsburgs which began in 1593 and ended by the peace treaty of Sitvatorok in 1606 persuaded both sympathetic and hostile observers that it was only a matter of time before the Ottoman order would collapse under the weight of internal and external pressures. Antagonists, both contemporary and of later years stressed the disaffection of the Empire's Christian subjects, focussing on the ''war of liberation'' marshalled by Michael the Brave of Wallachia with the support of the rulers of Transylvania and of the Habsburg Empire, of less powerful leaders such as Baba Novak and his hajduks, Grdan the voevod of Niksic, of clergymen in Bulgarian-inhabited territories, and above all of the peasant masses.(21) These manifestations were ostensibly indicative of the weakness of the Turks and of the crusading spirit of the anti-Ottoman forces. Even contemporary observers who had a better understanding of the multitude of factors which led to the decline of the Ottoman Empire and who had either propounded or accepted the view that Ottoman rule had been generally beneficial to the Jewish and Christian inhabitants of the Empire recognized at the beginning of the seventeenth century that their appraisal of conditions in the Empire may have been too optimistic if not actually incorrect. It seems therefore justifiable to ask what in fact was the *Pax Ottomanica* and what did it represent to the Christian and Jewish inhabitants of the Ottoman Empire.

To contemporaries the most beneficial features of Ottoman rule over Christians and Jews were religious toleration and good government. To later historians another positive element was added — the elimination of those aspects of feudal servitude which were apparent, if not yet fully developed, in the Christian-inhabited territories of the Ottoman Empire before the conquest. It seems appropriate to question the validity of these assumptions *per se* and as they relate to *Pax Ottomanica.*

The emphasis placed by sympathetic observers of the Ottoman Empire on religious toleration stems primarily from the fallacious assumption that the Turkish conquerors were *a priori* committed to destruction and or conversion of non-Moslems. After the Lutheran revolution and ensuing turmoil in western Christendom, acknowledgment of the practice of religious toleration in the Ottoman Empire was made primarily for political purposes related to religious pacification within the Christian West. Emulation of the Turkish example was deemed desirable for a variety of reasons, not always flattering to Ottoman practices, such as unification of Christendom to better fight the Infidel or disdain for the warring Christians who could not find solutions to religious problems in the manner of the contemptible Turk. Such views were seldom based on actual knowledge of conditions in the Ottoman Empire and rarely revealed genuine understanding of the advantages derived by non-Moslem inhabitants of the Empire from Turkish policies or of the reasons for the adoption of these policies by the Turks. The fact is that the Turkish rulers were tolerant of the Christian communities within their empire both for theological and for politico-economic reasons. Without recapitulating past and present historical explanations, it seems fair to say that coexistence with Christians was thought desirable mainly for strategic and economic reasons and was affordable from an economic and political point of view. This is not to say, however, that the Christian inhabitants of the Empire did not suffer during the age of toleration. The suffering was in all probability not of the moral or psychological nature assumed by critics of Turkish rule. The presumed humiliation of Christians by Moslems because of imposition of head taxes, of the *devşirme* system, and of other similar "discriminatory" measures is rooted in old and new prejudices and questionable assessments of the values of Balkan society. Rather, the suffering appears to have been a function of constant warfare and arbitrary demands made by massive armies, not always as disciplined as assumed by those who for one reason or another had to emphasize the ostensibly formidable military discipline and strength of the Turks. Abuses committed by the armed forces were the root cause of the discontent which manifested itself in the Christian millet by the second half of the sixteenth century although corollary negative governmental practices were contributing factors.

Supporters of the doctrine of *Pax Ottomanica* have repeatedly stressed, as indicative of Christian recognition of the values of religious toleration and good government, the constancy of migrations into Turkish-ruled territories from the Romanian provinces and certain areas of the Habsburg Empire which occurred during the sixteenth century.(22) Such migrations did indeed take place but were seemingly motivated not so much by factors related to religious tolerance or intolerance or, for that matter, to good or bad government as by the fortunes of war and by the immigrants likely knowledge of favorable economic conditions prevailing in protected areas of the Ottoman Empire. It would indeed appear that Christian attitudes toward Turkish rule cannot be explained in terms of religious toleration alone any more than in terms of the good government credited to the Turks during the period of *Pax Ottomanica.* For it was not a question of good government that distinguished the Ottoman Empire from the rest of Europe in the late fifteenth and during much of the sixteenth century as one of absence in the Empire of the forms of government which prevailed elsewhere in Europe.(23) The Ottoman governmental structure was far more primitive than those prevalent in contemporary Western and Central Europe. And it was precisely the simplicity of the governmental structure and the basic Ottoman *largesse* and *insouciance,* affordable in times of territorial expansion and economic affluence, which were most beneficial to the Christians during the Golden Age of the Empire. The absence of an elaborate institutional framework which could have given the Empire stability at all times proved detrimental to the majority of the Christians during the latter part of the sixteenth century when the shift in Ottoman military and economic fortunes occurred. But it was not detrimental to all Christians. In fact, it became increasingly beneficial to the clerical and commercial ''technocracy'' of the Christian millet which over the years had exploited the opportunities inherent in the Ottoman system and established and consolidated a power base which guaranteed the prolongation of the *Pax Ottomanica* for their benefit long after it had become obsolete for the Christian peasant masses. Perhaps it is not exaggerated to say that for the leaders of the millet the culmination of the *Pax Ottomanica* occurred when they themselves became the *de facto* rulers of the Christian peassantry and the guarantors of Ottoman solvency during the first half of the seventeenth century.

The realted question of the extent and quality of the masses' acceptance of the Ottoman order during the Golden Age of the Empire is more difficult to answer. The presumption is that for the peasantry the benefits of the *Pax Ottomanica* were most evident prior to the development of sedentary attitudes by the Moslem elite and the concurrent rise of the influence and power of a commercial, bureaucratic, and technocratic Christian establishment in the millet. It is reasonable to assume that the peasantry's socio-economic, political, and legal status originally improved with the replacement of a Christian feudal nobility by a Moslem service nobility and from the restoration by the rulers of the Ottoman Empire of the communal-patriarchal order whose effectiveness had been eroded in the age of ''creeping feudalism'' which antedated the conquest.(24) Whether the peasants recognized the sultans as their benefactors or greeted the new order with any degree of enthusiasm cannot be determined beyond reasonable doubt. But it would not seem unreasonable to interpret the historical evidence in favor of positive acceptance of the Ottoman order in preference to the contrary doctrine of mass rejection of the Turks because of religious, social, and national outrages experienced by the Christian inhabitants of the Empire through conquest and by subsequent negative actions directed against them by the illegitimate Infidel.

The status and attitudes of the Jews in the Ottoman Empire during the period of the *Pax Ottomanica* are easier to ascertain.(25)

Toleration of Jewish communities and even encouragement of Jewish migration into the Ottoman Empire are a matter of record since the fifteenth century. Even contemporaries critical of the Turks acknowledged that Ottoman policies toward Jews, particularly during the reign of Bayezid II when the massive emigration of Maranos occurred, were most favorable to the Jews. It is noteworthy, however, that neither contemporaries nor later historians deemed the favorable treatment of Jews relevant to understanding the fate of the Christian subjects of the Empire.

On the basis of limited data it seems fair to conclude that the Sephardic Jews were the privileged members of the Jewish millet largely because they possessed skills which were in great demand in the Ottoman Empire. Physicians, merchants, financiers, and diplomats were, after the end of the fifteenth century, mostly Sephardic Jews located usually in Constantinople and Salonika. The Ashkenazic Jews were also treated fairly by the Turks throughout the Golden Age of the Empire and the migration of such Jews from Germany and Hungarian territories into Ottoman-controlled lands occurred throughout the fifteenth and sixteenth centuries. In the absence of definite information little is known about the relations between the Jewish and Christian millets or, for that matter, between Jews and Moslems. The emigration of Hungarian Jews to Pleven, Nicopolis, and Andrianople after the seizure of Buda in 1541 apparently brought on anti-Semitic manifestations. Whether anti-Semitism as recorded in the sixteenth century was a function of the increase in the size of the Jewish population and influence in the Empire or of direct pressure exerted on the Porte by commercial and political rivals of the Jews such as Venice and the leaders of the Christian millet in Constantinople is unclear. It is known, however, that the resentment borne toward the ascendancy of Don Jose Nassi by Greeks and Venetians was shared by the Grand Vizier Mohammed Sokolli and that in the struggle for power in Constantinople the fortunes of the Jews took a turn for the worse in the closing years of the sixteenth century.(26) The gradual displacement of Jews by Greeks in the conduct of economic and diplomatic affairs at a time of, if not necessarily as a result of the economic and political crisis of the Empire did not, however, mark the end of religious toleration or of protection of the Jews' political and economic interests by the Porte. It was only in the seventeenth century that intolerance toward the Jewish, and for that matter also against certain segments of the Christian population becomes common in the Empire. These phenomena and manifestations are symptomatic of the end of the *Pax Ottomanica.*

For the Christians and Jews of the Ottoman Empire the period of the *Pax Ottomanica* was generally one of isolation from the crises which affected the rest of Europe during the tumultuous century-and-one-half which followed the conquest of Constantinople. The Turkish order and principles of governance were rooted in a past which was rapidly becoming obsolete throughout Christian Europe in the fifteenth and sixteenth centuries. Such peace as was provided to the inhabitants of the Ottoman Empire was ultimately based on the ability of the Turks to establish and maintain a viable empire by the use of methods and principles which could be applied successfully in the underdeveloped Orthodox Balkans. The Ottoman rulers permitted the Empire's rural inhabitants to engage in customary activities in a manner compatible with their traditional interests. And the Turks proferred similar treatment on Christians and Jews in urban centers. The *Pax Ottomanica* remained a reality as long as the patriarchal, theocratic, military-commercial state retained its ability to cope with changing international conditions. When the viability of the Empire became threatened toward the end of the sixteenth century the very foundations on which its underdeveloped order and society were built began to crumble to the detriment of Christians and Jews alike. The *Pax Ottomanica* may indeed be characterized as the last of the non-modern solutions to the problems of vast territorial empires of conquest. It was valid for the Christian and Jewish inhabitants of the Ottoman Empire but at best could have had but limited application elsewhere in Europe. It was, in short, *"bon pour les Balkans."*

NOTES

1. For a general discussion of the concept of *Pax Ottomanica* see L.S. Stavrianos, *The Balkans Since 1453* (New York, 1958), 112-114 with bibliographical references on pages 885-887.

2. Norman L. Jones, "The Adaptation of Tradition: The Image of the Turk in Protestant England," (Unpublished dissertation, University of Colorado, 1974), 4. A detailed summary discussion of West European reaction to the Fall of Constantinople may be found in Robert Schwoebel, *The Shadow of the Crescent: The Renaissance Image of the Turks, 1453-1517* (New York, 1967), 1 ff.

3. R. Wolkan, *Der Briefwechsel des Eneas 'Silvius Piccolomine* (Vienna, 1909), I, III, 199-202.

4. Schwoebel, op. cit., 9 and note 33 on page 26. See also Paul Coles, *The Ottoman Impact on Europe* (New York, 1968), 147 quoting a typical statement of Bessarion.

5. Bernard von Breydenbach, *Peregrinationes in Terram Sanctam* (Mainz, 1486).

6. M. Letts (Ed. and Tr.), *The Pilgrimage of Arnold von Harff* (London, 1946).

7. See, for instance Steven Runciman, *The Great Church in Captivity* (Cambridge, England, 1968), 186 ff.; Stavrianos, *op. cit.*, 112-113; Coles, op. cit., 145 ff.; M. Konstantinović, *Istorija ili ljetopisi turski spisani oko godine 1490* (Belgrade, 1865).

8. Typical of such works are I.C. Dostian, *Borba serbskovo naroda protiv turetskovo iga* (Moscow, 1958); B. Cvetkova, *Pametna bitka na narodite* (Varna, 1969); A. Grecu, "Rascoala Taranilor in Moldova in Anii 1563-1564," *Studii*, II, 1953.

9. See especially Halil Inalcik, *The Ottoman Empire: The Classicial Age 1300-1600* (London, 1973), 35 ff. and Runciman, *op. cit.*, 165 ff.

10. For a summary statement see Coles, *op. cit.*, 145-149.

11. An interesting collection of primary sources had been compiled by N. Reusner, Ed., *Epistolarum Turcicarum Variorum et Diversorum Authorum* (Frankfurt am Main, 1598-1600), 4 vols. On Luther's specific statements consult *D. Martin Luther's Büchlein vom Kriege wider den Türken und Heerpredigt wider den Türken im Jahre 1529* (Leipzig, 1854) as well as the perceptive analysis contained in K.M. Setton, "Lutheranism and the Turkish Peril," *Balkan Studies*, III, I, 1962, 136-165.

12. Exhaustive bibliographies of such materials may be found in C.D. Rouillard, *The Turk in French History, Thought, and Literature (1520-1660)* (Paris, 1938), 646-665 and S.A. Fischer-Galati, *Ottoman Imperialism and German Protestantism, 1521-1555* (Cambridge, Mass., 1959), 125-129.

13. The most comprehensive study of these accounts if Rouillard, *op. cit.*, 105 ff. Actual reports are found in E. Charrière, Ed., *Negotiations de la France dans le Levant* (Paris, 1848), vol. I. See also C.T. Forster and F.H. Blackburne Daniell, *The Life and Letters of Ogier Ghiselin de Busbecq* (London, 1881) and E. Alberi, Ed., *Relazione degli ambasciatori Veneti al senato* (Florence, 1840), 3 series, Vols. I-III.

14. The most readily accessible yet exhaustive collection of such materials is Eudoxiu de Hurmuzaki, Ed., *Documente privitoare la Istoria Romanilor* (Bucharest, 1887-   ). See also bibliographical references in Inalcik, *op. cit.*, 234-237.

15. An excellent summary of Montaigne's views will be found in Rouillard, *op. cit.*, 363-376. Bodin's views are scattered throughout *Les Six Livres de la Republique* (Lyons, 1576).

16. Inalcik, *op. cit.*; A.H. Lybyer, *The Government of the Ottoman Empire in the Time of Suleiman the Magnificent* (Cambridge, Mass., 1913).

17. See for instance C.C. Giurescu and D.C. Giurescu, *Istoria Romanilor* (Bucharest, 1971), 323 ff. or Mercia MacDermott, *A History of Bulgaria, 1393-1885* (New York, 1962), 22 ff.

18. For a summary of this tract see Coles, *op. cit.*, 147-148.

19. See in particular Rouillard, *op. cit.*, 69 ff. and Inalcik, *op. cit.*, 41 ff., 236, 242-243.

20. An excellent summary with bibliographical references is contained in Rouillard, *op. cit.*, 73-81.

21. An analysis of these phenomena will be found in S.A. Fischer-Galati, "Revolutionary Activity in the Balkans from Lepanto to Kuchuk Kainardji," *Südost-Forschungen*, XXI, 1962, 194-202. See also the excellent survey by C.M. Kortepeter, *Ottoman Imperialism During the Reformation: Europe and the Caucasus* (New York, 1972), 123 ff.

22. See for instance Kortepeter, *ibid.*, 152 note 7.

23. A good analysis of Ottoman institutions is contained in Inalcik, *op. cit.*, 55 ff.

24. *Ibid.*, 104 ff.

25. The most comprehensive discussion of the position of the Jews in the Ottoman Empire is by M. Franco, *Essai sur l'histoire des israelites de l'Empire Ottoman depuis les origines jusqu'a nos jours* (Paris, 1897).

26. *Ibid.*, 66 ff.

Béla K. Király

THE SUBLIME PORTE, VIENNA, TRANSYLVANIA AND THE DISSEMINATION OF PROTESTANT REFORMATION IN ROYAL HUNGARY

During the Renaissance, the Hungary of Matthias Corvinus (1458-1490) was still in effect a great power in East Central Europe, directly controlling provinces beyond its historical borders. Its policies and interests had to be reckoned with by friend and foe alike in the area and even, to some degree, beyond. By the coming of the Reformation, Hungary meant the lands of St. Stephen's Crown proper, including Transylvania, which had not yet become a separate political entity, and the associated triune kingdom of Croatia-Slavonia and Dalmatia, although the littoral's association was purely nominal. Hungary, however, had lost its lands west of the River Leitha and the medieval kings' traditional vassal territories, the banates *(bánságok)* that had served as Hungary's southern buffer zone, had already succumbed to the Turks.(1)

As Martin Luther in Worms in 1521 was uttering his historic ''I cannot and will not recant anything,''(2) Hungary's frontier troops were under Turkish siege in the fortress of Nándorfehérvár (Belgrade), which finally surrendered on August 29. The Turks thus broke through Hungary's southern line of defense. The simultaneity of Luther's rupture with Rome and the Ottoman penetration of Hungary's underbelly prefigured one of the most striking characteristics of the spread of Protestantism through Hungary: the interdependence of the Ottoman conquest of central Hungary and the dissemination of the new faith. Another major local factor, which, like the one just mentioned, overshadows other considerations, was the existence of Transylvania as a separate political unit and its impact on freedom of conscience and constitutional liberties in rump royal Hungary. The third theme, not so overriding as either of the foregoing but nevertheless highly significant, was the completion of the process that brought the gentry into the political forefront of Hungarian society. This last was accomplished in tandem with the final enserfment of Hungary's peasants, the process known to historians by Engels's term, ''second serfdom.''(3) These three interlinked phenomena form the focus of this report.

In a country like Hungary, which had a fairly well-evolved feudal parliamentary system, legislative acts are a perfect mirror of contemporary political, social and even international affairs. The following study will therefore quite closely follow the legislative activities of the time.

The Ottoman Empire completed its conquest of the Hungarian heartland during the first half of the sixteenth century. In direct relation, Protestantism also made great headway, and during the second half of the century Catholic Hungary became a Protestant land. Stephen Benjamin Szilágyi, a mid-seventeenth-century historian, wrote enthusiastically: ''With God's grace, the light of the Gospel, resurrected from darkness, shone once more throughout Hungary and Transylvania from 1517 to 1545 and the true faith could be freely propagated.''(4) The new faith reached its peak in the first decade of the seventeenth century in circumstances that amply support my main propositions, as we shall see.

Logically enough, a climax usually marks the start of a decline. Even before Protestantism reached its peak in Hungary, the Catholic church was making a major effort to win back its flock. The signal for this was the establishment of the Society of Jesus in Hungary in 1560. Its method was persuasion, polemics, education — that is, peaceful means, and little by little most Hungarians returned to the fold. The preeminent figure of the Hungarian Counter-Reformation was Péter Cardinal Pázmány, Primate of Hungary, a former Jesuit, who was born a Protestant in Protestant Hungary in 1570 and died a prince of the Roman church in a predominantly Catholic Hungary in 1637. The Counter-Reformation, however, was the aftermath of our present topic.(5)

The Ottoman Conquest of Central Hungary and the Dissemination of the New Faith

In 1521, the year Belgrade fell to the Turks, Maria von Habsburg, the sister of two emperors, entered Buda in medieval pomp as the consort of the young king of Hungary, Lajos II. The queen was enraptured with the new faith, as was her large retinue of German knights. The unreceptive Hungarian gentry was scandalized by their fascination with Protestantism and by their foreign dress, their alien way of life and their arrogance. Their outrage was not unlike what the French felt two and a half centuries later for Marie Antoinette, a great-great-grandniece of the queen of Hungary. The queen's court became a haven for the followers of Luther, whose doctrines had been introduced into Hungary even before Maria's arrival by George Margrave of Brandenburg, Lajos's uncle and tutor.(6)

Protestantism also enjoyed the support of another powerful group. Many magnates, especially in nothern Hungary, saw Protestantism as a new force for division.(7) They sought division because the more fragmented society was and the more anarchic the country, the less would be the power and prestige of the central government, leaving such oligarchs virtually sovereign in their own domains and free to deal with whomever they wished, be it the Habsburg dynasty, a national king or even the Turks.(8)

The gentry was diametrically opposed to these oligarchic interests and strove to preserve national unity, strong central power and an effective, unified national defense as their only shield against the Ottoman on-slaught.(9) They despised the queen and her suite for sowing the seeds of disruption and they loathed Protestantism, not so much for reasons of faith as for reasons of politics, because it . as a force for scission. Besides, the gentry believed the moral, political and financial aid of the Holy See vital to the coming struggle with the Turks. A Hungary in-fected by the new "heresy" would be denied papal assistance, while a people loyal to the old faith might count on Rome's support. They reasoned that this support had to be insured at any cost and they were overjoyed when Adrian VI (1522-1523), on his elevation to the throne of St. Peter, offered 100,000 gulden for the defense of Hungary and summoned all Christian monarchs to follow suit. The papal ambassador, Baron Antonio Burgio, and the nuncio, Tomasso Cardinal Vio, Arch-bishop of Gaeta, labored hard to help Hungary prepare its defenses. For some time Adrian VI's successor, Pope Clement VII (1523-1534), continued the same policy.(10)

The Hungarians repaid their benevolence. Within a year of Adrian VI's ascension, the Hungarian diet passed its first, harsh anti-Protestant law. This and another anti-Protestant enactment of 1525 were both patently xenophobic laws designed to curb the feared and hated aliens. The first one(11) laid down that Lutherans "and their patrons (influential foreigners) as well as those who subscribe to their beliefs, as declared heretics and enemies of the Holy Virgin Mary, shall be put to death and all their properties confiscated."(12) The second law, the last that the Hungarian gentry enacted against the Lutherans freely and on their own initiative, was equally draconian.(13) It inveighed against foreigners who smuggled the nation's riches out of the country and ordered them deported, but it stated that those willing to serve the king should be welcomed in without hindrance and paid for their services. All Lutherans, however, "shall be rooted out of the country and, wheresoever they be found, they shall be seized without restriction not only by the clergy but also by laymen, and they shall be burned."(14) This legal lynch law was a symptom of the gentry's jitters in the face of the Turkish threat. A great deal changed after Mohacs, however.

After Lajos II's death in that momentous battle, at a time when the first need was for unity, the country divided and elected two rival kings: Habsburg Ferdinand I (1526-1564), and the Transylvanian magnate János Zápolya (1526-1540). In the ensuing civil war Hungary was torn to pieces. Both monarchs were so weakened by the struggle that they had to buy peace by paying annual tribute to the Sublime Porte, King János from 1529 on and King Ferdinand from 1532. Amid such turmoil Protestantism went from strength to strength, for neither king could afford to implement the formidable act of 1525 and persecute the Lutherans for fear of losing support.(16) The Catholic hierarchy had been decimated at Mohacs and in the subsequent strife,(17) and in the absence of theological, moral and political leadership many of the uneducated lower clergy were won over by the dynamic new faith. At the same time, the vacant dioceses were left unfilled and the rival kings distributed these church lands thus made available to their lay supporters, further sapping the economic base of Catholicism, which even before Mohacs had been eroded by the impact of the Renaissance to the point where a contemporary churchman could lament: "Alas, the office of the bishop has degenerated to such a degree."(18) The towns, many of them ethnic German communities, had been strongly Lutheran since before the Ottoman victory. Since both kings badly needed the revenue from them, they left them alone. Lutheran preachers fanned out from them through the countryside, spreading their word and hurrying back to these urban havens whenever danger threatened. They were also safe in the Ottoman-controlled territories. A letter by Gál Huszár in 1557 noted: "Teaching the Testament meets no obstacles in the lands the Turks have conquered. The Turks treat those who preach it humanely."(19) The German regiments that were poured into Hungary contained many contingents of Lutheran soldiers, who also helped to spread the faith.

The masses' ready embrace of Protestantism was soon followed by the gentry.(20) Their militant Catholicism evaporated almost as soon as the dust of the Battle of Mohács had settled.(21) In May 1526, before Mohács, the Papacy had joined the League of Cognac with France, Venice, Milan and Florence.

Since France had already entered into a compact with the Sublime Porte, Hungary's major foe, the Pope's new alliance made him powerless in Hungary. The League's wars with the Holy Roman Empire diverted badly needed troops away from Hungary. After the Pope and the Emperor made their peace, the Pope did the Emperor the favor of excommunicating Hungary's last native king, János Zápolya.(23) This was the crowning blow and the Hungarian gentry now flocked to Protestantism. Besides these political factors in the success of Protestantism, there was also a strong intellectual impetus.

From 1522 onwards Hungarian students went in ever-increasing numbers to the University of Wittenberg in Saxony, where they sometimes studied under Luther himself or more often under his friend and ally Philipp Melanchthon.(24) These young men educated in the bosom of Lutheranism contributed substantially to the creation in Hungary of a Protestant school system that for centuries outshone all other schools in the country. By the middle of the century only one-fifth of Hungary's 150 schools were still in Catholic hands, and of the country's thirty printing presses all but one were serving Protestant interests.(25) During this period there also appeared a number of first-rate intellectuals whose influence on the growth of Protestantism in Hungary was enormous.(26) János Sylvester (c. 1504-?), for instance, translated the New Testament and in 1541 his version was the first ever to be printed in Hungarian. Mátyás Dévai Biró in 1529 became the first ethnic Hungarian to attend the University of Wittenberg. A follower of Melanchthon, he became a highly influential Protestant leader and religious polemist, whose most important work, *The Exposition of the Ten Commandments (Az tiz parantsolatnac . . . magyarázattya)*, was published in Kraków in 1538. He was a deputy to the Diet from approximately 1540 to 1545. István Szegedi Kis (1505-1572) earned a doctorate of theology at the University of Wittenberg and was Hungary's greatest Reformation scholar, several of whose works were translated and published in western Europe. Mihály Sztárai (d. c. 1579) put forward theological arguments in the form of dramas, two of the most notable of which, published in the 1550s, were *The Mirror of True Priesthood (Az igaz papság tüköre)* and *On the Marriage of Priests (A papok házasságáról)*. István Kopácsi (d. after 1562) transformed the high school of Sarospatak into one of the most advanced Protestant colleges, an institution that exists to this day. Imre Ozorai was a writer whose appeal lay in his use of Hungarian folk language. János Honterus

(1498-1549) brought Lutheranism to the Saxons of Transylvania and left an indelible stamp on the culture of the province.

For all these powerful objective factors, however, Catholic Hungary would never had been converted to Protestantism had there not also been compelling subjective forces at work. In the welling desperation of the wretched masses, there was a growing desire to find true spiritual consolation. The common people's yearning for an honest church had only been heightened by the Renaissance worldliness that had suffused Catholicism for several generations. This decay had shaken their faith in the old church and, now that it lay impotent, leaderless and impoverished, they sought an unsullied faith and turned with an open heart to this new one that seemed emotionally and linguistically to be speaking to them in their own tongue.(27)

The Impact of Transylvania
on Royal Hungary

The existence of Transylvania as a separate state contributed signally to the consolidation of Protestantism in royal Hungary. It set an example of religious freedom and eventually secured guarantees for royal Hungary against Habsburg suppression of the freedom of conscience and constitutional liberties. Formerly an integral part of the Hungarian kingdom, Transylvania was the nucleus of the large eastern sector that remained under King János's rule during the civil war of 1526-1538.(28) After János's death the succession passed to his son János Zsigmond in whose name the energetic queen mother Izabella, a Polish princess, ruled. With the fall of Buda in 1541, the Turkish occupation of central Hungary shielded the territory from the Habsburgs' forces. The gradual entrenchment and spread of Ottoman control severed Transylvania's traditional trade routes and connections during the late 1550s, and by the end of the century Habsburg influence in Transylvania had vanished.(29)

Between 1550 and 1571 a series of fundamental laws were passed that put Transylvania into the forefront of contemporary religious tolerance. The diet of Torda granted the Lutherans freedom of worship in 1550, stating: "Every man may hold to his God-given faith and under no circumstances shall one religion interfere with another."(30) In 1556 another diet secularized the incomes and property of Catholic dioceses. One year later the diet of Torda declared the Lutheran church an "accepted religion" *(recepta religio)*. According to this act, "Every man shall receive the religion of his choice unmolested; his church shall be free to choose its own preachers and to choose how its sacraments shall be taken; and no party shall resort to vengeance or violence in competition with another." This act allowed the Lutherans to set up their own senior church hierarchy and to hold synods. In 1564 the diet of Torda also declared the Calvinist church an "accepted religion." Finally the Transylvanian diet itself in 1568 legislated universal and complete freedom of worship, stating that, since faith was a divine gift born of hearing the Gospel, no obstacle could be put in the way of preaching it.(31) Transylvania thus became the most tolerant state of its time.

Its extraordinary freedom soon made Transylvania a magnet for religious extremists and in 1570 strict laws were passed to curb excesses. Acts of 1571 and 1576, however, extended "accepted religion" status to the Unitarian church. During these years some desultory and ineffectual efforts at Counter-Reformation were made under the Bathori princes who had come to power when the Zápolya dynasty died out in 1570: István (1571-1576), Kristóf (1576-1581) and Zsigmond (1581-1598, 1598-1599, 1601, 1601-1602). Prince Zsigmond, in alliance with Emperor Rudolf in the Habsburg war with the Turks of 1592-1606,(34) became so exasperated by his troops' zeal for the principles of the Reformation rather than the war that in a stunning address to them on June 2, 1597, he fulminated: "Had you spent as much time on your military training as you have on your Reform activities, you would already be in Constantinople. ... The work of the Reformation is not for peasants, cobblers, furriers or you treacherous damned sons of bitches." Then from trooper back to prince, he bade them the traditional general's farewell: "Valete."(29) It isn't recorded whether the men fought any better as a result, but such outspoken condemnation of the Reformation in Transylvania was the exception. Freedom of religion remained the rule.

Transylvania, the united principality of three nations — the Hungarians, the Szeklers and the Saxons,(32) was also the land of four religions — Catholic, Lutheran, Calvinist and Unitarian. As such it experienced an extraordinary political, international, cultural and economic upsurge. It would be interesting to assess to what extent Max Weber's thesis is applicable to Transylvania, which enjoyed a golden age under Calvinist princes.(33)

Transylvania now went beyond simple example in its influence on the rest of the lands of St. Stephen's Crown. Habsburg attempts to forcibly recatholicize those areas of Hungary under Vienna's control led to Zsigmond's deposition and drove Transylvania back into the Turkish fold. The assault on the Hungarians' freedom of conscience, constitutional self-government and individual rights was incarnated in 1604, when Rudolf arbitrarily attached to the laws passed by the Hungarian diet one not even considered by the deputies, banning their future discussion of all religious matters.(35) The act was illegal, of course, but Rudolf was determined to enforce it anyway. This effort to subordinate the Hungarians and reimpose Catholicism on them occasioned the first popular uprising against the Habsburgs in Hungary, which had as its newfound ally the principality of Transylvania. The protracted Habsburg-Ottoman war was now compounded with an uncompromising civil war. A threefold settlement was finally forced on the Habsburgs: the peace treaties of Vienna and Zsitva-Torok of 1606 and the legislation of the Hungarian diet of 1608, which together secured for Hungary religious freedom, constitutional autonomy and the right of habeas corpus.

The treaty of Vienna rescinded Rudolf's illegal enactment of 1606,(36) extending complete freedom of worship to all barons, magnates, nobles, the royal free towns and Hungarian garrisons in fortified frontier areas. It secured Hungarian autonomy by stipulating that the palatine(37) was to be elected by the Hungarian diet and "with his Hungarian counsellors shall have plenary power and authority in all matters seen to be necessary to preserve the kingdom of Hungary and the tranquillity and benefit of the inhabitants of the same."(38) This guarantee of the Hungarian government's administrative independence from all imperial institutions was the greatest prize the Hungarians won from the Habsburgs until the *Ausgleich* of 1867 (not counting, of course, the brief periods of independence under Ferenc II Rákoczy (1676-1735) and Lajos Kossuth (1802-1894)).(39) The third achievement of this remarkable treaty was the right that "no one shall be punished who is not legally accused and convicted in accordance with the law."(40)

The provisions of the treaty of Vienna were ratified by the estates of the Habsburg hereditary provinces and were further guaranteed by the Sublime Porte in the treaty of Zsitva-Torok.(41) Hungary's religious, constitutional and individual liberties thus became factors in the balance of power in the Danube basin.

The Hungarian diet of 1608 codified these guarantees and extended them. It granted freedom of religion to all communities, not just the royal free towns. It freed the Protestant churches from the tutelage of the Catholic bishops. It required the king to nominate two Protestant and two Catholic noblemen from among whom the diet would elect the palatine.(42)

Protestantism thus won an unconditional victory in Hungary. The solidity of this victory and the reality of Hungarian autonomy were dramatized on May 15, 1618, when Ferdinand, to secure his ascent to the Hungarian throne, signed a covenant of seventeen conditions that he was required to fulfill to be elected king. These conditions, which were in essence the guarantees in the diet's laws of 1608, were embodied in the coronation oath that he swore as King Ferdinand II in 1622.(43) The same ruler who expunged Protestantism almost completely from Bohemia and the Alpine provinces stood surety for it in Hungary.(44)

Consolidation of the Gentry's Predominance in Hungary and the Completion of ''Second Serfdom''

The least attractice concomitant of the success of the Reformation in Hungary was the consolidation of the political power of the gentry, the exclusion of the burghers from it and the completion of ''second serfdom.'' Protestantism is not perforce socially progressive, to say the least, but these retrograde developments occurred in association with its triumph in Hungary.

The gentry *(bene possessionati)* had been in the ascendancy in Hungary since before the Battle of Mohács. The doctrinal basis of their power had been incorporated in the *Tripartitum*, first published in 1517. Convinced by the *Tripartitum* of the unimpeachability of their privileges, the gentry had pressed continuously to expand their influence in affairs of state. Just before Mohács a diet had forced the king to include eight gentlemen among the members of his council, the executive branch of government in Hungary,(47) positions that had previously been open only to magnates and foreigners. In the decades following Mohács, the growing cohesion of the gentry, most of whom had converted to Protestantism, and their increasing appreciation of their power prevented Ferdinand I from enacting any meaningful Counter-Reformation laws in Hungary.(48)

So successful were their tactics that during the first decade of the seventeenth they managed completely to entrench their privileges at the expense of the burghers and serfs. Act VI of 1608 forbade the crown from creating new royal free towns without the consent of the diet. This measure gave the gentry control over any increase in the numerical strength of the burghers, the fourth estate, which would have been the only way the crown could have outmaneuvered the gentry by outnumbering them.(49) Another act of the same year defined the structure of Hungary's feudal system of four estates *(karok és rendek* or *status et ordines)*. The first estate was the prelacy, the second estate was the aristocracy of the barons and magnates, the third estate was the nobility, and the fourth estate was the burghers of the royal free towns.(51) The act thus wrote into law what had long been established by custom, but its real teeth were the inclusion of a ban that prohibited the king from summoning to the diet anyone who was not a member of one of the four estates. The king was thus prevented from packing the diet with officials or favorites and the gentry was assured of its majority in the assembly.

The gentry's flanks had been secured two years earlier by the treaty of Vienna, which had included a provision that the king was to give preference to those of noble birth when appointing prelates of the Catholic church.(50) This benefited the gentry by restricting members of the powerful first estate to those born into the second and their own third estate.

The socially most retrograde part of the gentry's climb to power was its assault on the peasantry. The *Tripartitum* had already bound the peasants to the soil and subjected them to the will of the lords. Numerous acts had been passed in the sixteenth century, however, alleviating the more brutal provisions of the *Tripartitum*. But in 1608 the gentry had drunk the sweet draft of the triumph of Protestantism, the confirmation of Hungary's constitutional autonomy and the securing of their own political power vis-à-vis the other estates, and now they wanted to ensure that the peasants would stay firmly under their own heel for good without risk of interference by the dynasty in the relationship of lord and serf. A seemingly insignificant piece of legislation, Act XIII of 1608, established that in the future the couties would have sole jurisdiction in matters pertaining to servile relations. (52) For the next one hundred and fifteen years the serfs were the concern only of the counties, which to all intents and purposes meant the upper gentry, their masters, who controlled the county administrations. Only in 1723, at the insistence of King Charles III (Emperor Charles VI), was a pious act promulgated enjoining the counties to protect the serfs from the excesses of their masters. Though it made the serf problem a national issue, it set the wolves to guard the sheep, who in fact were afforded no real protection until the decree of Maria Theresa's *Urbarium.*(53)

Conclusions

The Protestant Reformation in Hungary was far too rich in thought, development and consequences to allow of comprehensive treatment in a repot as brief as this. Some significant and typical aspects have had to be omitted altogether. These include the development of doctrine, which was more original, creative and colorful during the founding decades than at any later time; the separation of Protestantism into the three main currents of Lutheranism, Calvinism and Unitarianism, and the causes and effects of that division; the local organizational peculiarities in which presbyterian and episcopal principles and practices were curiously combined in both the Lutheran and Calvinist churches; and the scope and impact of lay activities in the affairs of the Reformed churches. These and similar issues are fruitful fields for further study, but even without exploring them, some valid conclusions may be drawn about the Protestant Reformation in Hungary:

+ It was a movement that was interdependent with the Ottoman advance into central Hungary and the development of Transylvania as a separate state.

+ The struggle for freedom of conscience was interdependent with the struggle for constitutional liberties and the freedoms of the individual, which had as a double-edged concomitant the consolidation of the gentry's predominance in the body politic, the blocking of further development of the political influence of the burghers, and the completion of the "second serfdom" of the peasantry.

+ Neither the Reformation nor the Counter-Reformation was imposed by force. Converts were won peacefully by persuasion, education and polemics; violence was an exception.

+ The administrative power of the state was not used to effect conversion to Protestantism except under János Zsigmond, who favored Unitarianism, and Princes Gabor Bethlen and György I Rákóczi of Transylvania, who tried to convert the Rumanians to Calvinism.

In sum, the direct and indirect consequences of Protestantism in Hungary were progressive for intellectual life, education, culture and constitutional liberty, and were retrogressive in the social sphere.

APPENDIX I
ABSTRACTS OF DOCUMENTS OF MUTUAL GUARANTY
OF EACH OTHER'S PRIVILEGES, LIBERTIES AND PEACE
BETWEEN THE ESTATES OF HUNGARY AND
THOSE OF THE HABSBURG HEREDITARY PROVINCES

I. *Extracts from the Peace Treaty of Vienna of 1606*

The Emperor and King will issue decrees on all items of the con-
vention (between the throne and Hungary) and they will be ratified by
the estates of Bohemia, of the Archduchies of Austria, of the
Margravate of Moravia, of the Duchy of Silesia, and by Archduke
Ferdinand together with the estates of the Duchy of Styria.

They will all "guarantee that His Imperial and Royal Majesty will
honor this treaty with the Hungarians in all its details and that the
neighboring provinces will do nothing that might violate the rights of
their neighbor (Hungary)." (§ 26) *(C.J.H. 1526-1608*, p. 977)

The Hungarians offer reciprocal loyalty to the king and to the estates
of their neighboring provinces. (§ 27) (*Ibid.*)

II. *Letters of Guaranty*

Letters of guaranty were exchanged between the estates of Hungary
and the estates of the neighboring Habsburg provinces. The letter of the
Bohemian, Moravian, Lusatian and Silesian estates was signed in
Vienna on September 16, 1606; the Hungarians, on September 23.
Both guaranteed the peace treaty between the Hungarians and the
Habsburg monarch signed in Vienna on June 23 and promulgated by
the Emperor and King on August 6, 1606. The estates mutually
pledged to keep the peace and honor all past treaties and agreements.
The Hungarians pledged their guarantee of the "future security and
freedoms *(pro futura ipsorum cautela et assecuratione)* of the estates of
Bohemia and its annexed territories, the Margravate of Moravia, the
Duchy of Silesia and the Margravates of Upper and Lower Lusatia."
(*C.J.H. 1526-1608*, pp. 979-983) The Bohemian letter stated in
conclusion that the estates, "freely and voluntarily assuming the
obligation, do assure the aforementioned Lord Bocskay (sic and all
the estates of Hungary and Transylvania that not only will His Sacred
Majesty honor this peace concluded with the Hungarians in all its parts
and keep it inviolate but also the estates of Noble Bohemia and its annexed provinces will attempt nothing against the Hungarians that might
violate their neighbors' law *(nihil contra hungaros, quod vicinitatis jus
laedere possit, attentabunt)*." (*Ibid.*, pp. 983-985)

APPENDIX II
ABSTRACT OF THE TREATY OF ZSITVA-TOROK OF 1606
BETWEEN EMPEROR AND KING RUDOLF
AND THE SUBLIME PORTE

GUARANTEEING THE ASSURANCES OF
THE HUNGARIANS FREEDOM OF CONSCIENCE
AND CONSTITUTIONAL LIBERTIES
CONTAINED IN THE TREATY OF VIENNA OF 1060

"Whatever else is conceded to the Most Illustrious Lord Bocskai is to remain as granted by the Treaty of Vienna *(Quod autem concessum est illustrissimo domino Bochkay* (sic), *illud maneat, juxta pacta Viennae facta)."* (§ 6) (*C.J.H. 1526-1608,* p. 993)

APPENDIX III

THE PACTA CONVENTA OF FERDINAND II

The "Seventeen Conditions" Guaranteeing to Hungary
Freedom of Conscience and Constitutional Liberties

1. Hungary's constitutional freedoms and liberties as guaranteed by the Treaty of Vienna and subsequent legislation will be honored.

2. All gravamina shall be settled by future diets which will be held at intervals not greater than three years.

3. Hungary and its annexed territories will be governed by their own inhabitants and no Hungarian troops will fight on foreign soil.

4. The fortified frontier zone in Hungary will be placed under Hungarian command.

5. The right of habeas corpus will be respected; only Hungarian judiciary will be entitled to practice in Hungary and they will be permitted to do so without administrative interference.

6. Freedom of conscience will not be infringed by the king or the lords.

7. The palatine will be elected.

8. The king will maintain the defenses of the fortified zone.

9. The privileges of the royal free towns and the mining cities will be preserved.

10. The Holy Crown will be kept in Hungary under guard by Hungarian laymen of both religions who will be elected by the diet.

11. No part of Hungary's territory will be ceded.

12. Peace with Bohemia and Transylvania and other neighboring provinces will be maintained in accordance with the Treaty of Vienna.

13. Domestic peace will be preserved and no foreign troops will be called in.

14. Territories, towns and fortresses occupied by Austria will be restored to Hungary.

16. The privileges of the *Hajdu* soldiery will be preserved.

17. Ferdinand shall not intervene in the governance of Hungary so long as his father Matthias II, (1608-1619) lives.

These conditions were then embodied in Ferdinand II's coronation oath. (Act II 1618, *C.J.H. 1608-1657*, pp. 175-183)

NOTES

1. Ozorai and Sói *bánságok* (Northern Bosnia); Macsói *bánság* (Northern Serbia); Szörényi *bánság* (Northeastern Serbia and Western Wallachia). See map in Bálint Hóman and Byula Szekfü, *Magyar Történet* (Hungarian History), 5 vols., Budapest: Egyetemi Nyomda, 1942, II, between pp. 152-53.

2. Harold J. Grimm, *The Reformation Era 1500-1650*, 2nd ed., New York: Macmillan, 1973, p. 114. The Hungarian delegation attended the Diet of Worms and appealed for the help of the Empire, but left the city empty-handed on April 20, four days after Luther's arrival. The delegation was headed by István Verbőczi (also Werbőczy), a leader of the gentry. Egyed Berzeviczy, "Magyarország az 1521-iki wormsi birodalmi gyülésen" (Hungary at the Imperial Diet of 1521, at Worms), *Századok* (Centuries, review of the Hungarian Historical Association, to be quoted below as Sz.), Vol. 39 (1905), pp. 452-56.

3. For the definition of "Second Serfdom," its evolution in Hungary and her neighboring countries, see Béla K. Király, "The Emancipation of the Serfs of East Central Europe," *Antemurale*, Institutum Historicum Polunicum Romae, Vol. XV (1971), pp. 63-85.

4. Stephen Benjamin Szilágyi, *Acta synodi nationalis hungaricae seu historica descriptio actorum synodalium* . . . Szatmár-Németi: 1646. Reprinted in Pál Finkei, "Magyar Prot.(estáns) egyháztörténeti kutfők" (Sources of the History of Hungarian Protestantism), *Sárospataki Füzetek* (Periodical of Sárospatak, a Calvinist scholarly journal), Vol. I (1857), pp. 161-80 (to be quoted below as SF). In 1521 the loss of Belgrade opened the main door to the heartlands; in 1526 the Battle of Mohács vacated the royal throne, decimated the Catholic hierarchy and destroyed a considerable portion of the army; in 1541 the seizure of Buda, the capital city, as well as the main central fortress, marked the partition of Hungary into three entities.

5. See Imre Révész Jr., "A magyarországi protestantizmus tudományos történetirása" (The Scientific Historiography of Protestantism in Hungary), *Protestáns Szemle* (Protestant Review, referred to below as P.Sz.), Vol. 36 (1924), pp. 110-12. Also József S. Szabó *et al.*, *A protestántizmus Magyarországon* (Protestantism in Hungary), Budapest: Bethlen Gábor Szövetség, 1928. Sándor Biró *et al.*, *A magyar református egyház története* (A History of the Hungarian Reformed Church), Budapest: Kossuth, 1949. Mihály Zsilinszky, *A magyarhoni protestáns egyház története* (A History of the Protestant Church in Hungary), Budapest: Atheneum, 1907. Károly Lányi, *Magyarföld egyháztörténetei Austria-házi korszak* (Church History of Hungary in the Era of the Austrian Dynasty), 3 vols., Nagyszombat: no publisher named, 1844. Imre Révész (Sr), *A magyarországi protestántizmus történelme* (A History of Protestantism in Hungary), Budapest: Magyar Történelmi Társulat, 1925, contains a comprehensive bibliography. The pre-Protestant religious dissident movements were rather strong in Hungary. Sects of Waldensians, Bogumils, Hussites and Moravian Brethren existed. Many of these movements of religious dissent blossomed particularly during the Peasant war of György Dózsa in 1514. S. Szabó in *A protestántizmus . . .*, pp. 10-11.

6. The same year, in 1521, Archbishop György Szatmári, Primate of Hungary, promulgated in all the churches of Hungary the papal bull con-

demning Luther's doctrine. Révész, A *magyarországi* . . ., pp. 11, 12. Vilmos Fraknói, *A Hunyadiak és a Jagellók kora (1440-1526)*(The Era of the Hunyadis and the Jagellonians (1440-1526), in Sándor Szilágyi, *A magyar nemzet története* (A History of the Hungarian Nation), 10 vols., Budapest: Atheneum, 1898, IV, 444-46. The two court chaplains of the queen, János Henckel and Konrád Cordatus, openly preached Luther's doctrines. S. Szabó, *et al., A protestantizmus* . . ., pp. 14-15. David Erdmann, *Luther und die Hochenzollerns,* Breslau: Max & Co., 1884, pp. 120, 128. Zsillinszky, *A magyarhoni* . . ., pp. 31-35. The soil for the Reformation was already ripe as early as the end of the fifteenth century. The widespread movements of religious dissent (see note 5), combined with an intensive contact with Byzantium, caused a remarkable lack of orthodoxy in Hungary. The University of Pozsony (Bratislava) (which existed between 1458 and 1490) flourished, and Hungarian students studied in Krakow, Vienna, Padua and Prague also (see note 24). Thus a considerable group of intellectuals emerged. Biro *et al., A magyar református* . . ., p. 25. These intellectuals were affected by humanism, were eager to learn, and as a matter of fact they became disillusioned with the Church hierarchy, for it was secular and economy minded, submerged in politics, was immoral and nepotic, many of them were also foreigners. The Renaissance Church was indeed dual in nature — one side was sophisticated and progressive, the other was decadent — and consequently it could not escape an internal clash. József Nagy, "A reformációt előkészítő körülmények Magyarországon" (Circumstances which Anticipated Reformation in Hungary), SF, Vol. 5 (1861), pp. 577-89.

7. Biro *et al., A magyar református* . . ., p. 45.

8. There were numerous barons and magnates, however, who supported Protestantism not for reasons of power and influence but because of devotion to the new faith: in Southern Hungary Péter Petrovics, the guardian of the young king; in the Transdanubian area Bálint Enyingi Török; in the Trans-Tisza region Gáspár Drágfy; in Northern Hungary the Révai and the Thurzó families; in Southwest Hungary the Batthyány and the Zrinyi families, to mention but the most prominent ones. Révész, *A magyarországi* . . ., p. 17. Zsilinszky, *A magyarhoni* . . ., pp. 36-45.

9. Révész, *A magyarorszagi* . . ., p. 12.

10. Baron Anthony Burgio, *Mohács Magyarországa* (Hungary of the Era of Mohács), translated by Emma Bartoniek, Budapest: 1926. See also Imre Révész, "Mohács és a reformáció" (Mohács and the Reformation), P.Sz., Vol. 35 (1926), pp. 475-86. Fraknói, *A Hunyadiak* . . ., IV, 451. In 1524 the queen's chaplain orally attacked the Pope. Representatives of the gentry retorted that whoever would speak against the Holy See or the Catholic faith would be cut to pieces; subsequently the queen dismissed the priest. *Ibid.*

11. Act. LIV. 1523. *Corpus juris hungarici 1000-1526.* Budapest: Franklin, 1899, p. 825 (quoted below as C.J.H.). Jenő Zoványi, "A *lutherani comburantur* és a *Corpus juris hungarici,*" P.Sz., Vol. 29 (1917), p. 626. Lányi, *Magyarföld* . . ., pp. 42-43.

12. This enactment was in fact the renewal of Mathias Corvinus anti-heretic act, which listed among the cases of treason the joining of ". . . some religious denomination which is openly practiced, though forbidden . . . ." Act. II. 1462. *C.J.H. 1000-1526,* p. 341. King Ulászló (Wladislaw) II (1490-1516) verbatim re-enacted Mathias Corvinus' law, as Act. IV. 1495. *Ibid.,* p. 567.

13. Act IV. 1525. *C.J.H. 1000-1526*, pp. 830-31. All the latter anti-Protestant laws were initiated not by the Hungarian estates but by Habsburg kings.

14. *Non solum per ecclesiasticas, verum etiam per saeculares personas, libere capiantur, et comburantur* . . . . See Jenő Zoványi, "A reformáczió Magyarországon a mohácsi vészig" (Reformation in Hungary up to the Disaster of Mohács), P.Sz., Vol. 3 (1891), pp. 70-88, 207-234; also Kálmán Révész, "Révész Imre a magyar reformáczió kezdetéről" (Imre Révész on the Start of Hungarian Reformation), P.Sz., Vol. 3 (1891), pp. 175-82.

15. King János' deal with the Porte was preceded by the Treaty of Fontainebleau between his and the king of France's plenipotentiaries on October 28, 1528. For the general description of the post Mohács evolution of Protestantism, see Zsilinszky, *A magyarhoni* . . ., pp. 46-71; also Jenő Zoványi, "A reformáczió Magyarországon a mohácsi vész után . . . 1526-1542" (Reformation in Hungary after the Disaster of Mohács . . . 1526-1542), P.Sz., Vol. 28, pp. 131-32, 227-40, 312-40.

16. Prior to Mohács the court did not execute the law either, but at that time the cause of nonconformity with the law was still the pro-Lutheran ways of the court. The still militantly anti-Protestant local gentry, however, in several instances and places took matters into their own hands and burned some preachers who illegally infiltrated from the West. In 1524 under strong gentry pressure the king issued some letters of reprimand to Lutheran towns but with little effect. Gradually the gentry's anti-Lutheranism also became more vocal than repressive. Fraknói, *A Hunyadiak* . . ., IV, 452. Károly Fabritius, *Pempfflinger Márk szdsz gróf élete* (The Life of Márk Pempfflinger the Count of the Saxons), Budapest: Akmadémiai értekezés, 1875, p. 134.

17. In the Battle of Mohács the following Prelates were killed: the Archbishops of Esztergom (who was also the Primate of Hungary) and of Kalocsa, the Bishops of Nagyvárad, Csanád, Pécs, Győr and Bosnia. S. Szabó *et al.*, *A protestántizmus* . . ., pp. 18-19. Lányi, *Magyarföld* . . ., p. 45.

18. Pongrácz Sörös, "Verancsics és a reformáczió" (Verancsics and the Reformation), *Katholikus Szemle* (Catholic Review, a scholarly journal), Vol. 14 (1897), p. 545. (Cardinal Antal Verancsics, Archbishop of Esztergom, Primate of Hungary 1504-1573, Ambassador at Constantinople and since 1572 *locumtenens* of Hungary.) Prior to Mohács one-third of the arable land was church property. Cardinal Tamás Bakócz (1442-1521), Primate of Hungary, born a son of a serf, owned one-sixth of Hungary's arable lands. S. Szabó, *et al.*, *A protestántizmus* . . ., pp. 12-13.

19. Biro *et al.*, *Magyar református* . . ., p. 51.

20. Révész, *A magyarországi* . . ., pp. 12-14.

21. The Transylvanian Saxons were already as a body Lutherans prior to the Battle of Mohács. Nevertheless, only after the fall of Buda in 1541, in other words only after they were assured against imminent Habsburg intervention, did they declare openly their conversion to Lutheranism. Biro *et al.*, *A magyar református* . . ., p. 45. Karl Kurt Klein, *Saxonica Septemcastrensia*, Marburg: N.G. Elvert Verlag, 1971. Calvinism, on the other hand, was considered the "Hungarian religion" for no ethnic group other than the Hungarian joined Calvinism in masses. Oszkár Jászi, *A nemzeti államok kialakulása és a nemzetiségi kérdés* (The Evolution of the Nation States and the Problem of Nationalities) Budapest: Grill Károly, 1912, pp. 365, 380. The Slovaks either

remained Catholics or were converted to Lutheranism. The Rumanian case was an interesting one. Honterus (see note 26) made great efforts starting in 1544 to convert Rumanians to Lutheranism. This effort resulted in the very first publications in the Rumanian language anywhere (Luther's catechism and four Gospels). Since 1577 András Tordai Sándor, Hungarian Calvinist bishop, founded several Rumanian Calvinist parishes. Soon the first Rumanian Calvinist bishop, Mihály Tordasi (alias Turdasi) was appointed and started the translation of the Old Testament into Rumanian. Religious publication in Rumanian, in Transylvania, introduced the use of the Roman alphabet into the Rumanian language. Princes Gábor Bethlen and György I. Rákóczi of Transylvania launched massive campaigns for the conversion of the Rumanians to Calvinism. After 1690, however, the Habsburg Counter-Reformation in Transylvania extirpated all the Rumanian Protestant parishes and a mass conversion to Greek (Uniate) Catholicism occurred. S. Szabó *et al., A protestántizmus* . . ., pp. 63-64. Emperor and king Leopold I (1657-1705) issued the noted *diploma leopoldinum* on August 23, 1692, granting equal benefits for Rumanian Orthodox priests with those of the Catholic priest in case of union with Rome. Consequently the council of Transylvanian Rumanian prelates in 1697 proclaimed the union. At another council held in 1700, 58 prelates and 1,563 priests of the Rumanian Orthodox church declared union with Rome; in response Leopold granted further privileges to them. Hóman and Szekfű, *Magyar történet* . . ., IV, 265-67.

22. An unsuccessful attempt of the Porte to ally itself with France in 1483 was followed by partial success in 1500 and in December 1525 the envoy of the king of France concluded in Constantinople an entente with the Porte. Sir Charles Petrie, *Earlier Diplomatic History 1492-1713.* London: Hollis and Carter, 1949, pp. 28, 50. Grimm, *The Reformation* . . . pp. 103, 165, 320. Révész, *A magyarországi* . . ., p. 13.

23. Révész, *A magyarországi* . . ., p. 13.

24. Révész, *A magyarországi* . . ., p. 11. In the sixteenth century 1,018 Hungarian students graduated in the University of Wittenberg, a substantial number indeed. Etele Thurzó, "A wittenbergi magyar tanulók anyakönyvéből" (From the Registry of the Hungarian Students at Wittenberg), P.Sz., Vol. 20 (1908), p. 242. The University of Heidelberg was attended prior to Mohásy by one; past Mohács, in the sixteenth century, by eight; and during the seventeenth century by nineteen students from Hungary. Jenő Zoványi, "Adatok a heidelbergi egyetem magyarországi hallgatóinak névsorához" (Data Related to the List of the Students from Hungary at the University of Heidelberg), P.Sz., Vol. 16 (1904), pp. 111-14. See also Vilmos Fraknói, "Adalékok a hazai és külföldi iskolázás történetéhez a XV. és XVI. században" (Data on the Education at Home and Abroad during the Fifteenth and Sixteenth Centuries), Sz., Vol. 9 (1875), pp. 667-77. From 1518 to 1560, the years Melanchton held a chair in the University of Wittenberg, 442 Hungarian students attended that university, practically all of them Melanchton's students. In Melanchton's correspondence there are to be found 23 Hungarian persons, mostly his former students, with whom he often corresponded. *(Melanchthonis Opera* in *Corpus Reformatorum).* See Vilmos Frankel (alias Fraknói), "Melanchton és magyarországi barátai" (Melanchton and His Friends in Hungary) Sz., Vol. 8 (1874), pp. 149-84.

25. Révész, *A magyarországi* . . ., pp. 26, 27. The most important process in the evolution of Reformation was, of course, the translation of the Bible into

Hungarian, which was a two-century long process. Two Hungarian Hussite ministers, educated in Prague, started the process by translating portions of the Old Testament during the years of 1416-1435 (the books of the four evangelists and various psalms). A Pauline monk, László Báthory, independently from these pioneers translated portions of the Old Testament during the last quarter of the fifteenth century. In 1533, the first book was printed in Hungarian (St. Paul's Letters), translated by a Viennese educated priest, Benedek Komjáthy. Three years later four Gospels, translated by Gábor Pesti Mizsér, on the basis of the *Vulgate,* were published. At last in 1541 the entire New Testament, translated by Erdősi (see note 26) was published. This was the first complete Hungarian language book ever printed in Hungary; the other Hungarian language publications in the past were being published abroad, while Latin and German language publications were being printed in Hungary. Erdősi consolidated the existing translations into a coherent full New Testament, and added his own translations and corrections wherever needed, on the basis of Erasmus' version of the Bible.

A more modern and more original publication was the Bible translated by a student of Melanchton, Gáspár Heltai (1490-1574). The draft was prepared in Kolozsvár (Cluj) by Heltai with the aid of István Gyulai, István Ozorai and Gergely Vizaknai. *A Bibliának első része . . .* (The First Part of the Bible), Kolozsvár, 1551. This publication, however did not have the expected effect, for it was not complete but even more because most of the Protestant ministers distrusted Heltai's Unitarian faith.

Simultaneously with the Heltai Bible the Holy Script was translated and prepared for publication in Debrecen by Péter Melius (also Meliusz) Juhász (1536-1572), but he could not complete the translation, so the work was continued after his death by Tamás Félegyházi, who himself died in 1586 so the work had to be taken up by György Gönczy, who published an incomplete version in the year of Félegyházi's death.

The first full Bible in Hungarian was at last published by Gáspár Károli (also Károlyi) (approximately 1529-1591) in 1590 by a printing shop operated by himself in Vizsoly. The effect of this translation was enormous. That is the basis of the presently used Bibles in Hungary. Its effect on literary modern Hungarian was as great as Luther's was on German. Zoltán Trócsányi, "A XVI. század magyar bibliafordítói" (The Hungarian Bible Translators of the Sixteenth Century), P.Sz. Vol. 46 (1937), pp. 517-27. Kálmán H. Kiss, "Egy adalék Károli Gáspár életéhez" (A Fact Related to the Life of Gáspár Károli), P.Sz., Vol. 3 (1891), pp. 103-106. László Németh, "A vizsolyi biblia" (The Bible of Vizsoly), P.Sz., Vol. 38 (1929), pp. 24-27.

26. In addition to those listed in note 25, the following leading reformers should be mentioned: János, Erdősi Sylvester (approximately 1504-1551), a humanist, studied in the Universities of Krakow and Wittenberg and became Professor at the University of Vienna. See Rabán Gerézdi, *A magyar világi líra kezdetei*(The Beginnings of the Hungarian Lay Lyric), Budapest: Szépirodalmi, 1962. Imre Révész, *Erdősi János a magyar protestáns reformátor*(János Erdősi the Hungarian Protestant Reformer), Debrecen: Város könyvnyomdája, 1859. S. Szabó *et al., A protestantizmus . . .,* p. 12.

Ferenc Dávid (approximately 1510-1579), the founding father of Hungarian Unitarianism, studied in Wittenberg, was Hungarian Bishop of Transylvania for the Reformed faith. From 1564 the court chaplain of János

Zsigmond. A prolific author, among his books were *De falsa et vera . . . cognitione,* Alba Julia, 1567; *A szentirásnak fundamentumából vett magyarázat* (Exposition Taken from the Foundations of the Holy Script), Alba Julia, 1568. Mostly it was due to his influence on the court that Transylvania became so tolerant with radical movemenᴛs such as the Anti-Trinitarians and the Anabaptists, at least for some time.

Mátyás Dévai (also Dévay) Biró (1500-1545), the first ethnic Hungarian to attend the University of Wittenberg; an outstanding ecclesiastic debater. His most important publication appeared first in Krakow in 1538, *Az tizparantsolatnac . . . magyarázattya* (The Exposition of the Ten Commandments). See Imre Révész, *Dévay Biró Mátyás életrajza és irodalmi müvei* (The Biography and Literary Writings of Mátyás Dévay Biró), Pest: Osterlamm, 1863. István Tüdős, ''Dévay Biró Mátyás,'' P.Sz., Vol. 3 (1891), pp. 342-360.

Mihály Sztárai (died approximately in 1579) studied in Padua, Italy; author of Hungarian Psalms, but most influential were his publications in the field of ecclesiastic polemics, e.g., *A popok házassága* (Marriage of the Priests), first published in Krakow, 1550; *Az igaz papság tüköre* (The Mirror of Genuine Priesthood), Krakow, 1550. See Tibor Klaniczay, *A magyar reformáció irodalma* (The Literature of the Hungarian Reformation), Budapest: Szépirodalmi, 1961.

István Kopácsi (died approximately in 1562) attended the University of Wittenberg and became a Protestant educator, developed the secondary school of Sárospatak into the most distinguished Protestant college of Hungary, which exists up to the present.

Gál Huszár (died in 1575), educator and ecclesiastic debater, founder of a Hungarian printing shop, translator of hymns and psalms. Kálmán Benda and Károly Irinyi, *A 400 éves debreceni nyomda* (The Four Hundred Year Old Printinghouse of Debrecen), Budapest: Szépirodalmi, 1961.

János Honterus (also Honter, alias Grass) (1498-1549), writer, publisher and a hymic scholar, the reformer of the Saxons of Transylvania. Studied in the Universities of Vienna, Krakow and Basel. The printing house he founded in Brasso in 1539 printed 31 books during its first fourteen years. Founder of the public library of Brasso. K.K. Klein, *Der Humanist und Reformator Johannes Honter,* Nagyszeben, Munchen: 1935. Béla Lakos, ''Honter János és a szászok reformációja'' (János Honter and the Reformation of the Saxons), P.Sz., Vol. 14 (1902), pp. 213-23.

27. Révész, *A magyarországi . . .,* pp. 12-13. Sándor Biró *et al., A magyar református . . .,* p. 25. The peasants felt ''. . . an utmost desire for a better world.'' S. Szabó, *et al., A protestántizmus . . .,* p. 14. Antal Ijjas, *Az egyház és az uralkodói abszolutizmus* (The Church and Monarchical Absolutism), Budapest: Pázmány Péter, 1941, pp. 5-20.

28. The Treaty of Nagyvárad, concluded on February 28, 1538, ended the civil war. On the effect of Transylvania on Reformation in royal Hungary see Count István Bethlen, ''A reformáció és Erdély'' (The Reformation and Transylvania), P.Sz., Vol. 29 (1917), pp. 592-608. József Pokoly, ''Az erdélyi fejedelmek viszonya a protestáns egyházakhoz'' (The Relationship of the Transylvanian Princes to the Protestant Churches), P.Sz., Vol. 8 (1896), pp. 545-61. The emerging Principality of Transylvania acknowledged her allegiance and vassal status to the Crown of St. Stephen, e.g.: in the Treaties of Nagyvárad in 1538, of Kolozsvár (Cluj) in 1551, of Speyer in 1571, at that occasion István

Báthori Prince of Transylvania (1571-1576, from 1576 to his death in 1586 king of Poland) swore "... on the living God, that I shall be obedient subject of His Majesty Maximilian, the constitutional king of Hungary . . . ." László Szalay, *Erdély és a porta 1567-1578*(Transylvania and the Porte 1567-1578), Pest: Leufer & Stolp, 1862, pp. 19-20. This last treaty in the sixteenth century to this effect was that of Prague in 1595.

29. Letter of Prince Zsigmond Báthori of Transylvania to György Király, the Commander of Nagyvárad, dated Alba Julia, June 2, 1597. SF., Vol. 7 (1863), p. 760.

30. Révész, *A magyarországi . . .*, p. 29. Biró *et al.*, *A magyar református . . .*, pp. 49ff. Lajos Rácz, "Vallási türelem Erdély- és Magyarországon XVI-XVII. század" (Religious Tolerance in Transylvania and Hungary During the XVI and XVII Centuries), P.Sz., Vol. 43 (1934), pp. 198-204.

31. Biró *et al.*, *A magyarországi református . . .*, pp. 50-51; Révész, *A magyarországi . . .*, p. 29. S. Szabó *et al.*, *A protestántizmus . . .*, pp. 38-56. Jozsef S. Szabó, "Zwingli hatása Magyarországon" (The Effects of Zwingli in Hungary), P.Sz., Vol. 40 (1931), pp. 689-694. Jenő Sólyom, *Luther és Magyarország, A reformátor kapcsolata hazánkkal haláláig* (Luther and Hungary, The Contacts of the Reformer with Our Country up to his Death), Budapest: Luther Társaság, 1933.

32. The three nations concluded their "union" in 1437; it was renewed in 1542 to remain in force up to 1848. See Benedek Jancsó, *Erdély története* (A History of Transylvania) Cluj: Minerva, 1931. László Makkai, *Erdély története* (A History of Transylvania), Budapest: Renaissance, 1944, pp. 221-71, 358-74. Karl Kurt Klein *Saxonica Septemcastrensia*, Marburg: N.G. Elvert Verlag, 1971, pp. 229-58. Elemér Mályusz *et al.*, *Erdély és népei*(Transylvania and Its Peoples), Budapest: Franklin, 1941, pp. 164-70. Sándor Szilágyi, "Az erdélyi alkotmány megalakulása a separatió kezdetén" (The Foundation of the Constitution of Transylvania at the Commencement of Separation), Sz., Vol. 10 (1876), pp. 36-48. The Sublime Porte jealously watched the Habsburg government not to dominate Transylvania, e.g., in 1571, after the death of János Zsigmond the Pasha of Buda Mustafa warned Verancsics (see note 18) not to interfere with Transylvanian affairs. László Szalay, *Erdély és a porta 1567-1578*(Transylvania and the Porte), Pest: Laufer & Stolp, 1862, pp. 6-7.

33. Max Weber, *The Protestant Ethic and the Spirit of Capitalism*, translated by Talcott Parsons, New York, 1930. Kemperer Fullerton, "Calvinism and Capitalism," *The Harvard Theological Review*, XXI (1928), pp. 163-91. See also András Fabó, *Rajzok a magyar protestantismus történelméből* (Sketches from the History of Hungarian Protestantism), Pest: Hornyánszky és Träger, 1868, pp. 9-83; Ferenc Váró, "Bethlen Gábor academicum collegiuma" (The Liberal Arts College of Gábor Bethlen), P.Sz., vol. 15 (1903), pp. 325-36, 397-411; Imre Révész, "Bethlen Gábor a kálvinista fejedelem" (Bethlen Gábor the Calvinist Prince), P.Sz., vol. 26 (1914), pp. 339-68; Jozsef Pokoly, "Az unitarismus Magyarországon" (Unitarianism in Hungary), P.Sz., vol. 10 (1898), pp. 28-44, 150-67, 228-46, 285-304, 375-92, 440-51.

34. The war of 1591-1606 is called in Hungarian historiography "The Fifteen Years War." On Rudolf's Counter-Reformation see Zsilinszky, *A magyarhoni . . .*, pp. 137-58.

35. Act XXII. 1604. *C.J.H. 1526-1608*, pp. 955-57. The same year István Bocskai concluded an alliance with the Ottoman Pasha of Buda. Both pledged mutual aid, not to attack each other's fortresses, and not to conclude separate

peace. Subsequently Bocskai could turn his full forces against the Habsburg troops. Antal Pálkövi, "Bocskay és a bécsi békekötes" (Bocskai and the Peace Treaty of Vienna), S.F., Vol. 1 (1857), p. 77. In 1605 the Sultán endorsed the above agreement. *Ibid.*, p. 263. Bocskai's letter summoning the Szekelys to rise on April 15, 1605, and his captain's transferring the summons to others November 11, 1604, in Imre Mikó, ed., *Erdély, történelmi adatok* (Transylvania, Historical Sources), 4 vols., Kolozsvár: Stein J., 1855, II, 317-18, 320-21. János Luczenbacher, "A zsitvatoroki békekötés" (The Conclusion of the Peace Treaty of Zsitvatorok), *Tudománytár* (Scholarly magazine of the Academy of Sciences), vol. 3 (1834), pp. 230-42. Arnold Ipolyi, "Adalékok a zsitvatoroki béke történetéhez" (Data on the History of the Peace Treaty of Zsitvatorok), *Uj Magyar Muzeum* (New Hungarian Museum, scholarly journal of the members of the Academy of Sciences), Vol. 2 (1851-2), pp. 148-61.

36. Act XXII 1606. *C.J.H. 1526-1608*, pp. 992-93. For the historical perspectives of the treaty see Zsilinszky, *A magyarhoni...*, pp. 158-71; Ferenc Márk, "Bocskay István és a bécsi béke" (István Bocskay and the Treaty of Vienna), P.Sz., vol. 16 (1904), pp. 217-25. Etele Thurzó, "A bécsi békekötés" (The Peace Treaty of Vienna), P.Sz., Vol. 18 (1906), pp. 357-75, 447-67. Géza Antal, "A magyar protestáns egyház külföldi érintkezései" (The Foreign Contacts of the Hungarian Protestant Churches), P.Sz., Vol. 20 (1908), pp. 65-84.

37. A specific Hungarian office, a kind of viceroy, head of the executive branch of the government, presiding officer of the House of Lords, Commander-in-Chief of the armed forces as well as presiding judge of one of the chambers of the supreme court of justice, indeed an extremely powerful office. See Király, *Hungary...*, pp. 83, 89, 93, 260, 265-66, 103, 181.

38. ... *per Palatinum, et consiliarios hungaros ... ad conservandum regnum Hungariae, ejusdemque regnicolarum quietum, et utilitatem videbuntur esse necessaria; plenariam potestatem, et facultatem habeat ... C.J.H. 1526-1608*, p. 962.

39. Ferenc II Rákoczy's regime declared the Habsburg dynasty dethroned in 1707, but his own reign came to an end with the Treaty of Szatmar in 1711; the Parliament of Debrecen proclaimed the Habsburg dynasty dethroned on April 14, 1849 but Kossoth resigned his presidential authority on August 11, 1849.

40. ... *nemo nisi legitime citatus, jurisque ordine convictus puniatur ... C.J.H. 1526-1608*, p. 966.

41. See Appendixes I and II.

42. *C.J.H. 1608-57*, pp. 10-11. These stipulations were re-endorsed by the Treaties of Nickolsburg in 1621, of Vienna (second treaty in this locality) in 1624, of Linz in 1645, this last secured the freedom of religion even to the individual serfs *(jobbágyok)*. The first *nádor* (palatine) of Lutheran faith was Baron Tamás Nádasdy (1498-1562), elected to this position in 1554. Mihály Horváth, *Nádasdy Tamás élete* (The Life of Tamás Nádasdy), Buda: 1838.

43. *C.J.H. 1608-57*, pp. 175-83; see also Appendix III.

44. Indeed Protestantism stayed. In early nineteenth century there were 1,971 Calvinist, 737 Lutheran and 110 Unitarian parishes in Hungary and Transylvania. (There were also 54 Unitarian affiliates — in other words, groups not having the status of parishes.) István Lassu, *Az austriai birodalomnak statistikai, geographiai és históriai leirása* (The Statistical, Geographical and

Historical Description of the Austrian Empire), Buda: A' magyar királyi universitás' betüivel, 1829, pp. 108-11. In late nineteenth century the religious affiliations of the various nationalities of Hungary were as follows:

Percent:	Rom. Cath.	Greek Cath.	Greek Orth.	Luth.	Calv.	Unitarians	Jews
Hungarians	56	2.1	0.2	4	30.8	0.8	5.6
Germans	66.5	—	0.3	20.2	1.3	—	11.4
Slovaks	68.8	5.4	—	23.7	0.5	—	1.1
Rumanians	0.3	36.5	62.6	—	—	—	2.9
Ruthenians	0.5	96.1	0.2	—	—	—	0.1
Serbs and Croats	62.2	0.4	37.0	—	—	—	0.1

Béla Bartha, "Statisztikai tanulmányok a magyar protestantizmusról" (Statistical Studies on Hungarian Protestantism), P.Sz., vol. 2 (1890), p. 39.

45. For the political and social status of the gentry *(bene possessionati)* see Király, *Hungary* . . ., pp. 24-42.

46. István Verbőczi (also Werbőczy) (d. 1541) published the *Tripartitum* (Work in Three Volumes) first in Latin in Vienna in 1517. The book was republished in countless editions both in Latin and in Hungarian thereafter. This work was intended to be codified as a law. Although it never has been enacted it was universally accepted in Hungary as the authentic codification of the rights and privileges of the nobility. That remained the lay bible of gentry power in Hungary.

47. Act XXXI *C.J.H. 1000-1526*, p. 851. Act XL obliged the queen to dismiss her foreign advisers and replace them with Hungarians. *Ibid.*, p. 853.

48. Between 1527 and 1547 ten Hungarian diets were held; none of them enacted anti-Protestant laws. In 1548 in harmony with the religious wars launched by Emperor Charles V, his brother Ferdinand intended to introduce anti-Protestant measures in Hungary also, but the gentry prevented it. The few legislations which the gentry could not refuse to enact for realpolitical reasons were so weak and contradictory that they did not hurt the Protestants at all.

49. For the political, social and economic status of the burghers see Király, *Hungary* . . ., pp. 43-50. See also Act VI. 1608. *C.J.H. 1608-57*, p. 20.

50. *C.J.H. 1526-1608*, p. 965.

51. *C.J.H. 1608-57*, p. 25 (post-coronation laws).

52. *Ibid.*, p. 28.

53. Király, *Hungary* . . ., p. 53.

BIOGRAPHIES OF CONTRIBUTORS

BROCK, PETER de BEAUVOIR, Professor of History, University of Toronto since 1966. Born in Guernsey, Channel Islands, January 30, 1920. B.A., M.A., D. Phil., University of Oxford, Ph.D., University of Cracow. Lecturer in History, University of Toronto, 1957-1958, Assistant Professor, University of Alberta, 1958-1960, Visiting Lecturer, Smith College, 1960-1961, Associate Professor of History, Columbia University, 1961-1966. Author of: *The Dawn of the Peasant Movement* (in Polish), Polish Peasant Party, London, 1956. *The Political and Social Doctrines of the United of Czech Brethren in the 15th and Early 16th Centuries*, Mouton, The Hague, 1957, *Essays of the Polish Great Emigration in England* (in Polish), Ksiazka i Wiedza, Warsaw, 1958, *The Genesis of the Polish People in England* (in Polish), Swiderski, London, 1962, *Pacifisim in the United States: From the Colonial Era to the First World War*, 1968 and *Pacifisim in Europe to 1914*, 1972, Princeton University Press, Co-editor of *The Czech Renascence of the Nineteenth Century*, University of Toronto Press, 1970, Author of *Twentieth-Century Pacifism*, Van Nostrand Reinhold, New York, 1970. *Nationalism and Populism in Partioned Poland*, Orbis Books, London, 1973.

DUKER, ABRAHAM G., Professor and Chairman, Department of Judaic Studies, Brookyln College of the City University of New York since 1972. Born in Rypin, Poland, September 27, 1907, B.A. City College, New York, 1930, Columbia, Ph.D., 1956. Managaing editor, *Contemporary Jewish Research*, 1938-1941, Professor of Social Science and President, College of Jewish Studies, 1956-1962; Professor of History and Social Institutions and Director of Library, Yeshiva University, 1963-1972. Lecturer, New York University, 1950-1951, New School of Social Research, 1950-1955. Managing editor of *Jewish Social Studies*, 1952-1956, editor from 1956. Lecturer, School of General Studies, Columbia University, 1953-1954, Graduate School, 1955-1956 and 1966-1967. Visiting Professor, Wayne State University, 1955. Author of: *Jewish Survival in the World Today*, Hadassah, 1939-1941, *Emerging Culture Patterns in American Jewish Life, The Psycho-Cultural Approach to the Study of Jewish Life in America*, American Jewish Historical Soc., 1950, *Jewish Education Committee*, New York, 1953, *The Polish Great Emigration and the Jews; Studies in Political and Intellectual History*, University

Microfilms, 1956, *Some Cabbalistic and Frankist elements in Adam Mickiewicz's Driady,* In: Studies in Polish civilization, Columbia University, 1971 and Polish Institute of Arts and Sciences, 1971.

FISCHER-GALATI, STEPHEN, Professor of History, University of Colorado since 1966, Editor East European Quarterly since 1967. Born Bucharest, Romania 1924. A.B., A.M., Ph.D. (1945, 1946, 1949 respectively) from Harvard University. Research Specialist (Eastern Europe), Department of State, 1950-53; Director of Research, Mid-European Studies Center, 1953-55; Professor of History, Wayne State University, 1955-1966. Research Associate, Russian Research Center of Harvard University, since 1963. Author of numerous books and articles of the history of Eastern Europe including *Ottoman Imperialism and German Protestantism* (Harvard University Press, 1959); *The New Kumania: From People's Democracy to Socialist Republic* (The M.I.T. Press, 1967); *Twentieth Century Rumania* (Columbia University Press, 1970).

HEYMANN, FREDERICK G., Professor Emeritus of History, University of Calgary. Born in Berlin, Germany 1900, studied at the University of Berlin, Gottingen, and Heidelberg, Ph.D. University of Frankfurt. Worked with the noted *Frankfurter Zeitung,* later in Prague (Czechoslovakia) and in England (1939-1946), taught in various institutions in the United States. In 1959 he developed the Department of History at the University of Alberta in Calgary, later called University of Calgary, served as the first chairman of this department. Member of the Institute for Advanced Study, Princeton, 1956-1958, and 1966. Visiting professor at the Universities of Iowa, Chicago and Bonn, Germany. Author of *John Zizka and the Hussite Revolution* (1955), *George of Bohemia, King of Heretics* (1965), both published by Princeton University Press, *Poland and Czechoslovakia* (1966), Prentice Hall and others.

HILLERBRAND HANS J., Professor of History and Dean of Graduate School of the City University of New York since 1970. Born Gersheim, Germany, September 13, 1931; Goshen College, 51-53; Ph.D. University Erlangen, 57. Professor of History Duke University 59-70. Author of *Die politische Ethik des Taufertums* Brill, 1962, *Bibliographie des Taufertums,* Gerd Mohn, 1962; *The Reformation,*

1965 & *The Fellowship of Discontent*, 1967, Harper; *The Reformation of the 16th Century*, Rand McNally, 1968; *Christendom Divided*, 'Vorld, 1971; ed., *Letters of Erasmus*, Harper, 1971; author, *The World of the Reformation*, Scribrers, 1973; *The Origins of 16th Century Anabaptism*, Arch. Reformationsgeschichte, 1962; *Thomas Muentzer*, In: Reformers in profile, Fortress, 1967.

KANN, ROBERT A., Professor of History in the Graduate School of Rutgers, The State University of New Jersey since 1947. Born in Vienna, Austria, February 11, 1906. Dr. Jur, University of Vienna, 1930, B.L.S. from Columbia University in 1940, Ph.D. Columbia University in 1946, Honorary Ph.D., Salzburg University, 1972. Member of the Institute of Advanced Study, 1942-45. Visiting Professor at Princeton University, 1966, at Columbia University, 1962-1964, 1966-1967, at University of Vienna, 1973-1974. Chairman, Conference Group Central European History, 1964. Corresponding member, Austrian Academy. Author of: *The Multi-National Empire* (2 vols.), Columbia, 1950, *The Habsburg Empire, a Study in Integration and Disintegration*, 1957 and *A Study in Austrian Intellectual History: From late Baroque to Romanticism* 1960, Praeger; *Sixtusffare und die geheimen Friedensverhandlungen Österreich-Ungarns*, Verlag Geschiches u Polit, 1966, *The problem of restoration, a Study in Comparative Political History*, University of California, 1968. Editor of *Marie von Ebner-Eschenbach-Dr. Josef Breuer, ein Briefwechsel, 1889-1916*, Bergland, Vienna, 1969, Author of *Kaiser Franz Josef und der Ausbruch des. Weltkrieges*, Bohlau, Vienna, 1971, *A History of the Habsburg Empire, 1526-1918*, University of California Press, Berkeley, 1974. Editor of *Theodor Gomperz, Ein Gelehrtenleben im Burgertum der Frank-Josefs-Zeit*, Akademieverlag, Vienna, 1974.

KIRÁLY, BÉLA K., Professor of History, Brooklyn College and the Graduate School of the City University of New York since 1964. Born in Kaposvar, Hungary on April 14, 1912. Diploma, Ludovika Military Academy, Budapest, 1935, Diploma, War Academy, Hungary, 1942, M.A. from Columbia University, 1959, Ph.D., 1966. Professor of military history, Supply Academy, Hungary, 1948-1949, professor and superintendent, War Academy, Hungary, 1950-1951, honorary member, staff and faculty, U.S. Army Command & General Staff

College, 1959. Visiting professor of history, Columbia University, 1971-1972, visiting scholar, 1972-1973. Author of: *Hungary's Army Under the Soviet*, Japan Institute of Foreign Affairs, 1958, *Hungary in the late Eighteenth Century*, Columbia University, 1968. *Farenc Deak*, Twayne, 1971.

LAMMN, NORMAN, Jakob and Erna Michael Professor of Jewish Philosophy, Yeshiva University since 1969. Visiting Professor of Judaic Studies, Brooklyn College, 19754-75. Born in Brooklyn, New York, December 19, 1927. B.A., Yeshiva College, New York, 1949. Ph.D. Yeshiva University 1966. Founder and first Editor, *Tradition;* Editor, *Library of Jewish Law and Ethnics*, Ktav Publishing Co. Author of numerous articles and books, including: *Faith and Doubt* (Ktav: 1971); *Torah Lishmah* (Hebrew; in Jerusalem, 1971); *The Good Society* (Viking, 1974); co-edited *The Leo Jung Jubilee Volume* (1962) and *A Treasury of Tradition* (1967).

SHAW, STANFORD JAY, Professor of Turkish and Near Eastern History, University of California, from 1968. Editor in Chief, International Journal of Middle East Studies, from 1966. Born: Saint Paul, Minnesota, May 5, 1930. Stanford University, 1947-52, B.A., (1951), M.A. in History (1952), Princeton University, 1952-1955, 1957-1958, M.A. in Near Eastern History (1955), Ph.D. in Near Eastern History (1958), University of London, January-June, 1955, University of Cairo and American University at Cairo, 1955-1956. University of Istanbul, 1956-7. Assistant Professor of Turkish, Harvard University, 1960-1965, Associate Professor of Turkish Language and History, Harvard University, 1965-1968. Visiting Professor of History, University of Washington, summer session, 1970. Member of the Institute of International Education, 1973-4, the Executive Board, American Research Institute in Turkey, 1964-1968, 1974, Associate Chairman, Near East Division, International Congress of Orientalists, Chairman, Publications Committee, Middle East Studies Association of North America from 1974, Director, Harvard University Near Eastern Summer program, 1963-1967. Author of *The Financial and Administrative Organization and Development of Ottoman Egypt. 1517-1798* (Princeton University Press, Princeton, New Jersey, 1962), *Ottoman Egypt in the Eighteenth Century: the Nizamname-i Misir of Ahmed Cezzar Pasha* (ed. and tr. with notes) (Harvard University Press, Cambridge, Massachusetts, 1962, reprinted 1964). *Ottoman*

Egypt in the Age of the French Revolution (tr. with introduction and notes) (Harvard University Press, Cambridge, Massachusetts, 1964). *Studies on the Civilization of Islam,* by H.A.R. Gibb (ed. by S.J. Shaw and W.R. Polk) (Beacon Press, Boston, Massachusetts, Kegan Paul and Co., London, 1962). *The Budget of Ottoman Egypt* (Near and Middle East Series, Columbia University, Mouton and Co., The Hague, Holland, 1968). *Between Old and New: The Ottoman Empire under Sultan Selim III, 1789-1807* (Harvard University Press, Cambridge, Massachusetts, 1971).

WILENSKY, MORDECAI, Professor of Jewish History at Hebrew College, Boston, Massachusetts, since 1946. Born in Kobryn, near Brest-Litovsky, (1914), 1934-1946 lived in Palestine. Hebrew University, Jerusalem M.A. (1938), Ph.D. in Jewish History, (1941), 1962-1967 — Lectures at the summer seminar of Hebrew Teaachers & Principals, Cornell University, Ithaca, New York, 1958-59; 1969-70; 1971-73, visiting professor at Haifa University, Israel. Author of: *The Return of the Jews to England,* Jerusalem 1943, *The Poetry of Isaac Luzzatto,* Tel-Aviv, 1944. *Hasidim & Mitnaggedim,* 2 vols., Jerusalem, 1970.